# When It Mattered Most

## The Forgotten Story of America's First Stanley Cup Champions, and the War to End All Wars

KEVIN TICEN

To Michaela, Annika, Anja and Lukas

# EDITOR'S NOTE

The timeline and all events in this book are factually accurate and have been retold through newspaper accounts. There is no video or audio of any of the contests other than black and white photographs of the participants. There are also no first-person accounts from any of the participants as they have all been deceased for more than fifty years. However, these games were played in vivid color at breakneck speed by complex human beings. In an effort to breathe life back into the games and humanity back to the participants, the author has used his experiences coaching and playing high level sports to interpret some words and actions of the participants and color has been added to the non-scoring plays of hockey.

# TABLE OF CONTENTS

Preface

## ACT I

## ACT II

# ACT III

## Epilogue

# PREFACE

The second half of the second decade of the Twentieth Century was as turbulent a time as the world has ever seen. The great monarchies of Europe clung to their last desperate breaths of life, losing to rampant nationalism and the first economic revolution. Bloody uprisings gripped Ireland and Mexico while the Austro-Hungarian Empire ripped apart along ethnic lines. To the east, the Czar's rule in Russia and the Sultan's rule over the Ottoman Empire were collapsing. America itself was struggling with its identity as the temperance and suffragette movements were picking up steam, nationalistic tensions were rising, and tempers roiled over America's role on the global stage.

Mankind was forever changed on June 28, 1914 in Sarajevo when assassin Gavrilo Princip gunned down Austrian Archduke Franz Ferdinand, heir to the Austro-Hungarian throne. That brazen act lit the fuse that began an unstoppable chain reaction of events. Within four years, more than eighteen million people had been killed and twenty-three million more wounded. The maps of Europe and the Middle East were redrawn. Kings and emperors gave way to presidents, prime ministers and chancellors and a new form of government led by the working class took shape.

More than five thousand miles from the battlefields of Europe, Seattle was a city trying to find its place after the Klondike Gold Rush. Alexander Pantages built a theater empire while William Boeing and John Nordstrom founded namesake businesses and Jim Casey's United Parcel Service took shape.

Professional sports were in their infancy, with baseball dominating the East Coast and upper Midwest of America and hockey ruling supreme in eastern Canada. Just prior to the turn of the century, Lord Stanley of Preston, Governor General of Canada, donated a challenge cup awarded annually to the best team in Canada. The cup grew in size over the years, first adding three tiered rings, and then five barrel rings, each inscribed with the names of those worthy enough to hold this trophy as champion. In the years to come, it became the centerpiece in the dreams of countless schoolchildren and the significance of winning it would render even the most hardened hockey veteran speechless.

In Seattle, a high-school dropout named Royal Brougham talked his way into a job at the Seattle Post-Intelligencer. He was soon named the newspapers' sports editor, a position he held for 68 years, making him one of the longest serving editors nationally and one of the most influential personalities in Seattle sports history. Second to perhaps only Brougham, Pete Muldoon established himself as an icon. So popular was Muldoon that the Seattle Times headline announcing his death ran above the Sports header. The Seattle Post-Intelligencer ran the story on page one, center column above the fold, a place never reserved for sports coverage in those days.

In the winter of 1917, as the U.S. was pulled into World War I, Muldoon molded the Seattle Metropolitans, a talented band of athletes, into an elite team. That elite team would battle the looming war, their own insecurities, and fierce opponents on both coasts of Canada to captivate a community and journey towards hockey immortality.

# ACT I

1916 Seattle Metropolitans Program Cover

Photo Credit: David Eskenazi Collection

"It is not the critic who counts; not the man who points out how the strong man stumbles, or where the doer of deeds could have done them better. The credit belongs to the man who is actually in the arena, whose face is marred by dust and sweat and blood; who strives valiantly; who errs, who comes short again and again, because there is no effort without error and shortcoming; but who does actually strive to do the deeds; who knows great enthusiasms, the great devotions; who spends himself in a worthy cause; who at the best knows in the end the triumph of high achievement, and who at the worst, if he fails, at least fails while daring greatly, so that his place shall never be with those cold and timid souls who neither know victory nor defeat."

> - President Theodore Roosevelt, Man in the Arena speech
>         April 23, 1910

# CHAPTER 1 – THE JOURNEY TO SEATTLE

The door gently closed behind him, sealing off the lingering aroma of a recently enjoyed family meal. Twenty-four-year old Frank Foyston stepped outside into the crisp, clear mid-afternoon air and started walking. Alfred and Clara Foyston's third son stood tall at 5'7" with warm gray eyes and dark blonde hair, always parted on the left. High cheek bones, a soft narrow jaw and well-proportioned features produced a handsome face that had always made him popular amongst the girls. His calm, secure, warm demeanor diffused any jealousy and made him equally admired by the boys. Frank never had the need to be great, just an insatiable desire to be part of something great that had always made his parents proud.

Peering through the front window of the farm house, his sister Jessie wistfully gazed out on the landscape as Frank began his journey. The seven Foyston siblings had a special bond that began as children and endured throughout their adult lives. It was always tough for them when Frank left knowing it would be months before they would see their brother again. With her elbows resting on the sill, she watched him cross the front yard with his bag slung tightly over his shoulder and his breath clearly visible against the frigid blue sky. Frank always walked with a purpose, wanting to get the most out of every step. He soon passed through the rock wall encompassing their Minesing, Ontario farm and out of sight.

Thursday, November 11 was still five weeks from the official start of winter but the seasons had changed that day. Fall had finally given way to winter and the beginning of hockey season. A forward for the Toronto Blueshirts the past three years, Foyston's journey once again took him the seventy-five miles to Toronto. He hopped the train in Barrie and arrived in the city late that afternoon where he met his close friend and Blueshirts teammate Hap Holmes.

Frank first played against Hap in 1910 in the Ontario Hockey Association with Frank's Barrie team competing against Hap's Parkdale

1

Canoe team. The pair joined the Toronto Blueshirts for the 1912-13 season, winning the Stanley Cup their second year. Winning the Cup was a dream come true for both boys and they forged a close friendship.

Hap, born Harry George Holmes, was the son of a blacksmith. At 5'10" and 170 pounds, he had an almost perfect build for a goalie. Large enough to be physically intimidating to opposing forwards but small enough to maintain the quickness and agility needed to repel rockets hit from every conceivable angle. Hap usually donned a ball cap, covering a large forehead and high, receding hairline. His big brown eyes sloped gently down towards lips often pursed in a smile. Hap was short for Happy. He had a dry personality that those who did not know him found boring but he was never angry so the boys had found humor in nicknaming him Happy. He spoke in quick, rapid fire bursts uttering phrases mostly logical in content and to the point. He was one of the best goalies in hockey and one of Frank's closest friends.

This year they met at Union Station rather than the Arena Gardens as Toronto was not their final destination. They were headed west. The pair boarded the *Imperial Limited* train for the 87-hour trip to Vancouver with excitement and trepidation. Looking for their seats, they hardly noticed the throngs of well-dressed men and women outfitted in the latest Edwardian fashions scurrying past them in the aisle.

Sitting down, both stared blankly out the window as the train pulled away until Hap finally broke the silence and began peppering Frank with small talk. Frank could sense his friend's nervousness. He felt the same. Although he was excited to see his teammates again and eager to get on the ice, the beginning of the season was always a time full of apprehension.

Leaving their families behind, the boys knew their lives would not be their own for the foreseeable future. They were playing in a new league, with new rules and for a new coach. Feelings of insecurity engulfed their minds. They thought they were good enough to thrive out west but did not yet know. Frank's tone and small talk calmed his friend, despite betraying his own inner unease. While he always had the ability to calm others, that familiar feeling in the pit of his stomach told him that hockey season was here. The boys' conversation slowly diminished until they were both asleep.

When they woke the next morning, the train was pulling in to the red brick station at Port Arthur. Their friends and Toronto teammates Eddie Carpenter and Jack Walker greeted them at the station. Jack was from Port Arthur and Eddie had spent the offseason living with Jack and working for the railroad.

As Frank and Hap descended the stairs to the platform, smiles and hugs flew between the four friends. After quick pleasantries were exchanged, the reminiscing and teasing began. A combination of laughter, pride and excitement produced a euphoric feeling within the boys. While their lives would not be their own, they would at least be together. Feelings of apprehension soon became unbridled joy. Anticipation for the season now brewed inside them.

Eddie and Jack were joining Frank and Hap out west but would not leave until Sunday. The four would meet again Wednesday afternoon in the capital city of Victoria. After their brief reunion, Eddie and Jack returned to the Walker residence while Frank and Hap hopped back on the train. The pair would spend the weekend traversing the Canadian Rockies landing in the coastal city Monday afternoon.

** 

Wednesday, November 17, 1915 was a warm and wet day in Victoria. A Pineapple Express from the Pacific had drastically raised temperatures but brought buckets of rain. As day turned to night, the crank began to turn aboard the S.S. *Princess Adelaide* and the ship pulled away from the Inner Harbor. Frank stood undercover on the main deck to avoid the rain crashing down around him. It had taken six days, but they were finally on the way to their final destination: Seattle. They were going to join a new team formed that year, the Metropolitans.

Looking out over the harbor city, Frank saw blankets of Douglas Fir covering the landscape. The Neo-Baroque British Columbia Parliament Building, with its green, oxidized copper dome stood to his right. The stunning Empress Hotel directly in front of him. Frank had been amazed by the landscapes he had seen traveling west, their beauty producing a calming effect. The feeling in his stomach had weakened but remained. It would not completely go away until their first practice. Tired, Frank walked back inside and found his three teammates sprawled on bench rows trying to catch some sleep. He sat down next to them, comforted that they were with him on this journey.

Jack and Eddie had played together for years and they were close friends. First for two seasons with Port Arthur Lake City in the North Ontario Hockey League and then with the Moncton Victorias of the Maritime Professional League. Eddie was tall and athletic at 6' and 170 pounds. With thick brown hair, hazel eyes and a serious look to his face, he was an imposing defender on the ice.

Jack had joined Hap and Frank in Toronto for the 1913-14 season and helped bring Eddie out last year. At 5'9" and 155 pounds, Jack was one of the best players in hockey. He had thinning brown hair, blue eyes and a square jaw that gave him the look of a fierce competitor. Off the ice, he was warm, engaging and had a quick wit that could quickly diffuse tension or make even Eddie's seriousness fade into laughter.

Jack had developed a technique on defense called the hook check and it made him one of the best defenders in the game. He would skate up alongside the opposing forward at full speed, quickly drop to a knee and knock the puck away. It was a high risk, high reward move for most. If the defender missed the puck, they were no longer in position to protect the goal. Walker never missed. He had an uncanny ability to read the weakness in the opponent's stickhandling that told him the exact moment to attack. He was also one of the best scorers in the game, scoring twenty goals to go with sixteen assists his first season in Toronto. His thirty-six points doubled Frank's eighteen. Jack was two years older than Frank and the two spent countless hours talking hockey.

The ship soon left the harbor and entered the Strait of Juan de Fuca. As the engine propelled the *Princess Adelaide* through the entrance to Puget Sound, all four men were asleep. Tomorrow morning, the boat would land at Pier 1 in Seattle, where Washington Street ended in Elliot Bay. While the hockey would ultimately be the same, America would be a new adventure for the boys.

**

Pete Muldoon first moved to Seattle in his early 20s to train as a boxer and immediately knew it was home. In just three years, he had become the amateur light-heavyweight champion of the West Coast but after his first few professional fights, he quickly realized there were better ways to make a buck. Returning to Canada, he began coaching, first finding success in lacrosse before getting a shot with his first love, hockey. He'd spent last season coaching the Portland Rosebuds but was now finally coaching the sport he loved, in the city he loved.

Muldoon was a handsome figure at nearly 6' tall and 180 pounds. With thick black hair, big brown eyes and an even bigger smile, Muldoon's charisma was captivating. He saw the greatness in people, often before they saw it in themselves. He had the deep emotional security formed from a strong, loving family but had experienced enough life to empathize with even the most broken of men.

Pete had grown up in St. Mary's, a town in southern Ontario, equidistant from Toronto and Detroit but he never fit in to the eastern sports scene. The east was more autocratic in its coaching style, more about size and power in its playing style. While Muldoon had the courage and inner fortitude that years of boxing had developed, he saw sport as his form of art. It was not the brutality and sheer force of will that he loved, it was the athleticism and creativity that attracted him to sports.

Out west, he'd found similar minds in the Patrick brothers, Lester and Frank. Transplants from Montreal, the brothers were innovators. They had founded and owned the Pacific Coast Hockey Association. Frank Patrick was the president and also played for and coached the Vancouver Millionaires while Lester played for and coached the Victoria Aristocrats.

Frank had given Muldoon his break in hockey, first hiring him as a trainer for the Millionaires before giving him the reins in Portland.

The brothers pushed conventional wisdom in all aspects of hockey and Muldoon loved their discussions. The Patricks believed more in the journey than the outcome. Fiercely competitive, it wasn't that winning wasn't supremely important to them, they just wanted to win the right way. And, they were most interested in elevating the level of play. As owners, they could have stacked their teams with the top talent to ensure success. Instead, they created a free market for players and shared their ideas with all of the league's teams. The Patricks wanted to win hockey games played at the highest level, games played for the Stanley Cup, and the only way to do that was to create a league based on the most competitive hockey.

Muldoon had been back home in Seattle for nearly a month overseeing the final construction of the new Ice Arena, located downtown on Fifth Avenue between University and Seneca streets. The beautiful new red brick building had opened to a capacity crowd on Friday, November 12. Almost two thousand five hundred people had come to watch a full program of skating, including Muldoon ice dancing with the beautiful Mary Nicholson. With a playing surface of two hundred feet long by eighty feet wide, more than eight hundred Seattleites had taken to the ice afterwards and enjoyed the free skate until ten o'clock.

Sitting at the desk in his sparkling new office, Muldoon prepared for the team's first practice. He had already signed six players and was looking for a few more, ultimately wanting nine on his roster. He had signed five of the best players off the Toronto Blueshirts team, forwards Cully Wilson, Jack Walker and Frank Foyston, defenseman Eddie Carpenter and goalie Harry "Hap" Holmes. Veteran forward Bobby Rowe would be joining them as well.

Rowe and Wilson had arrived separately in Seattle on Monday, November 15. Rowe spent the previous five seasons with Lester Patrick in Victoria, the past year-and-a-half as a reserve. He was college-educated, with thick brown hair parted smartly on the right. At 5'6" and 160 pounds, he was one of the smallest players on the ice but was lightning-quick and intelligent. Muldoon could sense that Bobby was going to make a great coach after his playing days.

Carol "Cully" Wilson was a stocky 5'8", 180 pound force on skates. Blond, blue eyed and with a smile that pulled slightly up to the left, Wilson's sense of humor made him popular amongst his teammates. His eyes were soft and inviting but had a look to them that told you there was also someone else in there. Cully had established himself as one of the top forwards in hockey last season but he played on the edge of rage. Once the puck dropped, he turned into a different person and Muldoon knew he needed to help Cully learn to control that rage rather than let it control him.

In his youth, Muldoon attended Stratford College, near his hometown of St. Mary's. He was highly intellectual and highly organized. The Metropolitans had now been practicing for a week and he liked the players he had, telling the *Seattle Post-Intelligencer* that "they are as good a bunch as I have ever seen together." He was not surprised by their skill level, they were, after all, the best players from the team that won the Stanley Cup two years ago. He was, however, surprised by their competitiveness and work ethic. They did not play like prima donnas, practicing every moment at breakneck speed. These guys played like their lives and careers depended on every play.

The hometown papers had anointed Jack Walker and Cully Wilson as the stars of the Metropolitans. The honor was well deserved as both were as good as advertised. Two years ago, Jack finished in the top-10 in scoring in the National Hockey Association. Last season, Cully had done the same. They were as talented a combination as there was in hockey and the sportswriters wrote about the pair almost daily.

While Muldoon agreed Walker and Wilson were great players, he saw something special in Frank Foyston. Foyston anticipated plays. He knew where everyone was on the ice at all times. He could handle the puck. He was fearless. And, most importantly, he was humble. Everything he did on the ice made those around him better. Outsiders might not always see it, but Pete did. He was just the type of player Muldoon needed to establish his system.

A week into practice, Muldoon named Frank captain, surprising only one person: Frank. He'd always been supremely talented, but it was all coming together this year. He continuously set the standard of play in practice and the others willingly followed. When a team's most talented players are also the hardest workers, the doors for greatness can be unlocked.

Still trying to add to the roster, Pete was in the process of signing two relative newcomers, young phenom Leo Haas from Michigan and forward Bernie Morris. The papers followed Haas with excitement. His Holton, Michigan team won the American Amateur Championship last season and Muldoon thought Haas was the best player in the Midwest. In fact, Pete thought they might be getting the best amateur player ever to sign with the PCHA.

Morris, on the other hand, was unheralded having missed most of the past two seasons. The previous year in Victoria, a badly sprained heel tendon derailed much of his year. He'd injured it in training camp but played through intense pain, desperately needing to make the club. Starting the first two games, he had scored a goal on opening night before the pain was too much and he missed the next six weeks. Forsaking rest, he frantically tried to play only to be a game time scratch over much of the injury. Finally healthy, he returned just prior to a February game against Muldoon's Rosebuds, scoring two goals and impressing the coach with his speed and accuracy. The only mention of Morris' in the press, however, was a small note in the Vancouver Daily World that Muldoon had secured his transfer from Victoria.

Sitting in his room at the Arena, Muldoon was preparing to sleep for the night. Before heading to bed, he glanced at the stack of newspapers that had accumulated on his desk. He'd been so focused on practice that he hadn't read them since the players started arriving two weeks before. He'd studied Law at Stratford and remained highly interested in world events.

Like most people, he was dismayed by the current state of affairs. The world was in turmoil. The Great War in Europe was now over a year old and no one could believe the carnage. Centuries old battle tactics had not meshed well with modern weaponry and the result had been a calamitous war. They had all seen countless friends and family fight in the conflict. The longer the war raged, the higher the likelihood that he and his players would be called to fight. They had registered for the Canadian military when the war began and if the U.S. joined the war, they would have to register for the American military as well. While the war was in a distant place, it was constantly on their minds.

Closer to home, the Mexican Revolution was in its fifth year and there was fighting close to the American border with Pancho Villa and his rebels waging a tough war in Mexico. In the United States, it was a conflicted time as many citizens wanted no part in the wars raging around the globe. They did not believe America should spend American dollars and American lives fighting a war in Mexico or Europe. Americans were additionally struggling with a massive influx of immigrants over the past few decades. In the 1910 census, a third of the U.S. population, almost thirty-two million people, was either foreign-born or had a parent born abroad. With a war fought on nationalistic lines raging, domestic tensions were high over fears of loyalty.

Muldoon picked up the November 17 *Seattle Post-Intelligencer* and began reading. On November 16, one day after Cully and Bobby first arrived in Seattle, a mine exploded thirty miles southeast of Seattle in Ravensdale. The mine, almost one thousand five hundred feet below ground, exploded when a pocket of gas ignited. Thirty-one of the thirty-four miners working were killed. It was tragic. Many of the men had wives and children. It took nearly three days to dig twenty-five of the bodies from the shattered mine. Some of Pete's players had worked in mines during the summer months and he was sick thinking of the danger involved.

As he picked up the next paper, the headline focused on the war. For months, they had read of a quick victory coming for both sides. Today, was Germany's day to declare a swift victory. The Balkans had been the flash point that began the war, and the fighting there was still intense. Germany and Austria-Hungary on one side and Russia, Italy and Serbia on the other. General Frederich von Bernhardi, a member of the German general staff, said the Allies were going to lose the Balkans, that Italy would be the first to quit, and that the war would be over soon. Muldoon was not so sure.

A few papers later he read that President Wilson was working on his December 7 speech to Congress. In his State of the Union, Wilson was going to request an increase in the size of the military, and he wanted the current generation to pay for it. At the onset of the war, the United States had a standing army of two hundred thousand soldiers, compared to nearly six million in Russia, more than four million each in Germany and France and three million in Austria-Hungary. Wilson remained steadfast that the United States had no role in a foreign war though the time had come to increase the size of the military to better reflect the uncertain times in which they all lived.

Reading the same paper, he learned that former Secretary of State, Philander C. Knox had given a speech in Philadelphia discouraging the "hyphenation" of American citizenship. Americans today seemed to be German-Americans or Italian-Americans or Irish-Americans. In his speech, Knox implored Americans to see past ethnic heritage and embrace America as a melting pot. These were confusing times, Muldoon understood. With the world at war, it was hard to trust the loyalties for many citizens. For example, were German-American's sympathetic to their motherland or new homeland? He did not have these answers.

Exhausted, Muldoon picked up the last paper in the stack, that morning's *Seattle Post-Intelligencer*. On the front page, he read "Gilmour Dobie Quits Position After Victory." Dobie was the University of Washington's football coach and had just finished his eighth consecutive season without a loss. His record at the University was an astounding 52-0-2. There had been rumblings of Dobie leaving for a week, but Muldoon was still shocked. Just yesterday, he had taken the boys to see the team play. On a cold, rainy Thanksgiving Day, they watched Washington destroy Colorado 46-0. Dobie still had one year remaining on his contract so many, including Muldoon, hoped calmer heads would prevail and that he would return.

As he finished reading, he set the papers in the garbage and laid down to sleep for the night.

**

The copper mine shrinking in the distance, Bernie Morris' mind raced between more thoughts than he could process. The train's rumble did little to calm his brain. The sun had set long ago but the moon provided plenty of light. He was glad to see the mine fade from view. He was sad Minnie and the baby were not joining him. He was worried about making the team. He was alone. Again.

Relationships were not easy for him and his marriage to Minnie was complicated. Olive would turn two in January and he wished they would be with him to celebrate. Minnie, however, chose to remain with her parents in Moose Jaw. He had not argued.

Pete Muldoon had wired yesterday asking him to come to Seattle. He played last season with Victoria, but the Aristocrats had not offered him a spot this fall. They won the league the year before his arrival but had imploded last season, finishing 4-12 and in last place. Lester Patrick was so frustrated he'd cut all but two players, himself and Bobby Genge.

Bernie was relieved to be getting this opportunity. Muldoon asked him to leave tomorrow and arrive by Tuesday but he was glad to leave everything behind and just play hockey again. He packed his belongings that day and left the high hills and mine of Phoenix, British Columbia. He entered America at the port of entry in Marcus, Washington, and then on to Spokane to catch the *Number 25*. The train left at 8:30 p.m. and his mind still raced hours later as they began the ascent up the eastern slopes of the Cascade Mountains. Exhaustion slowly overtook him and he fell asleep sitting upright in his seat, his head leaning against the window.

Bernie awoke as the train rumbled into King Street station in Seattle. It was Monday, November 29 and the weather was cold and clear. He was ready for practice and couldn't wait to get off the train. As he walked out of the station, the Smith Tower stood dauntingly in front of him. A white pyramid sat atop a finger of office floors housing men working on things he couldn't comprehend. He'd visited his uncle in America ten years before but had never seen a structure so tall. It intimidated him. When he turned around, he saw Mt. Rainier. He'd seen mountains most of his life but had never seen anything with Rainier's majesty. He took a deep breath and started walking.

He moved slowly up fourth avenue, tightly clutching his belongings. The internal tension overwhelmed him. He was tired of thinking and just wanted to get on the ice. At 5'7" and 145 pounds, Bernie's size blended in with the average citizen walking the streets that morning. His green eyes timidly looked down at the sidewalk as he walked. His brown hair slicked back with a face that did not carry an extra ounce of fat on it, the skin pulled taut over high cheek bones and a strong jaw line.

As he climbed the gentle slope, he was awestruck by the steep hills to his right and the water and mountains to his left. Even though he had never seen so much natural beauty, it did little to calm his mind. He needed to make this team. He needed to change the circumstances of his life. He needed to provide Olive all that he had never had. He just needed to get on the ice. It was the only place that made sense to him.

Finally arriving at the arena, he walked in the front door and was warmly greeted by Pete Muldoon, who was impressed Bernie had arrived a day early. Pete's huge smile and easy tone made Bernie feel more at ease. As Muldoon walked him to the locker room, he informed Bernie they were practicing today at half past one and to expect a crowd. The people of Seattle were thrilled to have professional sports in their city and had been attending practice in droves. The butterflies in his stomach immediately kicked back in. He was in a foreign country, in a big city playing with new teammates and now he was going to have to take the ice for the first time in front of a crowd. He needed to make this team. He needed to block out these thoughts and just get on the ice.

Entering the locker room, Bernie immediately felt even more intimidated until Bobby Rowe quickly ran over to greet him. The pair had spent much of last season on Victoria's bench. Bernie's insecurity again began to fade.

Behind Bobby were five players engrossed in a lighthearted conversation. They must be the guys from Toronto. The intimidation kicked right back in. He was fairly certain the player on the left was Jack Walker, one of the best players in hockey. With him was Eddie Carpenter, who towered nearly a half-foot taller than Bernie. Next to Eddie was Cully Wilson; he was the youngest of the bunch but had made a name for himself last season. To his right was Hap Holmes, the outstanding goalie. The final player must be Frank Foyston. Frank was another great forward. With Bobby, Jack, Cully and Frank all playing his position, Bernie wasn't sure where he fit in. How was he going to make this team?

Bobby had grown up in the same area as the former Blueshirts and began to call them over to make introductions. Before he could form a word, Frank was already leading the other men over to say hi. The look in Frank's eyes immediately put Bernie at ease. He had heard about Bernie's speed and scoring ability and was quickly praising his skills.

As the eight men stood in the locker room and talked, Muldoon slowly took command of the conversation, unofficially beginning their first team meeting. Pete talked to them about the type of team he wanted. He was going to put players in the best spots to maximize their talents. Pete believed in a team game rather than players hogging the puck and relying on individual rushes to score. Muldoon wanted them to play a combination game. He wanted them to maintain their spacing and create openings for each other. If each guy could play his best in a way that made those around him better, the Metropolitans were going to be tough to beat. Nodding in unison, the guys liked what they were hearing.

Excited to finally address the team, Muldoon's cadence was energetic and passionate. Looking the boys in the eye, he talked to them about the roster. He had built it on speed and athleticism, wanting the best athletes playing their fastest. He trusted his players to see the game and make decisions at full speed. They had never heard a coach talk to players like this or explain hockey in such simple terms. Although they wanted to glance around to gauge the others' reactions, Muldoon's energy and passion were so captivating that their eyes remained fixed on him.

Winning was like a wheel. The bigger the wheel, the more effort to get it going but the faster it would roll. He knew it was easier to make a smaller wheel, to make players conform to simpler strategies but that wasn't going to let them play their best hockey. He wanted the boys to push out, to play a game faster than their opponents could handle. To play this style, they were going to have to be in superb condition. They were going to continue to skate hard in practice.

Muldoon knew it was going to take some time to get the players to own the system, but their excitement was palpable. Finished, he walked back to his office to prepare for practice and left them alone.

Bernie could not believe the warmth of the environment. They all laughed so easily and told stories praising the men around them. He'd never felt so welcome in his life. He'd never felt like he belonged somewhere like this before. Much of the nervous energy left him and had been replaced by excitement. He quickly put on his gear and finally took the ice.

**

On Friday, December 3, Pete Muldoon named his team. He was moving Bobby Rowe from forward to play alongside Eddie Carpenter on defense with Hap Holmes in goal. Frank Foyston would play rover. Cully Wilson would play right wing and Jack Walker left wing. Bernie Morris had impressed them all and for now would be starting at center.

Practices had been intense but the team loved Muldoon. Pete brought in top amateur skaters to practice against but the Mets had been too fast for them. The flow to the game out west suited them to perfection and the amateurs couldn't keep up. Muldoon himself would often practice against the forward line, continuously pushing them to improve. They repeatedly practiced their combination work and they skated non-stop, wobbling home each night physically exhausted.

Leo Haas finally arrived the next day, two weeks late and complaining that the cable with his travel itinerary never reached him. Frustrated, Muldoon had pulled the offer but then relented and given Haas a second chance. If nothing else, the team needed a substitute.

Ticket sales for Metropolitans' games had been brisk. Many fans had already purchased tickets to all nine home games and the opening game had been nearly sold out for a week, reserved seats going for $1 per ticket. The players sensed the city's excitement. "Hockey's going to be good here," Cully Wilson predicted in the *Seattle Star.* "This rink won't hold all the crowds. And, the team will be a great one."

When Monday rolled around, the team announced that Mayor Hiram Gill would drop the first puck in Tuesday night's inaugural game. A confident Pete Muldoon and the Mets opened against Lester Patrick's Victoria Aristocrats. "We expect to win, but by a close score," Muldoon told the *Seattle Star.* "Victoria has a fast, tricky team, but I think our bunch has the edge."

For two-and-a-half-weeks, media interest in the Metropolitans had been high. Articles educating the populace on the rules as well as introducing the players had run almost daily in all three Seattle papers. The charismatic Muldoon was the antithesis of the tight-lipped Gil Dobie and the media loved him for it. Pete was quickly forming strong relationships with the writers covering the team, including a 21-year old sports reporter for the *Seattle Post-Intelligencer,* Royal Brougham.

Born in St. Louis, Brougham moved with his family to Seattle's Queen Anne Hill as a child. He attended the Warren Avenue School before moving on to Franklin High School. Brougham dropped out in 1910 to take a job as a copy boy in the sports department at the *Seattle Post-Intelligencer.* His folksy, honest personality helped him to quickly ascend the ranks from errand boy to trusted reporter.

The Warren Avenue School, coincidentally, would be torn down in 1959 to clear the grounds for the impending Century 21 Exposition World's Fair. The school house was replaced by the Washington State Coliseum, later renamed KeyArena and soon the future home for the NHL in Seattle.

Brougham had agreed to become the team's official scorer and was spending considerable time with Muldoon, eager to learn the rules of hockey and the nuances of each player. One rule that Muldoon had to explain to Royal was the new offsides rule. Incessantly tweaking the game to make play faster and better reward athleticism, the Patricks had changed the rule two seasons ago. Previously, all players had to be behind the puck or fervently trying to get behind the puck to avoid an offsides penalty. With the new rule, the league was going to allow forward passes between two blue lines painted near center ice. The players and fans loved the rule because it greatly increased scoring.

As Muldoon prepared for bed that evening, his mind raced going over the next night's contest. He hoped for a large crowd and that they gave that crowd a great game. And, he hoped they were in good enough condition to skate a full sixty minutes. He knew it was a long season but wanted the team to get out to a fast start and build some confidence. He couldn't wait to see his players compete.

As he looked at his night stand, he could see the stack of newspapers from the last week. Needing to get his mind off the game, he picked up the first newspaper and began reading. It had been a bloody week in the Mexican Revolution. President Wilson had kept American troops out of the conflict, but on Friday, November 26, Pancho Villa's rebels had been chased by the Obregon forces into the border town of Nogales. When a crowd of onlookers from the American side ran to the border to watch the fighting, U.S. soldiers quickly moved them back before Villa's snipers fired on the crowd, killing two soldiers and wounding eight. Under orders to only fire if fired upon, the American soldiers responded in force, killing twenty of Villa's men. The survivors fled into the hills.

It had also been a bloody week in the Great War. The Austrian Army had taken the town of Mitrovica in Serbia. Austria now had more than one hundred ten thousand Serbian soldiers in prison, nearly one-third of military aged Serbs. Reading further, he learned the Ottoman Empire was on the offensive. The Turks had launched a surprise attack in Gallipoli and now controlled a large section of Allied trenches. A Turkish submarine also sank a British passenger ship, killing twenty-five. The entire front page seemed to be dedicated to the war. There was truly fighting everywhere across the European continent. Sighing, Muldoon knew this was going to be a deadly war.

The last paper he read was yesterday's Sunday *Seattle Times*. One headline read "T.R. Pleads for Preparedness." Former President Teddy Roosevelt was leading the preparedness movement, an effort to modernize and ready the U.S. military for the Great War. Roosevelt felt strongly that the military rapidly needed more men and more training.

Finally tired, Muldoon threw the newspapers in the waste basket and laid down to sleep. Tomorrow, would be a big day.

**

Tuesday, December 7 had finally arrived. The boys all awoke to a wet and windy late fall day. The temperature that day was supposed to reach a high of forty-seven degrees with winds from the south. The headline in the *Seattle Times* read "Diver Fires on U.S. Ship." An Austrian submarine had fired on a Standard Oil tanker in the Mediterranean.

In Washington, D.C., the president was preparing to deliver his State of the Union address while in Seattle, Muldoon and the Metropolitans players were preparing to take on Lester Patrick's Victoria Aristocrats at the Ice Arena. Two thousand five hundred spectators were excited to jam pack the arena and witness the birth of major league sports in the city. The puck was set to drop at exactly 8:30 p.m.

At eight o'clock, Pete Muldoon sat at the desk in his office going over his roster for the night. His black hair was combed back and parted slightly on the left. A high collar and neck tie perfectly complimented his three-

13

piece suit. With eight players, he would only have one substitute, Leo Haas. It was early in the season, but Muldoon was confident that his players' conditioning would allow them to skate away from the Aristocrats late in the game.

Fifteen minutes later, Muldoon took a deep breath, exhaled and stood up. He slowly walked out of his office and into the locker room to address the team. As he entered, the boys looked great in their green, red and white barber pole sweaters, with "Seattle" written on the curve of a red "S" on their chests. The Patricks had decided to put numbers on the sweaters for the season. They wanted to sell game programs and thought numbers would make it easier for fans to distinguish each player. The mood in the locker room was excited but no different than any other opening day. The boys had been playing hockey for years so knew how to prepare themselves for the long season.

Muldoon briefly addressed the team. Tonight was going to be a fun night to show the people of Seattle how hockey was played. He wanted them to play hard. He wanted them to play fast. And, he wanted them to enjoy the night. He told them to get a break and take the ice.

Foyston gathered the team in the middle of the locker room and spoke a few words of encouragement. He was excited to compete with this group of guys and called the break. Cully was the first to take the ice, clearly excited and amped to play. Next, Bobby Rowe and the rest of the Toronto boys took the ice together, Leo Haas trailing close behind. Bernie Morris exited the locker room last.

In most locker rooms, a mirror hangs on the wall by the door so players can give themselves a quick check before taking the ice. Over the years, Bernie had developed the habit of looking at himself in the mirror as he exited in an effort to inject confidence into a mind desperately in need. Today, as much as he tried, there was no confidence to project. His eyes and posture betrayed him, exposing only nerves and trepidation. His breathing was rapid and his heart raced. Taking the ice, he was overwhelmed by the capacity crowd loudly screaming and cheering. It took a few minutes during warm-ups to settle his nerves, but he slowly got ready to play.

At exactly half past the hour, referee Mickey Ion called both teams in for the faceoff. Morris glided slowly to center ice first, waiting for the Aristocrats' rookie center, Michael O'Leary. The boys formed a circle around the pair, eagerly awaiting the puck. Ion escorted Mayor Gill out to center ice for the puck-drop. Play began. The Seattle Metropolitans began.

# CHAPTER 2 – DAWN OF A NEW CENTURY

The scorching summer sun sent waves of heat burning down on his trembling arms and legs. Dripping with sweat and gasping for air, Frank squatted down, wrapped his tiny arms around the bulky rock and hoisted it into position. Utterly exhausted, he collapsed in a heap as laughter erupted around him.

The dawn of a new century brings hope and promise of things to come. For nine-year old Frank Foyston and his six siblings, it meant a new fence surrounding the forty-acre family farm. In the first summers of the twentieth century, the boys' job was to build a rock wall around the farm. Whether they were playing sports or working the fields with their father, whenever they came across a large stone, they carried it to the growing wall encompassing the farm and cemented it in place.

An intense competition had sprung up between the boys to see who could find the biggest rock on the property and trek it to the budding wall. Today, Frank had carried a stone weighing more than his diminutive frame halfway across the farm. It was easily the largest stone that any of them had found and Frank beamed with pride. His brothers were amused, not an ounce of jealousy between them.

For the Foystons, the joys of childhood and a strong family life were abundant. The boys competed in everything they did and were the best of friends. Charles and Bert were the oldest, then Frank, Fred, Carlen, Harry and their sister Jessie. Their lives consisted of school, sports and working on the farm. They played baseball and lacrosse all spring and summer and hockey in the fall and winter.

The boys were building a baseball field on the farm when Frank uncovered the rock. He quickly ran to the barn to grab the tools necessary to excavate the stone as his brothers stood and laughed. The rules of the competition stated that for the rock to count, each boy had to handle the rock alone from extraction to insertion on the wall. Not one of the brothers thought Frank had any chance of trudging this behemoth the distance necessary to install it on the wall. He, on the other hand, never had an ounce of doubt.

Frank steadfastly dug around the rock and lifted it out of the ground. Quickly scanning the landscape, he chose a path to the rock wall where he could periodically stop and support the rock while he rested. A tree stump here, fence post there, boulder, farm equipment or whatever else he needed, Frank slogged the rock across the farm and into place. It was just like him to figure out a way to make the impossible, possible.

Despite being the middle son, Frank had the uncanny ability to bring them all together. He could reign in any of his brothers for the most egregious offense or could disarm their frustration with just the look in his eye. Although the boys played all sports, hockey was their favorite. They played non-stop. Before the ice was thick enough to skate on, the boys would stomp the snow into a compact, hard surface using two wooden posts on each end as goals. For pucks, they'd find a tree limb the correct diameter and cut five or six inch-and-a-half thick pieces giving them a few days' worth of prized pucks.

As they got older, they moved on to play at the Minesing Princess Rink that their father helped build. Bert, Frank and Fred soon formed the nucleus of the Minesing Green Shirts. Bert played cover point, Fred played center and Frank, with his left-handed shot played left wing. Their youngest brothers, Carlen and Harry, followed every move of the older boys.

Frank was quickly beginning to separate himself from the pack. Early one season, a group of boys working at the basket factory in Minesing formed a team and challenged the boys from the farms, including the Foystons, to a game at the Princess Rink. The factory workers looked down on the team of farmers, thinking themselves far superior. One of the local businessmen bet Frank fifty cents he wouldn't score ten goals against the factory boys. Frank scored eighteen.

Scouts were beginning to notice Frank and he was invited to join the Barrie Colts. Twice a week, he had to make the ten mile trip to Barrie for practice by horse and cutter, often taking an hour or an hour-and-a-half to get there depending on how hard the snow was falling. For games in the neighboring towns, he sometimes traveled all night to arrive back at the farm as the rest of the family was waking up for their morning chores. Soon, the Toronto Blueshirts of the National Hockey Association came calling.

**

The two-story brick building on Victoria Avenue East in Brandon, Manitoba served as both the Courthouse for the Western Judicial District of Manitoba and County Jail. The sand-colored exterior bricks stood in stark contrast to the depressing atmosphere inside. The drabness derived from dark wooden benches and desks reflecting scant rays of natural light.

Three weeks shy of his ninth birthday, Bernie Morris sat on a cold, hard bench inside the courtroom staring blankly at the wall. Eleven-year-old Thomas and seven-year-old Edward sat dejectedly on both sides of him. Breathing shallowly and quietly, the three brothers waited silently for the judge to finish speaking to their Uncle Thomas.

The boys' parents, Edward and Flora, sailed from Ireland in 1889, with one-year-old son Thomas in tow. Edward's older brother Thomas had emigrated to Brandon, Manitoba in the Canadian Plains years before and Edward had been eager to reunite. Flora gave birth to a set of twins shortly after their arrival in Canada, Lawrence and Hubert. The first of the Morris tragedies, it had been a complicated pregnancy and delivery and both boys survived only one day. Bernie was born almost exactly one year later, his brother Edward, two years after that.

Twelve months after Edward's birth, Flora was once again pregnant. On January 3, 1894, Bernie's brother John was born. It had again been a complicated delivery and Flora had not survived. Nearly five months after his third birthday, Bernie had lost his mother. They would bury John soon thereafter.

Their father Edward tried to nurture the boys as best he could, but it was not easy to run a farm and raise three children. Two months before the court hearing, on May 27, 1899, Edward too had tragically passed away. At eight years old, Bernie was now an orphan. His father had died without a will so Uncle Thomas and the boys were in court trying to gain control over Edward's estate. Bernie and his brothers had been in a fog since their father's passing.

The judge finished conversing with Uncle Thomas, closed the folder on his desk and nodded, dismissing Thomas back to the boys. Edward's estate, valued at $4,850, including the farm and the care of Thomas, Bernie and Edward had been passed to Uncle Thomas. Still in a daze, the boys gathered their belongings and despondently followed their uncle out of the courthouse.

Life without their parents was not easy for Bernie or his brothers. Their responsibilities on the farm increased drastically as they grew in size, leaving little time for school. After the eighth grade, Bernie withdrew from school and began working full-time on the farm. The brothers' only childhood outlets were the sports they played with the neighboring boys, hockey being their favorite. Bernie was always the fastest in any sport, especially on the ice. If he had a step on another boy, they never caught him. The ice was always the one place he felt good about himself.

Eleven years after taking the boys in, their Uncle Thomas died on

September 19, 1910. Barely adults, the Morris boys were now without any family and struggling to run the farm. It quickly became too much and they lost it, now needing to look elsewhere for jobs. Twenty-year-old Thomas moved to town and took a position as a clerk. Eighteen-year-old Bernie took a job in the factory making cigars while sixteen-year-old Edward moved to Moose Jaw in Saskatchewan and took a job as a machinist.

Bernie continued to play hockey and joined the Brandon Shamrocks late that fall, averaging a goal a game. The next season, he moved to Moose Jaw with his brother Edward and played for the Robin Hoods, scoring 21 goals in just eight games. Hockey was beginning to look like it might provide a future for Bernie.

In Moose Jaw, he met twenty-year-old Minnie and they had hit it off. Minniebelle Conwad was the oldest and only daughter of Samuel and Edith McMicken's five children. Minnie had been born a few months after her mom's eighteenth birthday and her stepfather Sam had married Edith five years later. Significantly older than her half-brothers and relied upon to help care for them, it hadn't always been the easiest life. Bernie decided to stay in Moose Jaw that offseason with his brother and Minnie.

When November came, Bernie took a job in the copper mines in Phoenix, British Columbia and starred for the local hockey team. When the season ended, he returned to Moose Jaw and Minnie. Within weeks of his homecoming, Minnie was pregnant and the pair quickly married. Soon, the two-time defending Stanley Cup Champion Quebec Bulldogs of the National Hockey Association offered him a contract to play the following season.. After more than twenty years of tragedy and struggle, Bernie's luck was finally changing.

**

Eliza Treacy glimmered with pride. Her son Linton was on his way. Handsome, charismatic and highly intelligent, she knew he was destined for great things. His charisma inspired those around him in a way that was different from the other boys. She loved watching them follow Linton's every word. He had just begun his first year away at university and had landed a job for five dollars a week in a law office. Her eyes sparkled when he told her the news. Eliza had always wanted him to go into Law. All their hard work was paying off and a remarkable future was within Linton's grasp.

Colonel Linton Treacy was born June 4, 1887, in St. Mary's Ontario, the fourth of five children born to Alexander and Eliza, second-generation Canadians. Alexander's parents had immigrated from Ireland, Eliza's from France. The Treacy's were a prominent family of carpenters and farmers that were early settlers to St. Mary's in the 1850s. A relative, George, had built a stunning stone mansion quarried from local limestone on Church

Street.    Alexander and Eliza worked hard to provide a nurturing environment for their children.

In addition to his studies, Linton loved sports. He excelled in lacrosse, baseball and was a tremendous skater. He starred as a goalie in the Ontario Hockey Association but his mom loved to watch him dance on the ice. She did not care to understand sports, but there was something beautiful about watching Linton glide across the ice with a partner.

Away at Stratford, Linton starred for a local baseball team. He was maintaining his grades and his job at the law office so didn't feel the need to tell his parents. Soon, scouts from the semi-pro teams came sniffing around campus. The team from Brandon offered him $150 a month to quit school and join their team. He didn't need the money, but compared to the five dollars he made each week at the law office, it was an astounding sum. And he was going to get to play ball. He accepted their offer with trepidation, terrified to tell his parents.

**

One lone table stood in the middle of the brightly lit locker room. Linton sat on the edge, gloves on, staring straight ahead as people rushed about the room. A single poster hung on the back of the locker room door. It read:

JACK LESTER vs. PETE MULDOON
10 Rounds Boxing Contest,
DREAMLAND RINK, TUESDAY NIGHT, JANUARY 17, 1911
Prices – Admission, $1; Reserved, $2; Ringside Seats, $3.

It had been a few years now since he left Stratford and he was finally used to seeing the moniker "Pete Muldoon." His parents had been surprisingly supportive of his desire to pursue athletics but had asked him to use a pseudonym. The Traecy's were hard working people and they did not want the family name sullied by an athlete's pursuits. It had hurt initially but Linton had too much respect for his parents not to abide by their wishes. He had chosen the name Colonel Pete Muldoon, but everyone just knew him as Pete.

Pete played one summer of baseball in Brandon before moving to Seattle to train as a boxer. The city was booming the summer he arrived, hosting the Alaska-Yukon-Pacific Exposition World's Fair on the University of Washington campus. He advanced all the way to the finals of the AYP boxing championships before losing to Los Angeles' Dick Allen, who outweighed him 237- to 160- pounds. That fall, he won the Pacific Northwest amateur heavyweight championship before winning the light-heavyweight AAU title in California.

19

He settled in Ballard, a neighborhood north of downtown and was fighting for the Ballard Athletic Club, located at Twenty-Second and Market Street. A massive construction project was just getting under way in Ballard a few blocks west of the club as Hiram Chittenden was leading efforts to connect Lake Washington to Puget Sound through a series of channels and locks. Now twenty-three years old, Muldoon was enjoying tremendous success boxing, gaining headlines and large crowds as the main event at smokers around the region. He'd turned pro last June and was 3-0. Jack Lester was going to be a good test for Pete. Muldoon was the faster, more skilled fighter but his 158-pounds was nearly thirty pounds lighter than Lester's 185. Heavily favored, Lester was 13-0-3 and managed by Tommy Burns, the former heavyweight champion who had lost his title two years ago to the legendary Jack Johnson. Burns was grooming Lester for a potential shot at the title.

The fight had been scheduled at the Dreamland Rink in Tacoma before immense fan interest had caused Muldoon's manager, Lonnie Austin, to change the venue to the larger Tacoma Theater. After a trip to Tacoma to inspect the theater, Austin deemed it unsuitable and the fight was moved back to the Dreamland Rink with Austin bringing in carpenters to turn the Dreamland into a tiered arena for better fan sightlines. Austin also arranged a special six-car Great Northern train to take spectators to and from Tacoma, beginning and ending its journey in Ballard. The train was scheduled to leave Ballard at 6:30 p.m., stop downtown at 7:00 p.m. before arriving in Tacoma at 8:15 p.m. After the bout, the train would depart Tacoma at 11:30 p.m., dropping off the last of its passengers in Ballard at 1:15 a.m.

A knock at the door signaled it was time. The activity, intensity and volume in the room spiked as Muldoon's handlers began to usher him out to the ring. The door swung open, bringing the sound waves of a capacity crowd coursing into the room. Muldoon, dressed in a black floor-length robe inlaid with gold designs began the slow walk down to the ring, passing through the wooden risers packed with screaming fans until he reached the canvas. Lester glared from the opposing corner.

Referee Jack Grant called both fighters to the center and the bell rang. Right away, it was evident Muldoon had too much speed for Lester as he electrified the crowd with his feet and constant jabs to the larger man's chin. The mass of fans cheered wildly every time Muldoon connected although Pete could immediately tell that the jabs were not fazing his opponent. Muldoon's strategy was to stay away from Lester, using his speed and jabs to exhaust the bigger fighter. At the end of the first round, the crowd was in a frenzy for Muldoon who had taken the round.

When the bell rang to begin the second round, a different Lester stormed out towards Muldoon. No longer waiting for an opportunity to land a punch against the quicker Muldoon, Lester attacked, suffocating his opponent and containing him at close range. Muldoon responded with a flurry of shots to the body and head before Lester grabbed Muldoon, forcing Grant to intervene and break up the pair. The crowd cheered the action wildly. As they resumed, Lester immediately charged again with the same result, this time landing a few punches before Grant once more intervened.

The third time Lester rushed Muldoon, Pete landed a combination before Lester sensed an opening and blasted Muldoon's chin with a vicious uppercut, immediately dropping him to his hands and knees. The crowd gasped as Grant pounced, counting, "one ... two ... three ... four ... five ... six ... seven ... eight," before Muldoon rose to his feet. As the fight resumed, Lester continued his barrage, charging Muldoon again. Pete fired off a lightning fast jab that Lester absorbed before the larger fighter "landed a staggering left on the jaw," dropping Muldoon to the canvas once again. Grant counted to seven before Muldoon was standing again, ready to fight. Lester immediately ambushed him once again but Muldoon quickly escaped the rush, using his speed to get away in an attempt to catch his bearings. Lester just reset and stampeded again, pinning Muldoon against the ropes. A crushing right cross to the chin dropped Muldoon again. Staggering to get back on his feet, Muldoon was saved by the bell at the count of nine.

During the break, Tommy Burns stood over his protégé, screaming above the crowd noise to continue the attack. In Muldoon's corner, the fight had not left Pete. It was only one round and he believed the fight was still his to win. His trainer, Ceis Fitzgerald, beseeched him to dodge Lester's advances faster and use his speed, continuously looking for an opening to drop the behemoth. The bell rang and round three began.

Lester immediately attacked as he had in round two. Jack charged and grabbed Muldoon before he could escape, throwing him to the canvas. Pete quickly popped back up as Burns screamed combinations for Lester to execute from the corner. Muldoon evaded Lester and moved around the ring, forcing the larger man to follow him with the mostly partisan crowd cheering Muldoon loudly. Lester charged Muldoon once again, with Pete popping Lester with a quick right cross as he escaped. Lester's momentum plus the force of the punch carried him into the ropes and then through them, landing forcefully on the floor and bringing the crowd to its feet. Lester sprang up immediately and was back in the ring ready to fight. On Grant's resumption, Lester charged again and landed a right to Muldoon's neck, dropping him for a fifth time in the fight.

Muldoon, shaken badly, rose again and proved to Grant that he was ready to fight. On Grant's signal, Lester attacked again showering a barrage of uppercuts and crosses to Muldoon's head. Burns screamed "follow up, follow up" as Lester punished Muldoon. A left cross started Muldoon falling towards the canvas once again before Lester landed an enormous right uppercut to his jaw sending Muldoon sprawling onto his back.

Muldoon amazingly rose again, ready to fight. Burns continued to scream instructions at Lester, yelling "Shift Jack, shift quick." Lester pounced again at Muldoon and landed a right, dropping him again for the seventh time in the fight. As Pete struggled to his feet, Fitzgerald threw in the ringside sponge, signifying he had seen enough. Grant waived off the fight and raised Lester's right hand in victory.

*The Seattle Times* wrote the next day that the fight "was simply one in which a very strong man, with no fear broke down the guard of a man who boxes cleverly with men of less strength." Muldoon had fought valiantly, never giving up despite being knocked down seven times in the fight. He was simply just not strong enough to stand up to the larger professional heavyweights.

Pete recovered quickly from the fight. He continued to be the Ballard Athletic Club's top performer and headliner at smokers around town. In April, Jack Tibbits was scheduled to fight Billy Ross in Yakima. Just days before the fight, Tibbits badly injured his arm and Lonnie Austin asked Muldoon to fill in.

Despite not having prepared for the fight, Muldoon pummeled Ross. Ross was tough and strong but a wild swinger and Muldoon was athletic enough to avoid his punches. Through the first six rounds, Ross had only landed one punch on Muldoon. In the seventh, Ross' landed his second punch of the night. It was a devastating blow and below the belt, immediately dropping Muldoon to the canvas where he was counted out by the referee. Pete was "winning by a city block when he was struck low in the seventh round and put out of commission." The fight doctor quickly examined Muldoon and declared the punch illegal. Referee Eddie Berry still gave the fight to Ross, enraging the crowd. The chief of police had been sitting ringside and was infuriated. According to the Seattle Times, "Berry escaped arrest but was given until the next morning to shake the dust of Yakima off his feet."

It was quickly becoming evident that boxing was not the future that Muldoon wanted for himself. The next spring, he was given an opportunity to train the professional lacrosse team in Vancouver. Coaching excited him and he gladly accepted the offer although he continued to box when time allowed. That winter, Frank Patrick offered him a position training both the Vancouver Millionaires and New Westminster Royals hockey teams who shared an arena. Soon, his pugilistic fires were extinguished by his passions for hockey.

# CHAPTER 3 – BIRTH OF THE PCHA

A westward expansion was occurring all over the North American continent. Vast wildernesses were becoming thriving metropolises. Gold and timber were in abundance and there were fortunes to be made for speculators of both.

In 1907, Montreal businessman Joseph Patrick purchased a sawmill and large tract of land in Nelson, British Columbia, and moved his family out west. His oldest boys, Lester and Frank were two of the best hockey players in Canada. Twenty-four-year-old Lester was coming off back-to-back Stanley Cup championships as the captain of the Montreal Wanderers. Frank had recently graduated from McGill University where he too had starred in hockey. At twenty-one years old, he was a prized recruit of the top professional teams. Their hockey dreams, however, would be put on hold to build the family business.

Joe's father had emigrated from Ireland in 1848, settling in Eastern Canada. A great potato famine had struck the island in 1845, decimating the food supply, economy and ultimately, Ireland's population. A million people would lose their lives to the famine and more than a million more would flee, causing the population to fall from a peak of more than eight million in 1840 to just above five million at the close of the century.

A lawyer in Ireland, Joe's father joined his sister and her family to farm the lands surrounding Montreal. Soon, his wife and three children joined him in Canada with seven more offspring, including Joseph, born thereafter. It was a happy childhood, but his father's plight had instilled a deep ambition in Joe nonetheless. A job as a clerk in a nearby general store soon turned into ownership of a rival store, then a lumber company near Quebec City that expanded into Montreal where he raised his family in prosperity. The business continued to grow until the spring of 1907 when Joe bought the swath of pristine British Columbia timberland and turned his business interests into an empire.

Upon arriving in Nelson, the boys were surprised to find a top local hockey team to join. Lester and Frank starred for the team while they helped their father run the timber business. Soon, the family helped finance a new arena in town. Four short years later, in the early months of 1911, Joe sold the thriving business for $400,000. Now wealthy and with experience growing a hockey club, the exceptional businessmen set out on a new adventure to build a major professional league out west. Thus, the birth of the Pacific Coast Hockey Association.

**

*December 3, 1913*
*Emmett Quinn, Montreal:*
  *Kindly notify all NHA club owners that Coast League waiver claim on all new players in our territory for this season with the exception of George Rochon and Bernie Morris, whom we have suspended. We strongly recommend your league to try out the new offside rule. The unanimous opinion of spectators, critics and players here is favorable.*
  *(Signed)*
*Frank A. Patrick*

Bernie was crushed. He thought his break had finally come when the Quebec Bulldogs had offered him a contract the previous spring. Bulldogs star Joe Hall had told him not to worry about the wire he received from Frank Patrick requiring him to report to Vancouver. Similar communications had been sent every year since the two leagues began competing over players. None had ever been enforced.

Bernie hopped a train back east, excited to finally sign his contract and play hockey at the major league level. However, the paper Quebec City officials handed him instead was a new missive from Frank Patrick. When they explained to him that it meant they could now sign any other western player except George Rochon and him, he was confused and devastated.

The NHA and PCHA had been warring over players since the first year of the Pacific Coast league. The NHA had imposed a salary cap for the 1911-12 season before they knew a rival league had sprung up out west. Initially, the NHA owners were not afraid of the coast league but the Patricks had two things the eastern owners did not: money and deep relationships with the top players. For many years, the best NHA players had been teammates and close friends of the Patricks. The brothers were simply using those friendships and offers of significantly larger salaries to recruit. It didn't take long for most of hockey's biggest stars to jump ship and head west that first season.

The NHA responded the next year by unsuccessfully trying to poach those same players, touching off a player war between the two rival leagues.

The Patricks leveraged that war perfectly over the next few years to legitimize the coastal league. The previous summer, the two leagues had finally reached an agreement to respect each other's rosters and, equally as important, to allow the winner of the PCHA to play the winner of the NHA for the Stanley Cup.

In addition, the agreement split the country in half, using Port Arthur as the line of demarcation. All unsigned players west of Port Arthur were property of the PCHA and all players east were property of the NHA unless the respective league waived their rights to that player. Because Moose Jaw was west of the line, Bernie was property of the coast league and they were not willing to waive their rights to him. Despite the fact he had committed to Quebec City before the leagues had reached their agreement, he was being suspended for signing with the wrong league. For the first time in their history, the leagues had reached a formal agreement and more importantly were enforcing it. Bernie was collateral damage.

He quietly went back to Moose Jaw and Minnie. He got a job in Regina and signed with the Regina Victorias, scoring two goals in his first game. Inconceivably, the Moose Jaw Robin Hoods protested the Saskatchewan Amateur Hockey Association, claiming he was their property. Bernie, once again, found himself suspended. The low point came on December 30, when he sat alone in the stands watching Regina destroy Moose Jaw 11-4. Six days later, SAHA President A. Eustace Hayden ruled that Bernie must play for Moose Jaw or not at all. Disgusted in the behavior of those in power, Bernie chose the latter. Two days later, Olive Irene Morris was born. If there was a silver lining, he had at least been home for Olive's birth. The next day, he left for another winter in the mines playing for the Phoenix team. For Bernie, it was a wasted year of hockey.

**

Nearly six thousand miles from the west coast of North America, a motorcade of black Gräft & Stift Double Phaeton automobiles rushed Archduke Franz Ferdinand and his wife Sophie up Sarajevo's cobbled Appel Quay. Morning rains had left a spectacular early summer morning for the future Austrian monarch. The fourth person to hold the title of heir to the throne during Franz Joseph's sixty-five years as Kaiser, Franz Ferdinand could be both boorish and prejudiced. His morganatic marriage to Sophie had added impertinence to his many characterizations so he was not the ideal successor to his uncle, nor to many in the monarchy.

He was in Sarajevo to conduct military exercises along the southern border of the Austro-Hungarian Empire as recent tensions throughout Europe had caused the major powers to drastically increase their preparedness. On the last day of his journey, June 28, he was to deliver a speech at City Hall in Sarajevo in an attempt to temper the nationalistic tensions rising in the southern dominions. It was also St. Vitus Day, a national day in neighboring Serbia that celebrated a fourteenth century war hero who had assassinated the sultan of Serbia's oppressors, the Ottoman Empire. To show his respect for the holiday, Franz Ferdinand had prepared his remarks that day in Serbo-Croat.

The Black Hand, an underground Serbian nationalist organization, had planted six assassins along the route that morning, each armed with a bomb and a pistol. As the motorcade drove to City Hall, it passed an assassin who hurled a bomb at the Archduke, missing badly. It hit one of the trailing cars, injuring a guardsman and terrifying the entire delegation. The assassin had been quickly apprehended and a major international crisis averted. Knowing they had missed their opportunity, four of the five remaining assassins fled immediately. Their leader stood dejected at the side of the road, in disbelief that they had failed their mission.

Believing it was an isolated incident, the Archduke planned to finish his official duties in Sarajevo with one stop added to the itinerary; he wanted to visit the injured guard in the hospital. A safe, direct route to the hospital was plotted and, as a final precaution, the head of the Archduke's guard stationed himself on the Gräft & Stift's running board nearest the heir presumptive.

As the motorcade sped up Appel Quay, the lead car made a wrong turn into a side street off Sarajevo's Latin Bridge. Immediately sensing the mistake, Franz Ferdinand's driver stopped to quickly turn around. Standing in front of the momentarily stopped car, on the opposite side from the head guard, happened to be Gavrilo Princip, the lead Black Hand assassin. Dumbfounded at his luck, he calmly drew the pistol from under his jacket and squeezed the trigger twice. He fired two shots that would kill the Archduke and Sophie. Two shots that would cause the death of eighteen million more in the greatest war the planet had ever seen. Two shots that would forever alter the western world.

**

It had taken a month, but on July 28, 1914, with the full support of its strongest ally Germany, Austria declared war on Serbia. The next day, Serbia's ally Russia mobilized against Austria. Two days later, Germany declared war on Russia prompting Russia's ally France to mobilize its army. After two more days, on August 3, France and Germany declared war on each other. The next day, Germany announced its intention to invade neutral Belgium, bringing Britain into the war to defend its ally. In the span of one week, over the assassination of an heir few saw fit to rule as monarch, virtually the entire continent of Europe was now at war.

Seven months later, like most of the world, Pete Muldoon was still in a state of disbelief at the war raging in Europe. When Great Britain declared war against Germany on August 4, it meant that all of the British Colonies, including Canada, were now at war. A letter had arrived for him today from England. The back of the envelope read:

*Robert Ellison, Sergeant – D Company*
*First Battalion, British Columbia Regiment, Canadian Expeditionary Forces*
*Salisbury Plains, England*

Taking a deep breath, he set the envelope on his desk and began to think about life. Quietly reflecting, he began to think about the past seven nomadic years: He'd left college and ultimately home for Brandon, then on to Seattle, up to Vancouver and now he was sitting in his office at the brand-new Hippodrome Ice Arena that had just been completed in Portland, Oregon.

At first, it was baseball. Then, his interests had turned to boxing and with that, he became infatuated with fitness. He parlayed that passion into a job training the lacrosse team in Vancouver, helping them win their first Minto Cup. He enjoyed helping the players improve physically and he loved to see their conditioning allow them to outplay their opponents late in games though he didn't love lacrosse.

Luckily, Frank Patrick had noticed the job he'd done with the lacrosse team and offered him a position training his Millionaires. He was hooked. He loved applying his knowledge to hockey and he had deeply enjoyed learning the finer points of coaching from Frank. Their discussions on hockey, however, had been his favorite. Frank saw the game on a different level than everyone else. Luckily, so did he and the two of them spent countless hours talking. He finally knew his place in the world, he wanted to train and coach a hockey team.

That offseason, the New Westminster team had folded and moved to Portland. Muldoon had been offered the chance to join them as their trainer and coach. It had been a dream come true. Now, two-thirds of the way through the season, the team was only a half game out of first place. He was pleased with the way they'd been playing though he'd found it difficult to get too excited with the war pervading most of his thoughts. With that, he took a deep breath, grabbed the letter and opened it.

A Canadian transplant like Muldoon, Robert Ellison had been one of the best soccer players on the West Coast. He played for the Celtics in Seattle while Pete was there boxing and the two had forged a close bond. The letter was dated January 15, a month ago, so Pete feared Robert was now on the front lines. Sitting up, he began to read:

*"You should have come along with us. We have had things kind of tough at times but have also had numerous good times to make up for it. We are now camping in huts,*

*which is quite an improvement over the tents, as a chap has a chance of drying his things.*

*Talk about damp. This place has Aberdeen, Washington backed off the boards for rain. And the mud is just about as bad as the brand we used to get in Winnipeg. Nick Carter, your old lacrosse player, is at present just recovering from a bad attack of cerebral spinal fever. In fact, he has been reported dead two or three times. I went to the hospital before Christmas and visited him, but since that time he has been isolated. There have been twenty four cases in camp, twelve of which died. So they have them under quarantine now for fear of contagion.*

*The English girls have taken a great fancy to the Canadians and about 1,000 or so of the continent have been married since coming here.*

*We are waiting here for orders to go to France. And this last week we have been getting the work slung at us. By all accounts, from the soldiers I have been talking to who are back from the front on furlough, the war is a good imitation of hell. Having got this far, we are all anxious to have the experience. I will be glad to get to the front because I was always, as you know, an inquisitive sort of fellow."*

        *Robert*

Pete set the letter back on the desk and exhaled deeply. He hoped for his friend's safe return and he hoped for a quick end to the war. Slowly standing up, he grabbed the letter and walked back to the locker room to address the team before practice. He quietly read them the letter, reminding the boys of the horrors of the war. Not that they needed a reminder. They all knew their play was a welcome distraction for all.

\*\*

It had been a little over four months now since a German U-Boat had sunk the *Lusitania* off the coast of Ireland, killing more than one thousand one hundred people, including one hundred twenty Americans. Germany had recently commenced unrestricted submarine warfare in the North Atlantic, sinking all military and commercial liners sailing for England. The Germans had discovered that in addition to the one thousand nine hundred passengers traveling from New York to Liverpool, the *Lusitania* would be carrying arms and munitions hidden deep within its bowels and therefore considered the *Lusitania* a military transport. The world, however, was outraged by the killing of more than a thousand innocent civilians and public opinion turned overnight to a strong anti-German sentiment, including in the United States.

While war tensions seethed in America, the Patrick brothers remained euphoric as the league was perhaps the strongest it had ever been. Frank's Vancouver Millionaires had won the league's first Stanley Cup in March. It had taken four seasons, but they had done it, a PCHA team reigned supreme.

In addition, construction was progressing on the new ice arena in

Seattle. After more than a year-and-a-half of painstaking work, there would be a Seattle team in the PCHA for the 1915-16 season. The team would be named the Metropolitans after the Metropolitan Building Company, who had helped finance the new arena on land owned by the University of Washington known as the Metropolitan Tract. Pete Muldoon had spent considerable time in Seattle prior to his work in Vancouver and Portland and had asked to coach the new team in the Sound City. Though the Rosebuds faded down the stretch after suffering injuries to two of their best players, Pete had kept them in the race until then and despite the injuries, it had been a highly successful rookie campaign for Muldoon. The Patricks had willingly obliged his request.

In Victoria, there had been talk of the military commandeering the Aristocrats' Ice Arena to use as a weapons and troop depot. The decision had recently been made to allow the Aristocrats to stay in their arena, finally making it a four-team league. With the crisis averted, the state of affairs in the PCHA was in harmony.

In Toronto, however, the state of affairs was in disarray. Blueshirts owner Frank Robinson had recently sold Frank Foyston and Harry Cameron to Eddie Livingstone's Toronto Shamrocks. Robinson had also cabled Hap Holmes with his offer for the season: there would be no salary, just a percentage of gate receipts. Robinson had been losing money the past few years so was trying to dump salary in Foyston and Cameron and was going to ensure he didn't go in the red again by only paying Hap and the others a percentage of what the team made. The Blueshirts were falling apart.

Bound by the player agreement, Muldoon feverishly scoured the western leagues recruiting players to join the Seattle team. At the same time, tensions began to escalate once again between the two major leagues. As part of the agreement struck two years prior, the Montreal Canadiens were to pay the Vancouver Millionaires $750 for star-player Newsy Lalonde. The money had not yet been received.

When Vancouver's best player, Fred "Cyclone" Taylor had shown up in Frank Patrick's office with multiple cables in hand, the final straw was broken. During the day, Cyclone worked in the immigration department for the Canadian Government offices in Vancouver. He had received a note from the government that he was being transferred back to Ottawa. In a separate cable, the Ottawa Senators had offered him a contract. Both men knew the Senators ownership had set up the work transfer to coax Cyclone into signing with them again. He quickly declined both offers and assured Frank he was remaining in Vancouver for the upcoming season. Infuriated that the Senators had broken the agreement, Patrick declared open war on the NHA.

Frank knew what was happening in Toronto so happily obliged Mr.

Frank Robinson's intention to cut salary for the upcoming season. When Frank was done, he left Robinson with only two salaries to pay that year. He had signed the other five players off the Toronto roster. Frank Foyston, Hap Holmes, Jack Walker, Eddie Carpenter and Cully Wilson would go to Seattle while Harry Cameron would join Victoria. Cameron later changed his mind and remained back east. The other five however, were soon on the *Imperial Limited* train bound for the West Coast.

The Metropolitans were now an immediate contender.

# CHAPTER 4 – FIRST HALF - 1916 SEASON

By December of 1915, Seattle was beginning to take shape. Isolated on the northwest reaches of the country, the region's stunning landscape has always inspired its creative spirit. Yet a deep-rooted need to be considered among the great American cities constantly burns below the surface of that grandeur.

Well into its first boom period, Seattle's population had exploded from just over 80,000 at the turn of the century to 240,000 by the close of the first decade. Five short years later, it was nearly 330,000. The gold rush brought wealth to the region and an intense desire to become more cosmopolitan.

In 1903, the Olmstead Brothers were hired to design a parks system master plan that was now nearing completion. Thirty new parks dotted the landscape offering activities for all. Citizens took leisurely strolls through the Washington Park Arboretum or Volunteer Park, while families picnicked and visited the zoo at Woodland Park.

Prideful locals took scenic drives in their new cars, rumbling up the series of Olmstead-designed boulevards connecting the city's parks and neighborhoods, complete with sweeping views of majesty in every direction. Each park and boulevard was constructed to offer the most panoramic views of the mountains and water encompassing Seattle.

Ingenuity, innovation and ambition coursed through the growing city. Along the shores of Elliott Bay, skyscrapers of steel and concrete rose towards the skies like the native Douglas firs they replaced only a generation before. Just north of downtown, the newest photoplays entertained in sparkling new theaters springing up alongside retailers where men and women shopped the latest fashions. The largest retailer, Frederick and Nelson, was planning a massive expansion, constructing a flagship store on Fifth and Pine while Carl F. Wallin and John W. Nordstrom's shoe store was well-trafficked a block away on Fourth and Pike.

A young entrepreneur named Jim Casey started the American Messenger Service in 1907 delivering packages and notes downtown via bicycle. By 1915, the business had changed its name to Merchants Parcel Delivery and was using Model T's to deliver goods purchased from those retail stores, efficiently organizing delivery vehicles grouped by neighborhood. Soon, Jim Casey's company would simply be known as UPS.

To the north, construction had just wrapped up on an airplane hangar on the eastern shores of Lake Union. In one month, thirty-four-year-old Bill Boeing would begin final assembly of his B & W seaplane, the first of his many airplanes that would come to define the region.

A larger construction project continued on Lake Union as laborers feverishly dug the Montlake and Fremont cuts that would connect Lake Washington and Lake Union to Puget Sound. When finished, Lake Washington would be lowered nine feet to the height of Lake Union, causing its outlet, the Black River, to dry up. The Ballard Locks were in their final stages of construction with plans to soon flood Salmon Bay, turning it into a freshwater reservoir that would serve as the homeport for the region's fishing vessels. Above the locks, smoke wafted into the breeze from smokestacks littering Ballard's many lumber and shingle mills. In Seattle, industry was booming.

With hockey, Seattle was now a major league city. It was a city bursting with pride, but a community desperately desiring an accomplishment all its own. By 1915, Seattle's greatness always seemed qualified. While its population boomed, it remained only the third-largest city on the Pacific Coast. Its largest skyscraper, the Smith Tower, was the tallest building in the country outside of New York. The University of Washington's storied football team was undefeated the past eight years yet had never won the national championship; the title each year awarded to an eastern team. Anticipation was high for the Metropolitans to finally give Seattle its crown jewel.

**

Bernie pounced first. He perfectly timed Mayor Hiram Gill's puck drop and the Mets were off. The mayor immediately slipped as players on both teams shot past him. He struggled to get off the ice before Mickey Ion dragged him out of harm's way and over the boards to his seat. Bernie pushed the puck up the ice aggressively before Lester Patrick quickly closed on him and the initial rush of the season was thwarted. The twenty-five hundred fans in attendance still did not completely understand the rules or know all of the players yet by name but they stood on their feet and cheered loudly nonetheless.

For the first few minutes of the game, the Mets looked slightly out of sync, struggling with the offsides rule and relying primarily on individual rushes. Victoria on the other hand, passed well and controlled the pace of play, scoring five-minutes into the contest to take a 1-0 lead.

As Seattle continued to flounder offensively, Cully Wilson's frustration overtook him and he was sent to the penalty box for fighting. Soon, the Mets began hopelessly firing long-range shots that were easily stopped. Thankfully, their defense kept them in the game and at the end of the first period, the score remained 1-0 Victoria.

The second period began much the same as the first ended with the Mets faltering on offense but playing well on defense. Five minutes into the period, the Mets offense finally stirred when Frank Foyston secured a loose puck in transition and shot up the ice past Victoria's defense. With the shake of his wrists, the puck was in the net. Foyston had scored the first goal in Metropolitans history and tied the game at 1-1.

Victoria soon regained the lead and held it until Jack Walker tied the score near the end of the period. Moments after the puck left his stick, Jack was blindsided and sent careening into the boards. He badly injured his ankle and needed to be replaced by Leo Haas for the remainder of the period.

Hobbled, Walker returned to start the third. The Mets passing game improved though they couldn't push through a goal. Cully Wilson's frustrations once again boiled over and he was twice sent off the ice for fighting. The first offense resulted in a three-minute penalty but the second time, an all-out brawl ensued as Wilson and Eddie Carpenter fought a pair of Aristocrats. Carpenter received a three-minute penalty while Wilson's third fight resulted in ejection.

With two of the Mets' best players in the penalty box and Walker badly injured, momentum swung towards the Aristocrats. With the clock nearing two minutes, Victoria's Ken Mallen grabbed a loose puck and started a mad rush towards Hap in goal. As he reached center ice, Jack Walker miraculously came out of nowhere to steal the puck and start it back the other way. Bernie Morris read Jack perfectly and sprinted up the right side, shooting past a defender who reacted a split second late. Three Aristocrat defenders collapsed violently on the injured Walker, who absorbed the hit and floated a flawless pass out to Bernie on the wing. The pass hit Bernie in stride and he blasted a shot past McCullough, 3-2 Mets. It was an incredible play by Walker and the crowd was in near hysteria. Sound waves reverberated off the ice as fans celebrated the goal. Bernie felt like he was on top of the world.

Lester Patrick and the Aristocrats frantically tried to tie the score, but Hap repelled three consecutive shots before the final whistle blew to end the game. Pandemonium ensued on the ice and then spilled into the locker room. The players were ecstatic and Bernie was relieved to have contributed in such a big way. They had not played well offensively but had found a way to win. Muldoon was in near disbelief at their individual talent and was excited for their prospects when they grasped the offense. The Seattle Metropolitans were now 1-0.

Three days later, the Mets traveled to Victoria for the back end of the series. It was their first away game and Muldoon was interested to see how the team would handle a hostile environment. The Mets jumped the Aristocrats, immediately going up 3-0 before eventually winning 4-3.

Victoria notched two goals in the third but couldn't push the tying score across. Although the offense still didn't perform to capacity and Cully Wilson was twice penalized for fighting, Bernie Morris had played superbly and the team found a way to win for the second consecutive game. Muldoon was hopeful to soon get the offense in rhythm and the fighting curbed. Regardless, the Mets were undefeated and returning home to play the Portland Rosebuds, who had swept the defending Stanley Cup champion Vancouver Millionaires.

**

Tuesday, December 14 was a beautifully clear day in Seattle with highs reaching the upper 40s. Washington had voted to go dry on January 1 and the city was bracing for the State's new Bone-Dry law. Initiative No. 3 prohibited "the manufacture or sale of intoxicating liquors in any place" as well as prevented advertising or solicitation of alcohol or its distribution in public places. The ordinance did however allow beer and liquor to be served in the home so long as there was no charge. Fourteen states were already dry with South Carolina set to turn dry on December 31 and Washington, Oregon, Idaho, Colorado and Arkansas the following day.

In the Ice Arena that night, the Mets hosted Muldoon's former Rosebuds team with the headline in the *Seattle Post-Intelligencer* sports section reading, "First Place in Hockey League at Stake Tonight." After just two games, the Seattle media was already talking about the standings. It was billed as a matchup of "irresistible force versus immovable object" as the Mets were fast and athletic while the Rosebuds were "a strong, heavy team."

The Rosebuds forward line of Fred "Smokey" Harris, Tommy Dunderdale, Charlie Tobin and Eddie Oatman was as intimidating as there was in hockey. They were extremely physical on defense and all of them could score. The previous season, Oatman had finished fourth in points and Dunderdale sixth, with Harris and Tobin close behind. Harris had easily led the league in penalty minutes, while Oatman could be one of the roughest players on the ice, often using his stick to whack opponents.

Their star, however, was Ernie "Moose" Johnson. The Moose had long been considered one of the best defensemen in the game having already won four Stanley Cups in his younger days back east. At 5'11" and 185 pounds, he was one of the larger skaters on the ice and one of the fastest. The twenty-nine-year-old was still one of the toughest players in hockey and he could deliver a vicious hit. Most players zigzagged the puck up the ice to avoid defenders while the Moose just liked to go straight ahead, taking out any poor defenseman in his way. He had no problem throwing his large body moving full speed into anyone else on the ice; in fact, he relished it. He had been one of the Patricks' biggest steals the first year they raided the NHA and had been an All-Star every year of the PCHA except one.

In twice defeating the Millionaires last week, the Rosebuds only allowed one goal. Frank Patrick remarked that the Rosebuds were "not only the best in the league at present but also the roughest." Muldoon, ever the optimist, still felt great about his chances at home, saying "I think this club will win by a small margin, but enough to win, anyway."

** 

At half past eight, Mickey Ion called both teams to center ice. The capacity crowd was on its feet, causing the arena to shake as Bernie Morris and Tommy Dunderdale slowly slid in for the faceoff. Immediately, Portland pushed the action as the Mets were again out of sync on offense and could not mount much of a charge. The Mets defense responded and neither team had a clean look at the goal until an errant Metropolitan pass went straight to the Rosebuds' Charlie Tobin who grabbed the puck on a breakaway and fired a shot into the back of the net. It was a good reminder how small the margin for error was at this level. It was just one bad pass but it had cost them a goal.

Not deterred when play resumed, the Mets continued to fly around on defense with Hap playing brilliantly, stopping everything Portland sent his way. A lightning fast, physical game unfolded as both teams banged into each other incessantly until the first period ended with Portland up 1-0.

When the teams took the ice for the second period, Seattle was better offensively but the Rosebuds continued to play tough on defense. Midway through the period, Jack Walker stole the puck and started a breakaway alongside Cully Wilson. As the pair approached, goalie Tommy Murray flung himself at the puck the exact moment Walker raised his stick to shoot. He somehow secured the puck while flipping both players over his body and sending them crashing into the net. Cully was incensed and rushed Murray before the pair was quickly separated and Wilson sent to the penalty bench for three minutes. Amazingly, Mickey Ion let the play stand. For the rest of the period, the Mets continued to improve on offense and began firing rockets at Murray without netting a goal. At the end two, the score remained 1-0 Portland.

Between periods, Muldoon was calm and reminded his guys how hard they had worked to make sure they would always be the better conditioned team. He knew the exhausted Rosebuds were going play even rougher in the final period, so Muldoon implored his guys to ignore Portland's antics and continue to play their game.

As the third period began, Foyston and Morris immediately took control of the game and the Mets pushed the action. A few minutes in, Morris created some space for himself and drove towards the goal, firing a beautiful shot past Murray and into the back of the net. The crowd immediately erupted as the boys piled on Bernie in celebration. After forty-five minutes of play, the Mets had finally broken through and tied the score, 1-1.

The arena continued to shake as Ion brought both teams in for the faceoff. On the drop, Bernie and Dunderdale fought hard for control. As both teams closed in, Bernie snatched the puck and shot up the ice, completely stunning the Rosebuds. Cully Wilson read the play perfectly and sprinted up the ice to Morris' right. Bernie closed hard on Murray who waited until the last possible second before once again aggressively lunging out to block the shot. Morris timed Murray perfectly and slid a pass to the wing, where Wilson buried a shot into the vacated net. Seventeen seconds after the tying goal, the Mets led 2-1 and an already raucous crowd was beside itself.

A split second late and visibly frustrated, Rosebuds rover Eddie Oatman slammed into Cully Wilson, smashing him with his stick and sending Cully into the boards. Wilson immediately popped up and dropped Oatman with one swing before pouncing on the Rosebud captain. It took most of both teams to separate the two as both were ejected from the game and fined $5. Oatman was led off the ice by his teammates with his head down and blood streaming from his forehead, earning himself five stitches for his cheap shot. Cully was walked off the ice by his teammates with a wry smile on his face "like that worn by the cat after he had swallowed the canary." Cully was not going to let anyone intimidate the Mets.

Despite Ion's best efforts to get control, the game remained chippy as both teams battled with everything they had. First, Dunderdale was sent off the ice for roughness, then Rowe and Carpenter for Seattle, then Johnson for Portland before Dunderdale was finally ejected for fighting a second time. At one point, only nine men were left on the ice.

Midway through the period, Moose Johnson grabbed the puck and powered up the ice, using his strength to throw defenders out of his way until he broke into the open and sprinted towards the goal. As the crowd gasped, Jack Walker chased him down, hurling himself into Johnson and knocking the puck away to prevent the goal. The force from the collision sent Walker flying into the boards, knocking him unconscious and leaving a pool of blood on the ice. He needed nearly two minutes before coming to his senses and returning to the game. It was an incredible effort, but the kind of effort that was beginning to define the Mets team. Despite Jack's valiant play, however, Portland broke through a few minutes later to even the score.

With the game now tied, fans shook the arena as both teams met at center ice with six-and-a-half minutes to play. Morris once again won the faceoff and flipped the puck to a still foggy Jack Walker who raced up the ice. The moment the defense collapsed on him, he delivered a perfect pass back to Bernie, who buried the shot. Fifteen seconds after they allowed the tying score, the Mets were back in the lead 3-2. An eruption of green, red and white ensued as the team celebrated wildly. They had immediately answered and Muldoon was beginning to see their mental fortitude. This team would not back down.

Portland furiously attacked the Mets goal after play resumed. With two minutes to play, an errant shot went behind the Mets' goal and both teams rushed to secure the loose puck. Jack got there first and started to skate around the left post when Tobin blocked his path. He quickly put his right skate in the ice, turned and sprinted around the other side of the goal, soon pulling away from the Rosebuds players. He swerved through Tobin and Dunderdale at center ice and directly into a waiting Moose Johnson, who launched himself toward Jack. Walker quickly dodged to his left as Moose shot past him and continued sprinting up the ice leaving only Murray to defend the net. He swiftly closed on the goal and fired the puck past the helpless goalie. 4-2 Mets. It was a dagger and the crowd was electrified. The players once again celebrated wildly as they knew they had just conquered the vaunted Rosebuds. The remaining ninety seconds ticked away as the Mets celebration once again poured into the locker room. On the other side, the frustrated Rosebuds stormed to their locker room knowing the teams would meet again Friday night in Portland.

It was the most intense game that any of them had ever played and certainly the most intense game any of the capacity crowd had ever witnessed. Bernie had played superbly for the third game in a row, and for the second time, he had scored the deciding goal. An unheralded player one week ago, Bernie was on the verge of becoming a star. Jack had awed everyone in the building with his play and Frank had been everywhere, controlling the game and the team out on the ice. Muldoon knew he had the right guys on his roster.

The city of Seattle was now officially hockey crazy. Three games into their first season, the Mets were undefeated and in first place. Portland was second at 2-1 and an intense rivalry was forming between the two American teams. Victoria beat Vancouver that night, leaving them in third at 1-2 and the defending Stanley Cup Champions were now 0-3 and in last place. Frank Patrick had retired from playing that offseason to focus on coaching and the Millionaires were not the same without him.

Muldoon felt great about the team, although he knew they still weren't rolling on offense. He also knew it was a long season and that they had a tough game later in the week at Portland and two the following week with Vancouver. Frank Patrick would return soon if the Millionaires continued to lose, Muldoon just hoped it would be after their series.

**

Two days later, the Mets and Rosebuds continued to demean the other in the press. Portland manager Ed Savage blamed referee Mickey Ion for the loss, claiming he had unfairly punished the Rosebuds players more than the Mets. He even implored President Frank Patrick not to schedule Ion for the upcoming game in Portland. Patrick quickly dismissed the request as Mickey Ion was regarded as one of the finest referees in hockey.

That morning, Vancouver released Roy Rickey, the only new player they had signed for the season. It was a strong indication that Frank Patrick was returning and unfortunately, most likely before the series with Seattle. The Metropolitans quickly signed Rickey. Muldoon thought he was a talented player, and Pete had finally had enough of Leo Haas. He still wasn't in shape and struggled to improve. Muldoon hoped Rickey would be able to develop and contribute soon.

The game in Portland Friday night began much as the first contest ended. It was fast and aggressive with both teams playing their best. Three minutes into the third period, Bernie Morris banged in a goal to tie the score at two. Four and a half minutes later, Bobby Rowe and Charlie Tobin were ejected for fighting. Because it resulted in an ejection, both teams were allowed to substitute. Portland subbed in Alf Barbour while the newly signed Roy Rickey made his Mets debut. Barbour immediately scored six seconds after entering to put the Rosebuds back on top.

Barbour knocked in a second goal two minutes later, and Portland tallied late to win 5-2. The Mets defense had played well until Rowe's ejection. It was patently clear how important Bobby was to the team. Muldoon was growing increasingly frustrated with seeing his best players lose their composure and spend their time in the penalty box rather than the ice. There was a time and place to respond harshly to physical play, specifically when trying to establish the tone of a game, but to lose one's cool and respond violently was not going to help them win. He needed to fix the problem soon. Although three goals had been scored after he entered the game, Roy Rickey had played hard the entire period. The guys liked what they saw from him and knew he just needed time to learn their system.

As teams took the next week off for Christmas, the league published the first stats of the season. After four games, Seattle and Portland were tied for first place at 3-1, Victoria was second at 2-2 and the defending champion Millionaires were now 0-4 and in last place. Lester Patrick led the league with six goals and nine points. Bernie Morris' four goals and two assists were good for third place while Jack Walker and Cully Wilson were tied for sixth. Although he'd scored only one goal, Foyston had played well all four games. Muldoon knew he simply needed to make a few adjustments to get Frank more involved in the scoring.

He also needed to keep his players on the ice. Cully Wilson led the league with twenty-nine penalty minutes, followed by Bobby Rowe in second with nineteen. Pete did not like having the league's two most-penalized players on his team, and four of the top-11.

The next week, Vancouver visited Seattle. And, as expected, the Christmas holidays had given Frank Patrick enough time to get in shape and he was back on the active roster for the Millionaires. Muldoon made a lineup change too, swapping Roy Rickey for Cully Wilson. Pete was not going to let Cully continue to play out of control. He was going to take away his starting spot until Wilson figured out how to rein in his emotions. He was too talented and too important to the team to continuously fight and spend his time off the ice.

From the opening whistle, Vancouver was a completely different team with Frank Patrick playing. He scored two goals and wreaked havoc defensively as the Millionaires won 6-4. The Mets offense continued to be out of rhythm although Jack Walker and Bernie Morris each scored two goals and most important to Muldoon, the Mets played a clean game without a penalty.

Early the next week, after the New Year's holiday, the Mets and Millionaires faced off in Vancouver. Muldoon made another lineup change trying to get Foyston more involved in the scoring, moving him from rover to center. Bernie went to right wing and Jack Walker slid into the rover position. Roy Rickey once again started for Cully Wilson. The change immediately worked as Foyston scored almost three minutes into the game, his first goal since the season opener.

Late in the period with the score tied at one, Cully Wilson subbed into the game. With the puck out on the wing, he drove towards the net, collapsing the entire Millionaires defense to stop him. Just when it appeared the rush had been thwarted, Cully slid a perfect pass out to Roy Rickey who immediately scored the puck to give the Mets a 2-1 lead. It was a normal pass, but that Cully had made it to the guy who had taken his starting job without hesitation impressed Muldoon and once again reinforced to him that he had the right guys on his roster.

Vancouver tied the score in the second and both teams traded goals in the third, setting up a dramatic finish. With just thirty seconds left on the clock, Vancouver's Si Griffis made an incredible play to knock a goal past

Hap and win the game. Despite the crushing loss, Muldoon continued to preach to his guys to trust the process. They had again played better on offense and he knew they were improving. Soon, the offense would click and be unstoppable. The Mets were also showing drastic improvement in their discipline, with only one 3-minute penalty for the night. Despite the effort, the team had now dropped its third in a row. Six games in, Portland was in first place at 5-1, Seattle second at 3-3 with Vancouver and Victoria tied at 2-4.

Finally feeling confident that Cully Wilson had learned the importance of staying on the ice, Muldoon returned him to his starting position for the next game, moving Roy Rickey back to the bench. Despite the move, the team dropped its next two games to Portland and Victoria. In the Portland game, they had completely fallen apart. Up 3-1 in the second, they once again lost their composure and allowed Portland to score five goals. All five were scored with men in the penalty box.

The team rebounded and played better in the Victoria game, but still lost after a bad call by the referee. After initially waving off the score, he awarded Victoria a goal when the puck had gone on top of the net rather than in it. He admitted the mistake after the game, but the damage had been done. Muldoon knew that great teams did not let bad calls affect them. Unfortunately, the Mets were not yet a great team. Seattle had now lost five in a row. Vancouver, on the other hand, was red hot since Frank Patrick's return, winning four straight and now sat only two games out of first place.

Muldoon began looking to sign another player as he had wanted nine before the season began. He was looking for "a big strong man who will work hard all of time" and thought he had finally identified the man. He had wired terms and was awaiting the reply.

Bernie continued to shine and was spending much of his time with Muldoon and Frank Foyston. Pete had an astounding ability to positively motivate his players. For someone with Bernie's emotional scars, it was the perfect fit. Pete had incredibly high standards but he rarely gave feedback from the negative and never tried to scare or intimidate his men. Great coaches repeatedly reinforce the positives to their players and push them to improve, continuously painting the picture of greatness. Muldoon, was a great coach.

Despite being six months younger than Bernie, Frank had become a big brother to him. When Bernie was stressed, he often became selfish. It was a defense mechanism that life spent as an orphan had taught him. There had never been someone to look after Bernie and provide for him. He had always had to fight for his basic needs. In this team, he had found the friendship and nurturing environment absent his entire life and he was thriving.

For the next game, Pete made another lineup change, moving Wilson to center, Walker and Morris to the wings and Foyston back to rover. The offense was improving but was still not where he wanted it. The move worked, as the Mets defeated Victoria 5-3 to snap their five-game losing streak. The team played well offensively, and, more importantly, without a penalty. At the halfway point in the season, Portland was in first place at 6-3, Vancouver, winners of five straight, was one game back at 5-4, with the Mets in third at 4-5 and Victoria in last at 3-6

On January 23, the league released the midseason stats. The headline in the *Seattle Post-Intelligencer* read, "Bernie Morris Best Scorer in Hockey League" with a picture of Bernie captioned, "Star Seattle Player." For a guy worried about even making the team six weeks ago, Bernie's circumstances had changed dramatically. He had scored more goals than anyone in the league, and his fifteen points tied him with Vancouver's Cyclone Taylor. The same Cyclone Taylor that many regarded as the best player in hockey.

Jack Walker was the only other Seattle player in the top-10 as the Mets ranked last in the league in goals scored and assists. They also ranked second-to-last in goals allowed, with that statistic perfectly mirroring the league standings. Cully Wilson still led the league in penalty minutes with forty-two, half coming against Portland though Bobby Rowe was now ninth and the only other Seattle player in the top-10. All of Rowe's twenty-one minutes had come against the Rosebuds, who now had the second, third, fourth and seventh most penalized players in the league.

Muldoon knew his guys were rapidly improving their composure and learning to ignore the noise around them. He instructed them "to take the bumps and refrain from roughing." Cheap shots, bad calls, illness or injury, it was all just noise. Great teams just play their game, they don't let anything change what they are doing on the ice. There is always an excuse to make or a reason to fight, but teams that want to win championships just expect those situations and play through them.

After playing above their heads for the first few games, the Mets had crashed back to earth. Muldoon had not expected things to be easy and was not discouraged. He knew these players could learn and they loved to compete. He just needed to keep them positive and focused on improving over the remaining nine games.

# CHAPTER 5 – SECOND HALF - 1916 SEASON

One week later, the second half of the season began. The Metropolitans had a tough stretch in front of them, playing a series against the defending champion Millionaires and then on the road at Portland. As Seattle arrived in Vancouver, Roy Rickey was approached by the military and asked to enlist. He was willing to fight if compelled but so long as he was able, he wanted to play hockey and chose to remain with the team. After the contest, Frank Patrick called it one of the best games he had ever seen, with Vancouver winning 3-2. Despite the loss, Muldoon continued to be encouraged that they were headed in the right direction.

Two days later, Vancouver made the return trip to Seattle. The Mets did not play well and the Millionaires won their seventh in a row, beating Seattle 4-2. Muldoon was upset with their effort all night and spent most of the game yelling instructions from the bench. Midway through the second period, Pete pulled Jack Walker to give his forward a breather. Soon, Muldoon's frustration boiled over and he yelled, "That guy's playing terrible" as he slapped the bench. Exasperated, he tapped Jack on the shoulder and yelled at him to get back in the game. Without taking his eyes off the action, Muldoon yelled "get in there for Walker, he's awful." Jack cracked a smile and sent Roy Rickey back to the bench.

After the game, Jack was the last to enter the locker room. He stormed in to yell at the guys about how poorly they played, telling them if they didn't play better, Pete was going to replace them in the lineup. If it continued, there would be changes. They were all tired of struggling so Pete wouldn't hesitate to substitute "Walker for Walker" if that's what it took to get them going. An immediate roar of laughter enveloped the locker room as the tension in the room instantly dissipated. The players, including Pete, had a good laugh. They all knew it would not be the last bad game they would play. It was clear this team had the resiliency to quickly process a bad game and move on. Walker for Walker became a joke the rest of the season. Pete did not mind the boys having a laugh at his expense, he just wanted them to play well. If there was another silver lining in the game, Frank and Bernie scored the two goals.

Eleven games into the season and it was only Frank's third tally. He was playing fabulously but his statistics did not reflect his output. Frank was one of the most aggressive players on the ice but he was so self-confident and so unselfish that he would readily sacrifice opportunities to score in order to get others involved in the offense. If Bernie or Jack had an opportunity to score, they took it. It wasn't that either played selfishly but if it was 50-50 shoot or pass, they were shooting. If Frank saw an opening, he attacked the defense and got the puck to the guy with the best chance to score, only shooting when he had the distinct advantage.

Frank had done wonders to get Bernie off to a fast start but now that Bernie had established himself and was playing great, Pete needed Frank to score or the opposing defenses could just focus on Morris. Regardless of the statistical start to his season, Frank was not the least bit frustrated. He simply played hard every second of every game and did what he thought best in each moment. Frank saw every play as a means to win games not as an indicator of his ability. Only truly great teams have a player like Frank at their core. Pete knew there was a combination that put all four of his talented forwards in the best position to score goals. He just needed to find it.

For the next game, the team traveled to Portland to play the hated Rosebuds. The Hippodrome in Portland had become the toughest place in the league to play. Muldoon knew the team was close to breaking out and, again, tweaked the lineup. He moved Bernie back to center and Cully to right wing. He now had Jack at left wing, Bernie at center, Cully at right wing and he still thought Frank had the biggest impact in the center of the ice so kept him at rover. Jack scored first, giving the Metropolitans an early lead but Portland was too tough at home and won 4-1. Portland was penalized twice for roughness but the Mets had maintained their composure and were not penalized once. They continued to compete through Portland's aggressive play. Although they had lost three in a row and eight of nine, Muldoon continued to be encouraged.

That same night in Victoria, Vancouver smashed the Aristocrats 16-4. Victoria jumped out to an early 3-0 lead but then, the lights suddenly went out in the arena for 15 minutes. When they came back on, it was all Vancouver. Earlier that week, Victoria had been told that the lights would be going out on the remainder of their season. The Canadian military used the port city as a shipping off point for weapons and soldiers. It was immediately commandeering the arena as a training facility for soldiers departing to the front meaning the Aristocrats would not be able to play in their arena for the last six games of the season. It was a crushing blow to

Lester Patrick and the city of Victoria.

Twelve games into the season, Portland was still in first place at 9-3. After winning eight straight, Vancouver was in second at 8-4, with Seattle in third at 4-8 and Victoria last at 3-9.

Late in the evening of February 1, snow began to fall on Seattle. First just a trace, it quickly became heavy, dumping snow on the houses of Beacon Hill and mills of Ballard. Soon, so much snow fell that the counterbalance trolley, climbing the steep southern face of Queen Anne hill was suspended. The skies continued dumping well into the next day until there were enough soft white flakes accumulated to collapse the dome of First Hill's St. James Cathedral, the seat of the Archdiocese of Seattle. It was a shocking sight, reminiscent of the images coming back from the European fronts. In total, more than a foot of snow fell on the city. All schools and amateur sporting events in the paralyzed city were canceled.

Just before the snow struck, Muldoon had received a return cable from the player in Colorado with his terms. He wanted transportation to and from Seattle and a full season salary despite only six games remaining on the schedule. Pete immediately declined. For a player that had not proven anything on the ice to request the highest salary on team told Pete everything he needed to know about this guy.

However, Muldoon wasn't done looking. He wanted a young, athletic player who just wanted to get better. He wanted someone who was going to push the guys in front of him and compete to help the team win regardless if he was starting or on the bench. A player that understood the competition for playing time was against himself rather than any of his teammates. Guys like that rapidly improve and usually end up as stars. He knew what his player looked like, he simply needed to find him.

After two days of being stuck in their rooms, it was finally time to play again as the newly orphaned Victoria Aristocrats arrived in the snow-covered city. Sitting in his office that day, Muldoon picked up the newspaper and began to read. Luckily, the collapse at St. James Cathedral hadn't structurally damaged the building. The church needed a new dome but they did not need to build a new cathedral.

The next article shocked him. The Canadian Capitol building in Ottawa had burned to the ground the previous night. At least five people were dead and two were still missing. The fire started in the reading room of the House of Commons with at least one explosion. The beautiful Gothic building was constructed between 1859 to 1865 with the cornerstone ceremoniously "laid by the then Prince of Wales, later King Edward the VII in 1850." There were rumblings that German sympathizers started the fire but authorities were not able to determine the cause.

The next headline read "Berlin Sorry, But Not Guilty of Illegal Act" in the sinking of the *Lusitania*. Germany feared the U.S. was moving closer to entering the war so they were willing to apologize for the sinking but were adamant it was not illegal, even if that meant war with America. Nobody in Germany "would regard a conflict with the United States as a slight matter" but would do so "if it cannot be avoided without sacrificing our self-respect and dignity." Ultimately, the apology and rescinding of its unrestricted submarine warfare policy kept the U.S. neutral and out of the war.

Last, Muldoon read that at 1:30 p.m. that day, the May B. II became the first passenger carrier to travel through the newly finished locks in Ballard. With snow still preventing streetcars from running, the boat picked passengers up at the foot of Madison Street downtown and took them through the locks to the city pier in Ballard. The first boat to pass through the locks that day was the Orcas, a tender used by the U.S. district engineer. Muldoon was happy to see a project that began when he first moved to Ballard to train as a boxer had reached an important milestone. After finishing that article, he threw the newspapers in the waste basket and began preparing for the game.

A second round of snow blanketed the city that morning and the season's smallest crowd was in attendance. If the Mets lost, they would be tied with Victoria for last place in the league, a place they did not want to find themselves.

Both teams struggled early with the atmosphere inside the cavernous arena. The Mets were down 1-0 midway through the second period before Eddie Carpenter took over, twice skating the length of the ice for goals, the second less than a minute before the end of the period. It was a great individual effort and sent the boys into the locker room with momentum.

Between periods, Muldoon decided to make a small adjustment in the lineup. He swapped Frank and Jack, putting Frank on the wing for the first time all season and moving Jack to rover. Nearly four minutes into the period, the Aristocrats evened the score but it was evident the Mets offense had better flow. Just over a minute later, Jack raced the puck up the ice and made a great pass to Frank for a goal to regain the lead. It was the exact play Muldoon had been searching for all season.

Quickly, Victoria evened the score again but the Mets' offense was now firing on all cylinders. Fifty seconds later, Cully Wilson took a pass from Bobby Rowe and found the back of the net. Two and a half minutes later, Roy Rickey blasted a goal. Two and a half minutes after that, Bernie took a pass from Jack Walker and buried the dagger, scoring the fourth goal of the period and giving the Metropolitans a 6-3 win. The six goals were a season-high. More importantly, all seven players logged a point. They had played Muldoon's offense to perfection and he finally figured out his best lineup. Pete could not wait for the next game.

The day before the game, they all woke to the headline, "Dobie Returns to His Position at Washington." The saga had been playing out since

Thanksgiving but Gil Dobie had lost out on some of the top jobs back east and Washington still hadn't found a replacement so he decided to return and honor the last year of his contract. Muldoon was happy Dobie was returning because he enjoyed taking the boys to see the football team play. He liked showing them how other great teams competed.

By February 8, the snow had abated and the crowds were back in the Arena as the Metropolitans hosted Victoria for the second straight game. It had been decided that Victoria would use Seattle as their home arena for the remainder of the season rather than send both teams on the road to a neutral site. The Metropolitans scored four goals in the first fifteen minutes on their way to a dominating 8-4 victory.

The only bright spot for the Aristocrats was their 20-year old reserve Jim Riley who "slammed one past Holmes" in the third. It was the second goal Riley had scored against the Mets that year in limited minutes. His first goal had impressed even the sportswriters but this one wasn't nearly enough as the Mets, for the second consecutive game, recorded a season-best in goals. And, for the second straight game, the entire forward line scored a goal, with Bernie scoring four alongside three assists. The offense that was the worst in the league at the halfway point in the season had scored fourteen goals in the last two games.

**

Three days later, a packed house jammed the Ice Arena to welcome the first-place Portland Rosebuds, winners of five in a row. Portland had entered their series the previous week against the red-hot Millionaires with a slim one-game lead over Vancouver. In danger of falling out of first if they lost both, they instead swept Vancouver, including a massive 1-0 win in Portland before 5,000 screaming fans to take a commanding lead in the standings.

Muldoon was excited to see his new offense compete against the Portland defense, "Wait until you see what we uncork tonight, my men are going after those boys from the whistle." The Rosebuds, on the other hand, didn't much care what the Mets had done to the last-place Aristocrats. They had beaten Seattle three straight games, outscoring them 15-6.

From the opening whistle, the Mets were a different team. Frank Foyston scored in the first and Seattle never looked back, handing Portland its worst defeat of the season, 8-4. The Mets absolutely dominated the best defense in the PCHA. Once again, all four members of the Mets' front line scored with Bernie again netting four goals. Equally important was that after two 3-minute penalties in the first, the Mets played the final two periods penalty free. Muldoon's boys had taken their hits and kept on playing. They were beginning to fire on all cylinders.

With just three games remaining for each team, Portland remained in first place at 11-4, with Vancouver second at 9-6. Seattle, winners of three straight, were now in third place at 7-8 with the orphaned Aristocrats in last place at 3-12. Although Portland snapped the Millionaires' eight game winning streak, Vancouver had still won nine of eleven since Frank Patrick's return. Seattle was only two games out of second place but closed the season with a series against Vancouver before finishing at Portland, the same stretch that handed them three consecutive losses in early January.

On Friday, February 18, the Metropolitans traveled to Vancouver. The Millionaires were 4-0 versus the Mets on the year. In all the recent talk of the Seattle forward line, Hap Holmes and the defense had almost been an afterthought. From the opening whistle, Hap played brilliantly as he "stopped a million shots from all sides, all angles and every degree of velocity." Frank scored twice, his fifth straight game with a goal while Bernie notched the other two goals as the Mets won, 4-1.

The next day, the Millionaires traveled to Seattle with their sights still set on second place, needing only a win. Lose, however, and they were tied with one game to play. Vancouver nonetheless had the advantage, closing the season with a home game against the struggling Aristocrats, while Seattle still had to travel to Portland, where the Rosebuds were 7-1 at home.

Vancouver's Hugh "Dutch" Lehman had long been regarded as the league's best goalie. Many observers saw these games as a direct competition between Hap and the fiery, impatient Lehman, who "wasn't happy unless he was in the limelight all the time." He loved making "the crowd yell, either for or against him. That didn't matter, as long as they yelled." Hap, was just the opposite. He was rarely, if ever, rattled and years later, Frank Foyston would remark that he didn't think he'd ever seen Hap excited.

Hap wore small, white canvassed pads that were the smallest worn by any goalie in hockey. The pads measured just 18-inches across and were wrapped tightly around his legs because the rounded pads made him more accurate deflecting the puck and more agile in the cage. Like everyone else on the Metropolitans roster, Hap's game was about quickness and athleticism.

Before every contest, Muldoon went over the game plan with the guys and they talked through their assignments. Although Hap never cared about the comparisons with Lehman and never placed more importance on the Vancouver games than any other, he was feeling particularly spry that day so took over the pregame meeting, saying, "If you want to beat that Dutchman tonight, don't go near him for five minutes or so. Just let him get anxious to start saving goals and he'll soon be out to the blue line to meet you." Laughter erupted in the locker room as the team took the ice.

From the puck drop, it was evident Vancouver planned to lock down the Mets forward line and led 1-0 after the first period. The Seattle forwards weren't getting anywhere near the goal and Lehman was getting antsy.

Early in the second period, Bobby Rowe drove the puck up the ice, weaving through the Millionaires defenders. On cue, Lehman aggressively came out of the cage to stop the rush. Bobby held the puck until the instant Lehman arrived, dumping a beautiful pass to Cully Wilson. Cully buried the shot and tied the score. Wry smiles adorned the faces above red, green and white barber pole sweaters.

Five minutes later, Eddie Carpenter made a similar rush up the ice. When Lehman came out once again to stop the puck, Eddie floated a perfect pass to Jack Walker who knocked it in, 2-1 Mets. This time, it was almost all out laughter. The Mets were playing a great game and feeling confident.

Almost seven minutes into the third period, Bobby Rowe took over. He picked up an errant shot behind the goal and sprinted up the ice, again weaving through defenders until this time, he found himself at the goal with Lehman remaining in his customary place in front of the net. It didn't matter, Rowe buried the corner of the goal, 3-1 Mets. He did it again two and a half minutes later as the Mets ran away from Vancouver 4-2. Royal Brougham wrote that the Mets had played their best game, "Playing together and displaying more effective combination attacks than any other game in which they were contestants."

The defense played brilliantly, allowing only thirteen shots on goal while the Mets took twenty-nine. Equally as important, the two defensemen scored two goals and notched two assists. It was just the game Muldoon was hoping to see. If the opposing team made a concerted effort to stop the forward line, this team was athletic enough and deep enough to still win. Bobby Rowe had been a forward most of his career and Eddie Carpenter would play forward on most other teams. The entire team was now firing on all cylinders. After almost being in last place a month ago, the Mets had won five straight and were tied for second place.

**

The first reports hit the newspapers in America on February 24. Seven German army corps had opened fire on heavily entrenched French soldiers at Verdun, France. One thousand two hundred twenty German guns rained artillery shells along a twenty-five mile front while the French valiantly returned fire. It was the beginning of an intense battle. According to reports from the front, Kaiser Wilhelm himself was in Verdun directing the attack. Three days into the German offensive, both sides were already reporting staggering losses. The French stated the German losses were approaching 50,000 people as the battle was "rapidly developing into the greatest of the war."

While the Battle of Verdun raged in France, Seattle traveled to Portland to close the season against the Rosebuds. It was another physical affair, with the Rosebuds committing five roughing penalties to the Mets three. Portland at home, however, was simply too much as a crowd of 3,200 saw the Rosebuds score the last four goals of the game and win 5-2.

It was a disappointing loss but everyone knew how tough Portland was at home and, luckily, Victoria shocked Vancouver 7-6 so the Metropolitans finished their first season tied for second place. Portland was the champion of the league and would soon travel east to face the Montreal Canadiens, winners of the NHA, for the Stanley Cup.

Immediately after the game, Portland manager Ed Savage approached Muldoon and asked the Mets to play an exhibition game in Seattle early the next week. The Rosebuds planned to travel north to Vancouver before catching the train east and wanted to stay sharp. Muldoon readily agreed as everyone in the Mets locker room wanted to get the taste of this defeat out of their mouth.

The Rosebuds finished 13-5, well ahead of the Mets and Millionaires at 9-9, with the Aristocrats in the cellar at 5-13. Bernie Morris lost the scoring title to Cyclone Taylor 35-32 but scored the most goals, beating Taylor 23-21. Jack Walker and Cully Wilson finished just outside the top-10 while Frank Foyston's late surge helped him climb into the top-20. Seattle scored the second most goals in the second half of the season and allowed the second fewest, a dramatic improvement over the season's first half.

Cully Wilson finally relinquished his "most penalized" title, finishing a distant second to Portland's Smokey Harris. The Rosebuds placed three in the top-5 while Bobby Rowe and Bernie Morris finished outside of the top-10. All in all, Muldoon was extremely pleased with how his boys handled themselves the last half of the season.

It was a leap year in 1916, so the Rosebud-Metropolitan exhibition game was scheduled for Tuesday, February 29. The Mets had the Rosebuds back at home and wanted retribution for their season ending loss. From the outset, it was all Seattle. 5-0 at the end of the first period, 11-0 at the end of the second. It was 14-0 before Portland scored their first goal as the Mets hammered the Rosebuds, winning 14-6.

Frank Foyston scored two goals while Bernie Morris punched in four scores. Cully Wilson, who had battled Portland the entire season, scored the remaining eight goals on the night. As he slowly skated off the ice, the left side of his lip pulled slightly up into a wry smile with a look in his eye letting every Portland player know that the Metropolitans were the team to beat next year.

After everyone exited the locker room, Muldoon sat alone. He was proud of everything his boys had overcome and impressed with their talent.

It had taken them a while to understand the system and to learn to control their emotions but they had done everything he asked and they always played hard. He never had to question their effort or desire.

After a full season together, he knew he had the right guys on his team, and, he knew what he needed to do to turn them into champions.

# ACT II

Seattle Ice Arena 1915

# CHAPTER 6 – OFFSEASON 1916

It was a tumultuous offseason around the world. In the early hours of March 9, just nine days after the Metropolitans inaugural season ended, Pancho Villa formed nearly five hundred soldiers into two columns and attacked the remote border town of Columbus, New Mexico, with its garrison of six hundred U.S. soldiers. Eighteen Americans were killed in the raid and the town badly burned before the rebels were chased back across the border, suffering more than one hundred casualties.

General John Pershing was immediately sent on a mission to cross the Mexican border and hunt down Villa. The expedition force eventually reached ten thousand soldiers as they chased the raiders deep into the Mexican interior. As the force reached Carrizal in June, a battle ensued with President Carranza's government troops rather than Villa's rebels that brought both countries to the brink of war. Wanting to avoid a conflict with Mexico while the war in Europe raged, President Wilson sought a diplomatic solution. Pershing's forces continued their search, albeit with strong restrictions. Most of the soldiers involved in the attack on Columbus were captured or killed though Villa ultimately escaped.

**

Monday, April 24 was Easter Monday in Ireland. Pete Muldoon, Bernie Morris, the Patricks and countless other North American citizens followed the news accounts in horror as an uprising gripped the birthplace of their parents or grandparents. One thousand six hundred Irish protesters seized the Dublin post office and other government buildings with Patrick Pearse, one of the uprising's leaders, delivering a proclamation declaring Ireland an independent republic.

In response, the British imposed martial law and a bloody repression followed, taking less than a week to crush the rebellion. Close to four hundred fifty Irish were killed and more than two thousand wounded while much of Dublin's inner city was reduced to ru. uprising were executed in May and more than th. arrested. Photos in the newspapers looked no di coming from the front.

The Olympic Games were scheduled to be held in Instead, they became the first Olympics canceled due fighting raged across the European continent. Fierce ba Verdun as the Germans slowly chewed up ground agai. .ich, forcing the allies to form a coordinated strategy to blun. German advance. In early June, a Russian regiment, led by General Aleksei Brusilov, began a massive offensive on the Eastern Front, overwhelming the Austro-Hungarian Army. Soon, Germany was forced to divert troops to aid Austria.

On July 1, British and French armies attacked heavily fortified German forces in an intense barrage along the Somme River, one hundred miles north of Verdun. The British reported more than nineteen thousand killed and fifty-seven thousand total casualties on the first day alone. Once again, the battle forced Germany to divert forces from Verdun.

Soon, the offensive at Verdun stalled as intense fighting raged on multiple fronts. In August, German General Erich von Falkenhayn, Chief of the German General Staff, was replaced by General Paul von Hindenburg in an attempt to breathe life back into the thinly stretched German Army. On September 15 at the Somme, the British used a new weapon for the first time in history, the tank. Less than a month later, the Battle of the Somme ended. Indicative of much of the Great War, in one hundred forty-one days of fighting, the line moved only five miles and caused 1.1 million casualties on both sides.

On September 20, the Brusilov Offensive ended with 1.5 million Austro-Hungarian casualties, ultimately decimating the Austrian Army. In its first successful campaign of the war, the Russian Army suffered more than five hundred thousand casualties itself.

As the fighting intensified, many Canadian athletes began to enlist. For much of the summer, the NHA feared it would need to cancel the season for lack of talented players and infighting amongst the owners. By late summer, the owners tenuously agreed to play, setting their differences aside and deciding to form a team of enlisted professional hockey players. The military sent the men to Toronto to train for the war and the NHA simply formed them into the 228th Canadian Battalion team, therefore completing the league.

Portland's Eddie Oatman joined the military and played for the 228th while Victoria goalie Fred McCullough signed up and departed immediately for the front. In early October, word came from Toronto that Frank Foyston was planning to enlist and play for the 228th. A few weeks later,

port came out of Port Arthur about Jack Walker. Both men
ely decided to delay their enlistment until after the season and
orted to Seattle.

**

At home, workers at the shingle mill in Everett went on strike in
October, upset over wages. The strike was organized by their union, the
American Federation of Labor. The Wobblies, members of a more radical
rival union, the Industrial Workers of the World, saw the strike as an
opportunity. The Wobblies traveled to Everett on October 30 to support
the striking workers and stand in solidarity against the mill owners resulting
in clashes with local authorities.

The following Sunday, Wobblies filled two boats in Seattle, the Verona
and Calista, and took the short trip to Everett for a return demonstration.
As the Verona began to dock, they were met by County Sheriff Donald
MacRae, his deputies, and a large pro-business contingent that yelled out
"Who are your leaders?" The response shouted in unison from the boat:
"We all are!" Moments later, gun shots rained out across the dock. The
*Seattle Star's* headline the next day read "7 Killed, 50 Wounded, Is Toll of
Sunday's I.W.W. Battle." When the boat returned to Seattle, seventy-four
Wobblies were arrested with one of the leaders, Thomas Tracy, charged
with murder. He was later acquitted.

**

Less than two weeks later, Americans went to the polls. It would be the
last presidential election without women voting in every state. On the
Republican ticket, Supreme Court Justice and former New York Governor
Charles Hughes ran against the Democratic incumbent, President
Woodrow Wilson. Taking more than two days to tally final votes,
California ultimately decided the election. When President Wilson's
plurality in the state reached a mere 3,100 votes on Thursday afternoon, the
Republican central committee conceded California's 13 electoral votes to
the president, giving him more than the 266 needed to win. In one of the
closest elections in history, President Wilson and his "He kept us out of
war" slogan had secured a second term, winning the electoral vote 277-254
and the popular vote 9,116,296 to 8,547,474. Montana, which had voted in
favor of woman's suffrage two years prior, elected the first woman to
Congress, Republican Jeannette Rankin.

**

It had been a tumultuous offseason for the league as well. The
Canadian military continued its use of the Victoria Ice Arena leaving the
Aristocrats once again without a home. Hockey enthusiasts in Spokane had

been clamoring for a team for years, so Frank and Lester moved the Victoria club there and renamed them the Canaries. Muldoon spent his summer in San Francisco, where he opened a sporting goods store and helped introduce hockey to the city. He returned in early October to join Lester in Spokane and get the city and arena ready for professional hockey.

While Pete Muldoon and Lester Patrick were in Spokane, Frank Patrick traveled to Toronto to present the NHA a new peace treaty. After some back and forth, both sides eventually signed the treaty. They agreed to once again respect each other's rosters and reaffirmed the schedule for the World Series, the best-of-five series played in March for the Stanley Cup. The Series location rotated each year between the home rink of the NHA and PCHA champion. After the inaugural trip out west to Vancouver in 1915, the Stanley Cup would be won on the Pacific Coast again this year for only the second time.

Upon Frank's return, the PCHA held its league meeting and adopted a few new wrinkles for the 1916-17 season. The teams agreed to add six games to their schedule, playing twenty-four games rather than eighteen and once again, the Patricks had some new rules to make the style of play more athletic. Previously, goalies had to stay on their feet to stop the puck but the Patricks decided to remove all restrictions. Goalies could now stop the puck any way they saw fit. They also decided to follow Major League Baseball and award a Most Valuable Player award, voted on by the four official scorers. Royal Brougham, the official scorer for the Metropolitans, listed Cyclone Taylor, Moose Johnson, Jack Walker and Lester Patrick as his MVP favorites from each team.

Over the past month, all four managers had been busy setting their rosters. In Portland, the Rosebuds had a few holes to fill. In addition to losing Oatman to the war, defenseman Del Irvin died of pneumonia on the trip home from Montreal after the World Series loss to the Canadiens. In their place, Portland signed the top three players from the Plains, including Del's younger brother Dick, who sat atop every PCHA team's wish list the past few seasons. All things considered, the Rosebuds looked to be equally as strong defending their coast championship.

Vancouver remained largely intact and had been given a gift that offseason. Gordon "Doc" Roberts had been a star in the NHA the past seven seasons, playing the previous six for the Montreal Wanderers while completing medical school at McGill University. He had graduated the previous spring and accepted a medical practice in the Vancouver suburbs. Frank quickly talked him into playing for the Millionaires and one of the best teams in hockey got that much better.

Lester Patrick, frustrated with consecutive last-place finishes, kept five of his starters, lost McCullough to the war and brought in a slew of players to compete for the remaining three spots on the Canaries. There was no complacency in his efforts to rebuild the roster and Lester was still one of the best players in hockey so they were going to be dangerous. In Seattle, Muldoon was excited to be the only team to return its entire roster intact though he was still looking for his elusive ninth man.

Bobby Rowe, Cully Wilson and Roy Rickey were the first to return to Seattle, in mid-November, while Jack Walker, Eddie Carpenter, Hap Holmes and Frank Foyston once again arrived together the day before the first practice. Jack and Eddie spent the offseason in Port Arthur while both Hap and Frank returned home for the summer. Bernie Morris spent the offseason with Muldoon in San Francisco, a far cry from the mines of his previous summers. His relationship with Minnie had deteriorated further, and she refused to move to Seattle. Bobby, Jack, Eddie and Frank rented an apartment together downtown with Jack cooking for the four of them plus Bernie on most days. All the players were excited to be together again.

As great as the 1915-16 PCHA season had been, all involved believed the 1916-17 season was going to be better. Frank Patrick issued a statement from the league office that each of the teams had "secured the best talent available, regardless of expense and I think that every team is stronger this season." In the *Seattle Post-Intelligencer*, Royal Brougham wrote "With four of the best teams ever assembled in the history of the sport on the coast, followers of the popular ice sport are holding their breath and waiting for the start of what should be a banner hockey year." The first practice of the season was scheduled for November 22, and anticipation was high for the most competitive season yet.

**\*\***

The night before the first practice, five thousand miles from Seattle, the slowly leaking demise of one of the largest and most powerful European empires became a rupture. At half past nine in the evening of Tuesday, November 21, the second-longest reigning European monarch took his last breath. From his modest bed in Schloss Schönbrunn, eighty-six-year-old Kaiser Franz Joseph died ten days short of the sixty-eighth anniversary of his ascension to the throne.

The immensely popular, humble Kaiser had by many accounts led a tragic life. Charming and courteous as a teenager, he grew to become pragmatic and taciturn as an adult. He had been lucky enough to marry the love of his life, Sisi, only to see her struggle with the pressures of court life and ultimately withdraw from him. His only son Rudolf's liberal views caused much consternation but that paled in comparison to Rudolf's murder-suicide in 1889 that left him without his son and heir. Sisi never emotionally recovered from Rudolf's suicide. She was assassinated less than a decade later.

Franz Joseph's brother, Archduke Ferdinand Maximilian was executed by firing squad as Emperor Maximilian I of Mexico in 1867 and his brother Archduke Karl Ludwig, died of illness in 1896. Maximilian was heir before Rudolf's birth and Karl Ludwig after his death. Karl Ludwig's son Franz Ferdinand became heir upon his father's death. Franz Ferdinand's nephew Karl was now Kaiser. It had indeed been a life full of tragedies.

In 1900, Vienna was the sixth largest city in the world. Sixteen years later, it was draped in black in mourning. The New York Times wrote "the death of the universally beloved venerable monarch has accomplished what all the horrors and varying fortunes of the war failed to do – it has wrapped the hearts of Austrians in earnest, thoughtful, sincere grief and has sombered the gay Austrian capital amid scenes reminiscent of Old-World cuts on America in mourning for Lincoln." Scholars have since written that "the mood at his funeral ceremonies showed that his death was seen as a symbol of the downfall of the centuries-old Habsburg Monarchy." The empire of Maria Theresa and the empire whose cultural splendor produced the likes of Mozart, Beethoven, and Strauss was clinging to its last breaths. It had truly been a tumultuous offseason.

# CHAPTER 7 – DECEMBER 1916

As November turned to December, nine thousand fans packed the stadium at the University of Washington to watch the football team win its ninth consecutive coast championship, defeating Cal 14-7. In Spokane, Lester Patrick finalized his roster and felt confident that this would be the team to get the Canaries back to the top of the standings after two disappointing seasons. He signed Lloyd Cook from Vancouver, who finished fourth in goals scored last season, and Ran McDonald from Portland, who finished just in front of Frank Foyston in the stats. And, in an intense competition, Lester kept Cook's younger brother Leo over his reserve from last season, Jim Riley.

Muldoon immediately snatched up the young and talented Riley, hopeful he had finally found his ninth player. Pete now had four players on his roster discarded from other PCHA teams: Riley, Bernie Morris and Bobby Rowe from Lester Patrick's organization and Roy Rickey from Vancouver. Under Muldoon's tutelage, Bernie had development into one of the best players in the league. Muldoon gave Rowe's career a second life by moving him to defense and Roy Rickey was quickly developing into a top player as well. Pete wasn't just a good game manager, he was a good coach. He knew how to put each player in position to maximize their strengths, and more importantly, he knew how to improve their weaknesses. In Jim Riley, he saw a big, strong, athletic skater with as much talent as anyone on the team.

On Friday, December 1, Spokane opened the season at Portland and shocked the defending champions, 5-4. In memory of Del Irvin, Portland began the game with only six men on the ice, leaving Irvin's position on defense open for the first few minutes of the game. The Rosebuds led heading into the final period but ran out of gas in the third and gave up three late goals. In true Portland fashion, it was a rough game. Mickey Ion handed out seven penalties for forty-six minutes, thirty going to Tommy

Dunderdale.

The next night, the Mets played at Vancouver with a capacity crowd anticipated for the season opener. It had been a week-and-a-half since the Metropolitans first practice and excitement in the city was high. "With the 1916 football schedules completed and the moleskins put aside for another year, Seattle's sport-loving population now is turning its attention to ice hockey" read the *Seattle Times*.

Frank Patrick was not going to make the same mistake he made last year and was on the ice for the first game in top shape. He knew he had an extremely talented team and he wasn't going to take any chances this year. He believed he had the best goalie in the league in Hugh Lehman, and as good of a defense as there was in hockey with captain Si Griffis and himself.

As excited as Patrick was about his defense, his forward line was better. Center Mickey MacKay was the fastest skater in the coast league and a skilled scorer. Playing alongside MacKay was perhaps the greatest tandem ever assembled. Many experts thought Cyclone Taylor was the best player in hockey while others thought it was Doc Roberts; Frank didn't care as he had both. The Millionaires remaining wing, Barney Stanley, was emerging as a star himself. They were going to be a tough offense to stop.

Muldoon knew he too had a very talented team and he knew his best lineup that maximized each man's ability. His starting seven was as good as any in hockey, Roy Rickey was now playing as well as the starters and Jim Riley had the potential to soon be one of the best players in the league. Riley was quickly getting up to speed, and because eight of the nine players were in their second year with him, Pete had been able to install the next phases of the offense. He was teaching them to pass to open spaces which allowed them to play faster and made them tougher to defend. He was also teaching them how to be champions. To do that, he needed to teach them how to compete as champions, how to play to the same high standard every moment of every game. In essence, how to play against the game itself.

Playing against the game means chasing a loose puck with the same intensity in the fourth game of the year as in the final game of the World Series. It means defending the net the same way down ten goals as you would up one. It means never letting how you feel dictate how hard you play. Every game, every period, every minute is played the same.

Championship teams play at the same level every game. They bring their A-game against the best teams, competing to the final whistle and they bring their A-game against the worst teams, winning big. Average teams, however, play against their opponents, playing well against great teams while playing down to the level of mediocre teams, barely squeaking by inferior opponents or letting them hang around long enough to win late.

Championship teams play every moment with the same purpose, intent and passion regardless of the situation so that when the pressure is most intense, the game remains the same to them. Average teams, on the other hand, ramp up for big games and leave their championship ambitions to chance. They need things such as luck and momentum to break their way without the ability to overcome when neither is on their side, ultimately relying on those outside influences to determine their fate. Muldoon wasn't going to let this team leave their season up to chance. They were going to be the masters of their fate.

Teams that can play against the game will play their best when it matters most, when the stakes are the highest. It doesn't mean they'll win every game, it simply means they'll treat every moment the same, treating each as a championship moment. If the Mets could do that, they would be champions to Muldoon regardless of the outcome.

As the team left Seattle for Vancouver, reporters asked Muldoon if the Mets were going to return to Seattle as winners. The usually talkative and optimistic coach deadpanned, "I can tell you better after the game." Upon their arrival in Vancouver, Pete snuck the team past the media and up to their rooms. He was done with words for the moment and wanted their play to do the talking. After their strong finish last season, he was sure they had the team to win the league this year. Pete was ready for his boys to take it right at the Millionaires on opening night and send a message to the rest of the league that 1916-17 was going to be the year of the Metropolitans. He was supremely confident that they were ready.

**

At exactly 8:30 p.m., Mickey Ion called both teams to center ice for the faceoff. Five thousand screaming fans had been waiting the entire offseason for this moment and were cheering wildly. Bernie Morris and Mickey MacKay waited patiently as Ion slowly slid in to center ice and dropped the puck. MacKay snatched the disc first and was off quickly, pushing toward Hap in goal before passing to Doc Roberts out on the wing. The pass found Doc in rhythm and he quickly launched a shot on goal. Hap made a great save and the Mets took the puck back up the ice to set up their offense.

From there, the contest quickly evolved into a fast-paced game. With two of the best goalies in hockey playing well, it remained scoreless past the seventeen-minute mark when Barney Stanley had the puck out on the wing. He sensed an opening in the Mets defense before attacking the goal and firing a shot. Hap made another great save sending the puck careening back out onto the ice. The deflection went straight to Mickey MacKay who quickly redirected the puck to Cyclone Taylor who had anticipated the play and snuck behind the Mets defense in front of the net. Hap lunged back for the puck but it was already in the net. 1-0 Millionaires. Vancouver had a lot of scorers out on the ice and it was going to be tough to stop them if they continued to pass so well. The Mets couldn't take a split second off on defense or the Millionaire forwards would find an open space ready for the puck.

Seattle tried to push the action on the resumption of play, hoping to keep the puck on their side of the ice for the remainder of the period. They were getting good looks and took multiple shots but Lehman continued to play superbly and blocked everything. Doc Roberts finally grabbed the puck with fifteen seconds left in the period and sprinted up the ice. He was past the Mets defense in the blink of an eye and one-on-one with Holmes. A quick flinch of his shoulders brought Hap lunging out of the cage to stop the shot while Doc calmly flicked the puck into the vacated net. With ten seconds left in the period, it was now 2-0 Vancouver. It was a crushing goal to end the period. The Mets had again relaxed for a split-second and the Millionaires made them pay. The defense could feel the pressure mounting.

When the second period began, the pace of play was slower as both teams were still working their way back into shape and conserving energy for the third period. The Metropolitans took the offensive and began pelting Lehman with shots. He blocked everything before securing one and passing it out to Cyclone Taylor who grabbed it and sprinted up the ice. Cyclone swiftly broke through the forward line, forcing the defensive line to close on him and stop the puck. The moment Bobby Rowe arrived, Taylor skipped a pass out on the wing to Doc Roberts who wristed a shot past Hap and into the back of the net, 3-0 Vancouver. Not yet twenty-three minutes in to the new season, the Millionaires offense appeared dominant as they were annihilating the shell-shocked Mets.

Muldoon soon began to sub Jim Riley for each forward, giving them a chance to catch their breath. Pete wanted to push the tempo and exhaust the Millionaires so the Mets would have fresher legs and win the game late. Almost ten minutes into the second period, Seattle finally got on the board when Jack Walker finished off a beautiful combination play by driving the puck into the goal. 3-1 Vancouver.

Frank Patrick quickly recognized and countered Muldoon's strategy by getting aggressive and sending their defensemen up the ice to attack the goal. It was a simple adjustment, but he wanted to increase their numbers to keep control of the puck on their side of the ice and neutralize Seattle's fresh legs. Five minutes later, Doc Roberts netted his third goal of the evening. Three and a half minutes after that, Frank Patrick stole the puck, passed to Mickey MacKay who passed back to Patrick who pounded the puck past Hap and into the goal. It was 5-1 Millionaires and the Vancouver offense looked invincible.

In the final period, Vancouver dropped their entire team back on defense and suffocated the Seattle offense. After almost six minutes of relentlessly attacking the goal, the Mets finally broke through when Eddie Carpenter brought the puck up and slid a perfect pass over to Jack Walker in front of the net. Jack quickly buried the shot but that was all the Mets would get on the night. Vancouver tacked on a late goal to make the final 6-2.

It was not the opening that any of them envisioned for the season. It was only one game, but it had been a crushing defeat. The Mets had been outplayed and outcoached. Vancouver's forward line had played flawlessly. They had matched the Mets speed and created options with their passing. Seattle was going to need to drastically improve to achieve their goals for the year. They had not played aggressively and had been back on their heels for most of the night. Muldoon still thought his guys playing their best game would beat the Millionaires playing their best, but it was now obvious that there wasn't much margin for error. He needed to get his guys to the point where their average game was good enough to beat the Millionaires best game. That task, however, was not going to be easy.

The next day, the Mets were criticized in the Seattle papers for being overconfident. If there was one positive, they had managed to stay out of the penalty box for the night. Other than that, Vancouver dominated every facet of the game.

By Monday afternoon, the team was back in Seattle and out on the ice for practice. As Muldoon met with the media, he admitted that they had been overconfident and not played well. While it was disappointing, many young teams fight overconfidence so he was just as happy to get it out of the way now rather than later in the year when it could spell doom for their season. Despite the way the team played overall, however, Pete was extremely happy with Rickey and Riley. Both men held their own out on the ice which allowed Muldoon to sub and keep the team fresh for the third period noting "their entrance into the game made a great difference in the last part."

He also admitted that the Millionaires were going to be a force. Most pundits had predicted that the coast championship would come down to Portland or Seattle, although it was now quite evident that Vancouver was going to challenge as well.

Despite the thumping by the Millionaires, the team's mood remained positive. In a Monday story headlined, "Seattle Hockey Team is Spurred on by Trouncing," the *Seattle Times* wrote, "rather than to discourage, defeat often spurs a team to do greater things. This is the spirit that prevails today in the camp of the Metropolitans hockey squad."

Muldoon knew they weren't going to win every game so he didn't panic. The best teams know what their best game looks like and they strive to play that well every night. They know the real competition is with themselves and not against an opponent. The Metropolitans had failed that test miserably the first game of the season. Pete wasn't excited they had played so poorly but he knew the most important thing was that they continued to improve so they would be playing their best hockey at the end of the season. He hoped this game would cure them of any overconfidence and keep them focused on themselves.

He put the guys through a tough workout that day, spending significant time at the end on their shooting. They had not shot the puck well against Vancouver and he knew they were going to need to be better against Portland.

The next day, twenty-five hundred screaming fans packed the Ice Arena to see the Mets' bitter rivals from Portland. Frank Foyston had injured his leg in practice the day before so Doc Kelton had heavily wrapped it; Foyston was noticeably slower out on the ice. The Mets struggled again right off the bat, and Portland jumped out to a 2-0 lead. Hap seemed to be having trouble with the new goalie rule and was uncharacteristically making mistakes. For the second game in a row, he allowed an easy goal as time expired at the end of a period. He aggressively came out of the net to stop the shot only to see Charlie Tobin instead float a pass over to Smokey Harris, who buried the vacated net as time expired.

When the second period started, both teams found their groove and a fantastic game unfolded. Ten hard-fought minutes into the period, Bernie Morris scored on a well-placed pass from Bobby Rowe, and the Mets were within one at 2-1. On the resumption of play, both goalies locked down their nets and despite the best efforts of each offense, the margin remained one goal going to the final stanza.

The teams traded goals to open the third, before Cully Wilson finally broke through and beat Tommy Murray to tie the score with five minutes left to play. For the remainder of the game, both offenses unleashed a barrage of shots on goal but both goalies stood tough and neither team pushed across the game winner. Regulation ended with the score tied 3-3.

It had been a physical game but clean with Cully playing spectacular on both ends of the ice. Only three, three-minute penalties had been handed out thus far, but the fights that had consistently plagued the two rivals had been avoided.

As the teams went in to their locker rooms before overtime, many of the capacity crowd stood on their feet rocking the arena. The *Seattle Times* reported that "seldom are the lovers of the puck game furnished with such soul-stirring excitement." As one woman in the front row was asked to sit down, she whipped around and yelled at those imploring her to sit, "I can't sit down while this is going on, and I don't see how anybody else can." "She remained standing and there were hundreds of others that followed."

When the puck dropped to begin the sudden death overtime period, both teams played in mid-season form. They had both used their substitutes throughout the game so while everyone was tired, the pace remained fast. A few minutes into the period, Tommy Dunderdale checked Cully Wilson aggressively and the first fight of the evening erupted. Both players were ejected after order was restored. Because they were ejected, each team was allowed to sub in a reserve. Jim Riley replaced Wilson and Stan Marples replaced Dunderdale.

Eleven minutes into the period, Frank Foyston stole the puck and raced up the ice. Approaching the goal, he slid a perfect pass over to Jim Riley who promptly scored the game-winner. Riley's first goal as a Metropolitan sent the crowd into a frenzy and sent the defending champion Rosebuds packing with their second loss of the young season. Big Jim had held his own replacing Cully and helped the team win a great game 4-3.

Spokane beat Vancouver that night to hold down first place at 2-0 while the Millionaires were tied with Seattle at 1-1. After two games, the Mets had scored the fewest goals in the league and were tied with Portland for the most goals allowed. It was not the start that any of them had imagined, but Muldoon was pleased at how well they played against Portland and was confident they had righted the ship.

Their next two games were Friday at Portland and then at home against Vancouver. The Mets were still looking for their first ever win in the Rose City and despite Frank Foyston's injured leg, the team was feeling good. The following day's *Post-Intelligencer* stated that the Mets had "picked up a lot of confidence by their victory Tuesday night and will be a hard team to beat from now on" though it was now clear that there was no weak team in the league. "The Seattle men realize that the other teams in the league are unusually strong this year and that they will have to do some fast stepping to win the championship."

Three days later, it was quickly evident they had not righted the ship as Portland jumped out to a 2-0 lead halfway through the first period. The Mets tied the score early in the second only to see Portland run away with the game, easily winning 5-2. Portland was now 4-0 against the Mets at home and had won five of their eight overall meetings. Three games in and Seattle had allowed fourteen goals to only eight scored. They all knew how tough it was to win at Portland, but Muldoon had hoped for a better showing.

The following Tuesday, the Mets hosted Vancouver looking to avenge the opening day loss and climb back to .500 in the standings. The *Seattle Post-Intelligencer*'s sub-headline read, "World Stars to Play" with the article stating that "several men who can be termed the best hockey players in the world will come down with the Vancouver men today." The *Seattle Times* simply wrote, "The Vancouver players are regarded as the most spectacular in the league." Superlative after superlative were gushed upon Doc Roberts, Cyclone Taylor and Frank Patrick. The Millionaires were loaded with blue-blood talent so Pete knew how gifted Vancouver was, but his guys had put in a great week of practice and he was confident they were going to take the Millionaires at home.

Frank Foyston's injured leg was not healing so Muldoon decided to start Jim Riley in his place and rest his captain. On the Vancouver side, Cyclone Taylor had come down with appendicitis the day before and remained in a Vancouver hospital awaiting surgery. Despite their absence, it was a magnificent game. Jack Walker scored twice, and Roy Rickey, Cully Wilson and Bernie Morris all notched goals. The work in practice was beginning to pay off as the offense finally started to hum. The Millionaires, however, had matched the Metropolitans scoring and for the second time, the Mets were headed to overtime.

Frank Foyston immediately checked in for the first time, replacing Bobby Rowe and giving the Mets another scorer on the ice. Twice, he made brilliant plays to score goals only to have both waived off by the officials. Minutes later, Mickey MacKay slapped one past Hap and won the game for Vancouver. Despite another loss, the Mets had played great and Foyston made a herculean effort to play the overtime period. It was a disastrous start to a season teeming with high hopes, but they were nonetheless a talented team and there remained plenty of time to turn it around. What was worse, perhaps, was that even without Cyclone Taylor, Vancouver still looked like a force on the ice, scoring seven goals.

Four games in and the Mets were tied with Portland for last place at 1-3, two games behind first-place Vancouver and Spokane who were tied at 3-1. The Mets had the most anemic offense in the league, scoring a paltry fourteen goals, three fewer than Portland, ten fewer than Spokane and twelve fewer than Vancouver. Defensively, they were equally inept, having allowed twenty-one goals, an average of more than five per game. In total, they had allowed one less than Spokane, one more than Vancouver and three more than Portland.

Individually, Jack Walker led the team with seven points, tied with Lester Patrick and Mickey MacKay for fifth place in the league. Bernie had three goals with three assists in the four games while Frank's injured leg had derailed his season to date. His only points of the season were from two assists. Vancouver, on the other hand, had the three top scorers and all four of their forward line were in the top-5. Doc Roberts led all scorers with ten points, one more than Cyclone Taylor.

As much optimism as everyone maintained through the first few losses, many on the outside now thought this season was on the brink of disaster. Muldoon, however, still believed in his guys and continued to push them at practice. They needed to simplify and play faster, especially on the defensive end. Royal Brougham wrote, "Happy Holmes, has been working hard to get in the best of shape," but Pete knew his goalie was going to be fine, telling Royal that before too long in the season, Hap would rank as the best goalie in the league. Pete knew they had played well and were close. He knew if they could get Frank healthy and continue to play hard that they would soon turn the corner and start winning. They just had to keep competing.

Sitting at his desk, Muldoon looked over and noticed the stack of newspapers accumulating. It had been a busy first few weeks of the season and he'd once again lost touch. He picked up the first paper to see what he had missed since the season began. On December 5, President Wilson had given his annual State of the Union address to Congress. As he entered the chamber, there was a long ovation congratulating him on his reelection. The president opened his speech proposing new railroad legislation and was beginning to speak about Puerto Rico, saying, "The present laws governing the island and regulating the rights and privileges of its people are not just," when a huge banner in suffrage yellow was unexpectedly unfurled over the balcony. It read, "President Wilson, what will you do for women's suffrage."

The president looked up at the banner, "smiled broadly and without hesitation or interruption turned his eyes back to his manuscript and continued his address to its end without further demonstration." Afterwards, the suffragists said the banner "was their protest against the president's plea with Congress for broader suffrage for the men of Puerto Rico, while he did not mention their own issue in his address." Wilson had initially been against women's suffrage but, in the past year, he had begun to change his mind.

Meanwhile, it had been a turbulent few weeks in London. First, David Lloyd George had threatened to resign as war secretary. Then, in a stunning series of events, Prime Minister H.H. Asquith resigned after eight years leading the country. Casualty numbers from the Battle of the Somme coupled with lingering frustration over Britain's early campaign in Gallipoli had ultimately led to Asquith's downfall. In Gallipoli, what should have been a sure victory over the Ottomans in the Dardanelles, had instead been a bloody slog. The newspaper reports suggested the King would first offer the Prime Minister position to Andrew Bonar Law. If he declined, David Lloyd George would be next. Law did indeed decline and Lloyd George was named Prime Minister on December 6.

\*\*

Friday night finally arrived with Lester Patrick and the first-place Spokane Canaries in town. The Mets had a great week of practice and Muldoon was optimistic, "We have practiced more for tonight's game than any other since the Seattle team was organized." But, for the first time, Muldoon also dropped the hammer on his guys. Through all of last year's streaks and the opening of this season, he had remained positive, but he was not about to change his standards. He let the boys know that he believed in them but that it was time to perform telling the *Seattle Star*, "If we do not win tonight, some changes will be made in the squad."

Hap put in another great week of work, asking Jim Riley to stay an extra hour after practice every day to shoot goals at him. The players knew how much work Hap was putting in and hoped it would begin to show up in the games. If they were going to get their season back on track, it was going to begin with Hap and the defense shutting down some explosive offenses.

Frank's leg was finally showing improvement and he was back in the lineup. From the opening faceoff, a different Seattle team was out on the ice. The boys looked like the team all of them thought they were going to be when the season began. Fast and athletic with a swarming defense, the Mets flew across the ice with confidence. At the end of the first period, both goalies had defended their nets superbly and the game remained scoreless.

The second period began much the same as the first ended, with fast, defensive hockey. Thirteen minutes into the period, Cully Wilson finally broke through on an assist from Frank and scored the first goal of the night. Thirty-three minutes of goal free hockey was the longest drought in the two short years of the Seattle Ice Arena. The game remained a spectacular defensive contest the last seven minutes of the period, ending with Seattle still up 1-0.

When the puck dropped to start the final period, the Mets depth and conditioning began to kick in. Three minutes into the period, Frank took a pass from Cully and scored his first goal of the season. One minute later, Jack found the back of the net and extended the lead to 3-0. The Mets continued to play phenomenal defense and stymie the Canaries' offense.

With five seconds left in the game, Big Jim Riley put his extra work to use and blasted the final goal of the night. Hap recorded the PCHA's first shutout of the season as the Mets easily won 4-0. Rickey and Riley played significant minutes off the bench, with Rickey losing five teeth in a collision with Lester Patrick. He remained out on the ice and continued to play hard. It had been a total team effort. The Mets won with depth, they won with superior conditioning, they won with athleticism and most importantly, they won with toughness. Muldoon knew this game was coming and his team had set their standard of play for the year. He couldn't wait to get back out on the ice next Tuesday and do it again.

The next night, Portland beat Vancouver at home, holding the high-powered Millionaires offense to only three goals. Without a doubt, Portland was the toughest place in the league to play and the Millionaires had shown their first cracks offensively without Cyclone Taylor. His appendix had been removed and he was going to be out four to six weeks.

Portland's win had brought all of the teams to within one game in the standings. Spokane and Vancouver were still in first place at 3-2 while Portland and Seattle were close at 2-3.

The Mets continued to practice hard, with Muldoon saying, "Our team is up and coming now." Lester Patrick told the media that his squad had struggled with injuries in their last game so promised the Mets would see a different Spokane team on Tuesday. Seattle had now played every team in the league and Muldoon thought Portland was still the team to beat. "I realize that Vancouver has a powerful team, but the Uncle Sams seem stronger." The Uncle Sams was a nickname left over from when Portland was the only American team in the league. To most in hockey, however, the question remained how Vancouver would handle the extended loss of Cyclone Taylor. Plus, the Millionaires defense was not as physical as Portland's so Muldoon believed the Rosebuds would be the team to beat.

The Mets practiced Monday morning and then took the train to Spokane that afternoon. That same day, the Battle of Verdun finally ended. Three days short of ten months, it was one of the longest battles of the war. All told, there were close to seven hundred thousand casualties on both sides with nearly three hundred thousand killed. When the battle was finally halted, the lines were in almost the exact same positions as when it began ten months prior and without a strategic objective achieved other than mass bloodshed.

**

In their first trip east of the Cascade Mountains to the Inland Empire of Spokane, the Mets found a city booming similar to Seattle, with a population that had grown from nearly 37,000 in 1900 to 104,400 in 1910 and now stood at more than 150,000 residents. Precious metals had been discovered in North Idaho near the end of the nineteenth century and Spokane had an abundance of wealth within its populace, boasting an estimated twenty-six millionaires in 1910. The stunning new Davenport Hotel had recently been completed downtown and Spokane's most famous native son, thirteen-year-old Bing Crosby, was a few months away from seeing his idol Al Jolson on stage at the Auditorium Theater. It was a performance that would give rise to perhaps the most successful recording career in history. At the Spokane Arena, the Metropolitans were looking to build on their victory over the Canaries Friday night to climb out of the cellar for only the second time in the young season.

As the puck dropped, play picked up right where it left off in the last game with both teams playing fast and aggressive. Hap was again superb, repelling shots from every angle. Ten minutes in, Spokane's Sibby Nichols made a rush on goal and fired a shot that Hap blocked, athletically sprawling out on the ice to make a great save. The deflection miraculously went straight back to Nichols, who quickly flicked it back into the net. Holmes tried in vain to get back into position to block the put-back, but it had just been an unlucky bounce. It was a great effort, but Spokane took a 1-0 lead nonetheless. Bernie soon scored on an assist from Cully Wilson to tie the score.

The third period opened with the game still tied and immediately, Spokane began to play physical. The Canaries knew Seattle liked to skate fast and pull away from their opponents late in games so began to play rough to get the Mets out of their game. Neither team could push a goal across until Foyston somehow broke through and gave the Mets a 2-1 lead. The Canaries' physical strategy began to work as Cully Wilson was soon sent to the penalty box, with Frank shortly joining him; his first penalty minutes of the year. Upon his release, Cully quickly earned himself another three minutes off the ice and the Mets were forced to play five-on-seven for most of the last half of the period. Incredibly, Hap prevented the Canaries from capitalizing. Despite being shorthanded, Bernie scored his second goal of the night on a beautiful pass from Jack Walker and clinched the 3-1 win

The Mets had once again taken the Canaries' best shot and kept their offense in check. The Spokane newspaper lamented, "if every well-meant Spokane shot that hit some portion of Harry Holmes' ample padded proportions, or his club, had counted, Spokane would have been victorious over Seattle in tonight's encounter." Hap had once again played brilliantly. Muldoon said "it was the best game of the year. Harry Holmes played a wonder game at goal, and it was his work that went far to give victory to the Mets. All of the boys played their best, and I look for them to keep right on winning." It had been an ugly, physical struggle but the Mets had found a way to win. They were showing the ability to win different styles of games and were feeling good about the direction they were headed. They had the next week off for Christmas and were excited to continue to practice hard and get healthy.

Vancouver beat Portland that week at home and after a quarter of the season, remained in first place at 4-2. Seattle and Spokane were tied for second at 3-3, with Portland just a game behind them at 2-4. Hap's streak of one goal surrendered over the last two games was the fewest allowed in a two-game stretch in the history of the PCHA. As the teams took a few days off for Christmas, tragedy struck the league. Rosebuds manager Ed Savage had been in an automobile that was sandwiched between two streetcars in Portland. Two people were killed and Savage suffered a fractured skull in the accident. Dick Irvin's former coach Frank Scott was brought in from Winnipeg to manage the Rosebuds until Savage could recover.

**

After the break, the Mets welcomed the Vancouver Millionaires back to Seattle on December 26 with a chance to move into a first-place tie with a win. The *Seattle Star* wrote that the team, "after a more or less disastrous start, had rounded down to the form that made it a factor" last season. Muldoon told the *Seattle Post-Intelligencer*, "I have the best team in the league. The boys ought to win three-fourths of their games, the way they are going now. Every one of the boys is skating like champions, and I look for them to step into the lead Tuesday night." Pete's plan was to take Frank Patrick out of the game offensively and force the forwards to beat them. "We have it all planned so that Frank Patrick will be unable to slip over any of his sensational stuff, and my men will watch every man on the rival team as well. Patrick is a star, but he can't shine if he can't get the puck."

As the game started, Vancouver immediately took control and pressed the action. Three and a half minutes into the period, Frank Patrick broke through the Seattle defense before dumping a beautiful pass to Doc Roberts for a 1-0 Millionaires lead. Seattle had prepared for the exact play the entire week and Frank Patrick still made it look easy.

Mickey MacKay won the ensuing faceoff and charged the Seattle goal. As he pulled up to set the offense, Bobby Rowe swept in and hook-checked the puck away and started a mad dash back up the ice. As he closed on Lehman, "he brought the house down with a well-placed shot between Lehman's flags" and quickly tied the score. The capacity crowd was instantly on its feet and back in the game. It was a perfect response from Bobby and immediately snapped the Mets back to life.

When play resumed, Seattle took control of the game and maintained the puck for most of the period. Almost thirteen minutes into the session, Bernie Morris had the puck out on the point before attacking the net. Frank Foyston read the play instantly and crashed from the left side as Bernie floated him a perfect pass in stride. 2-1 Mets. It was a beautiful play and something they had also practiced the entire week. With less than thirty seconds remaining in the period, the pair executed the same play and made it 3-1.

The Mets continued to play their game and pulled away from Vancouver over the next two periods. When the final whistle blew, Frank Foyston had scored five goals while Bernie added a goal and three assists. Seattle had once again played a complete game, winning 7-2.

" 'Didn't I tell you my boys were champions?' smiled Manager Pete after it was over and one of the largest crowds of the season had left the Arena. 'We're going to be hard stopping now.' " Pete had stuck with his guys through a tough start when many had given up on them. He was extremely proud of their work to turn it around. He knew his players had already experienced their taste of overconfidence so felt strongly they would be able to stay focused for the remainder of the season. It wasn't going to be easy, but he liked their chances.

The only thing that could derail the season at this point was injury as Cully Wilson had hurt his knee in the second period and needed to be replaced by Jim Riley. Riley had played fantastic filling in for Cully with Royal Brougham writing that he "banged around the ice like a veteran, his aggressiveness stopping many rallies." While they were all excited how well Riley had played, they were worried about the extent of Cully's knee injury as he was a crucial member of the team. His penalties frustrated Muldoon but they all knew his spirit helped define the toughness of the team. He was a special player and they all hoped the injury was not serious.

The next morning, Pete took Cully to see Doc Kelton. The injury was worse than expected and he was going to miss four to six weeks with a badly sprained knee ligament. Muldoon had experienced his Portland team falling apart two seasons ago due to injury so had put a premium on depth with this team. While he had hoped it wouldn't matter, the Mets' bench had indeed come into play though Muldoon was confident Jim Riley and Roy Rickey would fill the void. The Mets had now won three in a row and were tied with Vancouver and Spokane for first place at 4-3 with Portland in last place at 2-5.

After Hap's last three games, the Mets had now allowed the fewest goals in the league with twenty-four, seven less than the next closest team. Offensively, the Mets remained in last place with twenty-seven goals but had scored the most goals in the league over the past four games, netting twenty. After their disastrous start, they were showing everyone that they were the best team on both sides of the ice. Doc Roberts was still leading the league in scoring with seventeen points but Bernie Morris had moved into third with twelve and Frank Foyston and Jack Walker were now tied for sixth with nine.

On December 30, the Mets traveled to Vancouver looking to extend their winning streak to four games. The night before, Portland beat Spokane at home in an ugly game marred by penalties and fights so the winner of the Mets-Millionaires game would end 1916 in first place. Vancouver scored first and led 2-1 after the first period before the Mets tallied four unanswered in the second and the beginning of the third period to pull away. The teams traded late goals as the Mets won their fourth straight, this time besting Vancouver 7-4. Jim Riley, starting in place of the injured Cully Wilson, notched four goals on the night with Bernie Morris scoring the remaining three. The Vancouver Daily World reported that "the Mets looked like the class of the league." After a 1-3 start, they were now 5-3 and in sole possession of first place. Vancouver and Spokane were tied for second at 4-4 and Portland was in the cellar at 3-5.

**

That same night in St. Petersburg, Russia, Felix Yusupov invited Grigori Rasputin to his beautiful palace on the Moyka River. Rasputin's dead body was found in the Neva River a few days later. There was trouble brewing in Russia.

# CHAPTER 8 – JANUARY 1917

The headline in the New Year's Day edition of the *Seattle Times* simply read, "What Does the New Year Hold for the World?" It was certainly the question on everyone's mind.

The headline in that day's *Seattle Star* sports section was a little less grave, perhaps even inspiring. It proclaimed "1916 Was Woman's Year in Sport" with the article stating, "the most remarkable performances in the world of sport in 1916 were achieved by women." Aviation, much like auto racing, was a sport on the rise. Ruth Law's non-stop flight from Chicago to Hornell, New York, a distance of 668 miles, bested Victor Carlstrom's record for the longest flight by 216 miles. Her flight took five hours and thirty-eight minutes, an average of 118 miles per hour. According to *The Star*, "Miss Law's long cross-country flight is one of the high spots in the history of aviation."

In golf, Atlanta's Alexa Stirling "winning the national golf championship for women was one of the remarkable performances of the year." In tennis, Molla Bjurstedt won her second of four straight U.S. Open championships while swimmer Olga Dorfner was the U.S. Champion in the 50- and 100-yard freestyle. She would soon become the first American woman to set a world record.

The men had their accomplishments in 1916 as well. In golf, Chick Evans won both the U.S. Amateur and U.S. Open. It was the first time a golfer won both titles in the same year, a feat only matched since by Alexa Stirling's close friend Bobby Jones. Tennis player, R. Norris Williams, a survivor of the *Titanic*, won his second U.S. Open.

The Boston Red Sox followed their 1915 World Series championship by winning the pennant again in 1916. Boston's Babe Ruth was the American League pitcher of the year while Philadelphia's Grover Cleveland Alexander was regarded as the best pitcher in the National League. Cleveland's Tris Speaker won his only American League batting title, the lone year Ty Cobb didn't win the crown between 1907 and 1919. Cincinnati's Hal Chase won his sole batting title as well, taking top honors in the National League.

In hockey, the storied Montreal Canadiens won their first Stanley Cup by defeating the Portland Rosebuds in five games. In just their second year of existence, the Metropolitans were hoping to soon win their first. There was, however, a lot of season left before the Mets needed to even start thinking about that ambition. First, those same Portland Rosebuds were coming to Seattle the following day for the first game of 1917.

The next morning, they all woke to the headline, "Rasputin, Monk and Dark Force of Russia, Murdered." Reports coming out of St. Petersburg said, "Grigori Rasputin, the Russian monk who is reputed to exercise great influence over the czar, is dead." News sources said his body was found on the banks of the Neva River with many reporting his "assassination under dramatic circumstances." It was at least the third time news of his murder had been reported in the West though this time it appeared to be credible.

According to the news reports, Rasputin "was a monk of no great literary ability or of descent, but of a commanding personality. He was regarded with fear by many not only because of his undoubted influence in court circles, but apparently because of supernatural qualities imputed to him or claimed by him." Many in the inner circle of Russian politics blamed him for their current state of affairs with the reports noting that "every shortcoming of the government, no matter how naturally evoked through the extraordinary circumstances of the war, has been laid at the door of Rasputin."

There was indeed trouble brewing in Russia.

\*\*

With the teams back from the break, it was time for hockey again. Muldoon had given the team a few days off for the holiday in the hopes of resting their legs and conserving energy for the stretch run. The Mets opened against their bitter rival to the south with the *Seattle Times* writing, "The enemy is back again and the 'just before the battle' atmosphere is pervading the Seattle hockey circles" with the *Seattle Star* adding "the Portland team has always put up an aggressive game with the Seattle boys and attracts the largest crowds of any visiting squad." It was going to be an epic beginning to 1917 for the city of Seattle and their beloved Metropolitans, winners of four straight.

Portland immediately took control of the game as the Mets looked out of sync. Hap reverted back to his early season form, and three minutes in, the Rosebuds had taken a 2-0 lead. Jim Riley struggled mightily, and the Rosebuds were clearly the more aggressive team. They added another score before the halfway point and the first period ended with Portland up 3-0.

In the second period, the Mets stormed back to pull within one goal, but the game soon became physical and then spiraled into a downright brawl. In the third period alone, six penalties were handed out. The Rosebuds capitalized on the rough play and won 7-4. Hap played his worst game in more than two weeks. Frank scored two goals on the night but also received two penalties, the second touching off the skirmish after almost hitting Portland's goalie in the face trying to score on a loose puck.

According to the *Seattle Star*, "The melee started like the dinky pop of a fire cracker, but before the final had been reached the contest was raging like a second siege of the Dardanelles." Royal Brougham wrote it was "a wild battle that started in whirlwind fashion and ended like a miniature Verdun" saying "the bitter feeling between the two aggregations culminated in a near riot near the close of the contest." It was a fierce rivalry, but a fairly one-sided rivalry with Portland now the victors in six of their nine all-time meetings.

It was just one game, but it was deflating to lose to a rival, especially in a physical contest like this. They were going to need to quickly regroup. Spokane and Vancouver had a bye so Seattle maintained a half game lead in the standings at 5-4 with both the Millionaires and Canaries at 4-4 and Portland only one game back at 4-5. Nine games into the season and it was the closest race in the history of the league.

The Metropolitans made their second trip to Spokane three days later. The offense sputtered again as Spokane climbed out to a 2-0 lead in the middle of the second. Once they got some breathing room, the Canaries played physical and a fight soon erupted between Sibby Nichols and Frank Foyston. Both men received twenty minutes in the box. It was Foyston's second consecutive game with a penalty and the Mets fell apart without him, allowing three goals and losing 5-1. Spokane moved into first place at 5-4. Portland beat Vancouver and was now tied with Seattle for second at 5-5 relegating the Millionaires to the cellar at 4-5, having now lost four straight without Cyclone Taylor.

The next day in the *Post-Intelligencer*, Muldoon acknowledged that Spokane had played a great game and that "our boys were not in their best form. Either the strain of the Portland clash was too much for them, or they were lost on the strange ice, for the defense was not up to snuff." During the current skid, Eddie Carpenter had played his two worst games as a Metropolitan but Muldoon was confident he would snap out of it before their next game. The Mets were going to get a reprieve this week with two home games and home crowds. And Cully Wilson, who had begun to move better, was going to practice Monday though Doc Kelton thought he was still a week or two away from playing in a game. The *Seattle Times* reported that "although Riley has been filling Wilson's position creditably Cully's absence has been very noticeable."

The league released stats that day for the Sunday morning newspapers.

Doc Roberts and Dick Irvin led the league in scoring with eighteen points, one ahead of Bernie Morris. After a slow start, Frank Foyston was now tied for fifth with fourteen points. Jack Walker and Cully Wilson were just outside the top-10 at ten and eight points, respectively.

In penalties, Portland's Tommy Dunderdale led the league with sixty-five minutes. Cully Wilson was fourth with thirty-three minutes on eleven, three-minute penalties. Cully was an aggressive player so he was going to get some penalties but he was learning to control his emotions. He hadn't been penalized any additional time this year for fighting other than the overtime game against Portland. The Mets desperately needed him to return soon.

Overall, the Mets had been penalized the least of any of the four teams with just twenty-one penalties though they were third in penalty minutes with eight-eight, sixteen more than Vancouver. Spokane had been penalized one hundred thirty minutes and Portland was once again running away as the most penalized team with one hundred fifty-three minutes.

As Tuesday arrived, it was clear that Cully Wilson's knee was not ready and he once again did not dress for the game. The *Seattle Times* summed up the importance of the game perfectly, "Three things may happen to the Seattle Hockey Club tonight in its scheduled battle with the Spokane puck-chasers. Either the Metropolitans will jump out in front in the league standings, will tie with Portland for first place or will drop back into the ruck where the climb to the top of the heap will be more arduous."

To say it was a must-win game was a little much, but they were nearing the halfway point in the season. Coming off two straight losses made it as critical a game as they had yet played. Win, and they were back in first place. Lose, and they could potentially be tied for last place. They hadn't played well the last two games but were feeling confident after three good days of practice.

A big crowd greeted both teams that night and, right from the start, Frank Foyston took control. A minute-and-a-half in, he grabbed the puck near center ice and split the defensemen for Spokane. A subtle hesitation move got Canaries' goalie Norm Fowler off-balance, and the puck was soon in the corner of the net to give Seattle a quick 1-0 lead and some breathing room.

Near the end of the period, Frank stole a pass and made another brilliant rush up the ice to score a goal. It gave the Metropolitans a 2-0 lead and renewed sense of confidence on their way to a much-needed 3-1 win. Frank had simply taken over the game and willed the Mets to victory. "The Seattle win was not a result of brilliant team play," Brougham wrote, "but one of individual prowess." "The Seattle leader pulled two of the cleverest plays ever seen on the local ice." The *Seattle Times* agreed, "Captain Frank Foyston put the game away for Seattle all by himself in the first seventeen minutes of play."

Once the Mets had taken the lead, the two defensemen played brilliantly and Hap shut down the goal. Brougham wrote, "covering the game without mentioning Bobby Rowe would be doing the hard-working defenseman an injustice." Bobby played one of his best games of the year, as had Jim Riley. On the heels of their two worst games, the team responded with one of its best games.

There are ebbs and flows to every season, and the Mets had just experienced a low point. Flat spots where the team simply doesn't click or perform as well as it can and the internal pressure mounts as each player tries to put the team on their shoulders and right the ship. Unfortunately, trying to put the team on your shoulders is counterproductive. It usually speeds up the game and leads to forcing the action which leads to even more pressure and soon, a flat spot becomes a slump. Every team experiences flat spots, the best teams simply prevent them from becoming slumps.

Championship teams typically have a great player to make the plays when it matters most. Players that lessen the pressure on their teammates, thereby allowing the team to perform its best. Soon, a flat spot becomes a winning streak.

Great players don't do anything extra, they don't force the action. They simply trust they will succeed and just play. The game remains slow to them which allows their best performance. They anticipate plays rather than react to them, seeing the holes to exploit and opportunities to score rather than frantically committing to a bad course of action. Frank Foyston was that guy for the Mets. Tonight, in a critical game, he didn't put the team on his shoulders, he just went out and played and scored two goals that gave the Mets a quick lead and removed the pressure. It allowed the entire team to cut loose and play at full speed for the remainder of the game. Frank was continuing to grow into one of the best players in hockey.

In Vancouver that night, the Millionaires snapped their four-game losing streak by beating Portland so the Mets now stood alone in first place at 6-5. Vancouver and Spokane were a half game back at 5-5 with Portland again in the cellar, only one game back at 5-6.

The next day, Muldoon broke his tradition of giving the team a day off from practice following a game. He brought Jim Riley, Roy Rickey, Cully Wilson and Hap Holmes in for practice. They faced Vancouver on Friday night and Pete wanted to make sure his guys were still playing their best. Despite his recent lapse, Hap had been playing brilliantly for a few weeks and Pete was going to continue to push him. Muldoon used one of his old boxing techniques to improve Hap's hand-eye coordination, setting up a speed bag for him.

Cully's knee continued to improve so Pete wanted to keep his shooting sharp and increase his conditioning. Muldoon wanted him in game shape once the ligament could handle cutting on the ice at full speed. The Mets were going to need him to step in immediately and provide a spark. In Rickey and Riley, Muldoon knew his two young reserves were close to being stars and he was going to take every opportunity to push their development forward. If the Mets were going to compete for the Stanley Cup, both were going to play big roles.

Before the game, news broke that Frank Vance of the Seattle Athletic Club was forming a women's hockey team to take on a squad coached by Pete Muldoon. Pete learned of Vance's plan, and thought it a good idea to form his own team. Muldoon knew that Cully Wilson's wife played hockey as did Frank Foyston's sister, Jessie. Frank immediately cabled Jessie to invite her to Seattle.

Friday night's game against Vancouver was another big one, marking the halfway point in the season. With a win, the Mets would climb to two games above .500 for only the second time all season and end the first half atop the standings. Pete told the *Seattle Times*, "We must go over the hump two games to the good and we intend to do it." Jim Riley started in place of Cully Wilson, who had practiced all week but still couldn't play.

Referee George Irvine dropped the puck at exactly half past eight. Each team scored two goals in the first period, with Bernie netting both Mets' goals. Midway through the second period, Frank and Mickey MacKay traded goals to knot the score at 3-3 before Seattle began to pull away. First, Frank scored his second goal and then Big Jim Riley added one of his own to end the period with the Mets up 5-3.

When the third period started, it was all Seattle. Bobby Rowe scored first with Bernie tacking on another twenty seconds later. Then, Eddie Carpenter scored his first goal of the season, then Jack Walker, then Morris, Foyston, and Morris again to make the final an astounding 12-3 Seattle victory. It had been the most complete game the Mets played all season with all seven players recording a point on the evening, six scoring goals. Bernie led the charge with five goals and two assists including two goals directly from the faceoff. Eddie Carpenter played his best game of the season and Jim Riley had again played superbly.

The Mets finished the first half on top of the standings with a 7-5 record. The Canaries beat Portland in Spokane to remain in second place at 6-5, with Vancouver in third at 5-6, having lost five of their last six. Portland, still in the cellar at 5-7, was just a mere two games out of first place.

Bernie Morris was now leading the league in scoring with twenty-four points, two ahead of Doc Roberts and Dick Irvin. Frank was in fourth at nineteen points. Irvin currently led the league in goals with eighteen, three in front of Bernie and Roberts. The Mets were now leading the league in goals scored with fifty-six, one ahead of Portland and four in front of Vancouver. They had also allowed the fewest goals with forty-four, four less than Spokane and nine less than Portland. Halfway through the season, Muldoon had the best offense in the league, the best defense, the best scorer in Morris and the best goalie in Hap, allowing almost a goal less per game than the next closest goalie.

Seattle would need to continue playing well with two tough games the following week against Portland, first on the road and then at home. The Mets had still never won a game in Portland, and, after beating the Rosebuds in overtime the second game of the season, had lost two straight to the Uncle Sams. Muldoon was worried about the upcoming games but the Mets had played brilliantly the last two outings and they were hopeful Cully Wilson would finally be healthy enough to return.

As Pete sat and finished contemplating the first half of the season, he once again grabbed the stack of newspapers accumulating on his desk. On January 10, Buffalo Bill Cody passed away. His body was to lay in state at the Colorado capitol building for four hours the following day. President Wilson had wired condolences to the family, and retired General Nelson Miles wrote that "Colonel Cody was a high-minded gentleman, a brave American and a great scout. He performed great work in the West for the pioneers and for the generations coming after them and his exploits will live forever in history."

In Washington D.C., a dozen women representing the Congressional Union for Woman Suffrage were picketing outside the White House with signs that once again read, "Mr. President, What Will You Do For Woman Suffrage." The women were going to picket the White House "until March 4 when the suffragettes plan to bring their campaign for a federal amendment to a close with a big parade."

The temperature was "so cold on January 10 that White House officials invited them into the executive mansion to get warm." According to the newspaper reports, "the invitation hardly could have been extended without the authority of the president or Mrs. Wilson." The suffragettes had refused, but on a few occasions the police had looked the other way to allow the women to enter the White House grounds and protect themselves from the icy winds blowing on Washington. Later, President Wilson tipped his cap to the women while departing the White House. Although he still wasn't ready to support a constitutional amendment to bring suffrage to women, they had earned his respect.

Last, he read that General Pershing's punitive expeditionary force would be leaving Mexico immediately. A new policy regarding Mexico was to be announced early the next week. The government was hopeful to send the ambassador back to Mexico City and resume normal diplomatic relations with Carranza's government.

Muldoon gave the team Saturday off with practice on Sunday and Monday before departing for Portland Tuesday morning. Muldoon told the *Seattle Times* the Portland games were "among the really important games of the season" while Royal Brougham wrote in the *Post-Intelligencer* "that Seattle is up against a really crucial series." When the Mets fought to the top spot in the standings in December, the Rosebuds decisive victory snapped their four-game winning streak. The Mets only remained in first place because the other teams did not play.

In Monday's practice, however, disaster struck. Eddie Carpenter had tweaked his back in Friday's game against Vancouver and made it worse on Monday. Doc Kelton was not sure if he was going to be able to play. Worse, though, was that Jack Walker and Jim Riley had collided at full speed leaving Walker with a severely sprained ankle. The *Seattle Times* wrote that Walker "probably is the most valuable hockey player in the league" and that Doc Kelton "has forbidden Walker to play." Jack could not walk without a severe limp, meaning skating at full speed was completely out of the question. Both Eddie and Jack told the papers they were going to play, but not many believed they could. Cully Wilson was almost back but Doc Kelton wasn't sure he could withstand a full game therefore leaving the Metropolitans in the precarious position of not having enough healthy players to field a team.

Pete didn't waste a second fretting about the injuries. His plan was to move Bobby Rowe to rover and start Roy Rickey on defense, then spend pregame figuring out if Cully Wilson or Eddie Carpenter were able to fill the last spot. Regardless of the lineup, Muldoon told the *Seattle Times* the Mets were going to send everyone forward in the first period to overwhelm the Portland defense and get out to a quick lead. If they were successful, they would drop everyone back on defense for the last two periods and run out the clock. Muldoon knew Jack was one of the best players in the league, but he also knew how talented the rest of his team was and that winning championships wasn't always about your best versus their best. It's often about finding a way to win with the best you have on that particular day against their best. And, he still had a lot. Regardless, he was excited for the challenge.

As the team arrived in Portland, Jack Walker talked Doc Kelton into at least dressing and trying to loosen up his ankle. Cully Wilson was going to suit up as well and Doc Kelton worked fastidiously to get Eddie Carpenter ready. The Portland newspapers ran the Rosebuds' record against the Mets that day, reporting "the locals have triumphed over Seattle in two of the three games played between the two teams this season, and the fans think the Puget Sounders are liable to suffer defeat again, as the Buds play like champions of the world on their home ice."

A few minutes before the puck was set to drop, the starting lineups were announced. Both Jack Walker and Eddie Carpenter were starting. So long as they were able to hold their weight on their skates, they were going to play. Moments before the game began, however, Portland manager Frank Scott filed an official league protest over the officiating. Mickey Ion was set to referee the game without a judge of play. Portland was frustrated in general with the refereeing in the league, claiming they were unfairly punished more than the other teams and wanted a second official alongside Ion. They proposed a local amateur step in to work the game but Muldoon vigorously opposed the move as he did not want an amateur referee working a professional contest. This incensed the Portland squad and things spiraled from there.

From the outset, the Rosebuds were completely disjointed on both ends of the ice. The Seattle injuries prevented the Mets from coming out fast, so an awkward game unfolded. More than eleven minutes into the first period, Jack Walker finally broke through and made a great pass to Bernie Morris who netted a goal to give the Metropolitans a 1-0 lead. Two minutes later, Morris secured the puck and raced up the ice to score his second goal of the night. A late Rosebud goal near the end of the period made it 2-1 heading to the intermission.

The teams traded goals in the second period, with Seattle's coming from Frank Foyston on another great Jack Walker pass. In the third, the Mets forward line took over the game. Frank scored two goals on assists from Bernie before Jack put the finishing touches on a brilliant night, scoring the final goal to give the Mets a 6-2 victory and their first ever win in Portland.

Jack played the entire sixty minutes on a painfully sprained ankle, registering a goal and two assists. Bernie had two goals with two assists and Frank scored three goals on the night. Eddie Carpenter battled through the first two periods before being replaced by Roy Rickey midway through the third. He also registered his first penalty of the year. As injured as he was, he had played aggressively and given everything he had. Muldoon knew both men were going to be extremely stiff the next day and hoped they could recover in time to play again on Friday.

The Oregon papers heavily criticized the Rosebuds effort, writing that the "Portland players failed to get together or play together. The Portland team was not there at any stage." The next day, the Rosebuds filed another official protest, this time against Mickey Ion himself saying they would not come up to Seattle to play on Friday if Ion refereed. In addition, they would forfeit their remaining games if both protests were not taken seriously. Muldoon, clearly vexed, said "Ion certainly has not favored Seattle in any game in which he has officiated." Frank Patrick simply called Ion the best referee in hockey but promised to take the protest seriously and removed Mickey from the Seattle-Portland contest Friday night. He decided to referee the game himself with Si Griffis as judge of play.

On the afternoon of the game, Frank Patrick called a meeting of himself, Mickey Ion, Pete Muldoon and Portland's Frank Scott. The meeting quickly devolved into a shouting match with Mickey Ion eventually resigning his post in frustration. Portland's protest was unsubstantiated and overturned, but they ultimately won in that Mickey Ion was done. All involved were exasperated by the behavior of the Portland franchise.

Doc Kelton once again worked feverishly on Eddie Carpenter, Jack Walker and Cully Wilson. The Mets had a week off after the Friday game; if he could get them ready to play tonight, the trio would have plenty of time to rest. Shortly before the teams took the ice, Doc Kelton cleared all three to play. For the first time in weeks, Muldoon had a sore, but complete roster at his disposal.

At half past eight, referee Frank Patrick, judge of play Si Griffis and the Seattle Metropolitans stood alone at center ice. The Rosebuds wanted to drive their impertinence home so made the largest Seattle crowd of the year wait a few extra minutes before exiting the dressing room. When they did arrive, an intensely focused Metropolitans team was ready.

Bernie scored late in the first to get the Metropolitans on the board, but Portland grabbed a 2-1 advantage eight minutes into the second period. From there, Bernie, Frank and Jack dominated the contest. On the ensuing faceoff, Bernie snagged the puck, raced up the ice and made a beautiful pass to Frank for the tying goal, immediately answering the Portland rally. After that, two quick Jack Walker scores put the Mets ahead before Frank knocked one in to make it 5-2 at the end of the second. In the third, Portland scored another goal but not before Frank and Bernie each rounded out hat tricks for the evening to give Seattle a commanding 8-3 victory.

Jack Walker was a warrior. He could barely walk, but he'd skated his way to three goals and two assists in the sweep of the Rosebuds. Frank scored six goals in the two wins while Bernie scored five with three assists. And, perhaps the best news of the series was that Cully Wilson entered the game in the third period on Friday.

Heading into their bye week, the Metropolitans were on a four-game winning streak, outscoring their opponents twenty-nine to nine during the stretch, and sat in first place at 9-5. Vancouver thumped Spokane the next day, and after bottoming out in last place in early January, the Millionaires had won two of three to climb into a tie with the Canaries for second at 6-6. Portland remained in last place at 5-9. The Mets were now two games up on the closest teams, the largest lead in the standings since the fourth game of the season.

**

On Tuesday, January 23, they all awoke to the *Seattle Post-Intelligencer's* headline of "Wilson Speech Startles World." President Wilson addressed the Senate the previous afternoon in a "revolutionary peace address," delivering his Peace Without Victory speech. "Whether the United States shall enter a world peace league and, as many contend, thereby abandon its traditional policy of isolation and no entangling alliances, was put squarely before congress and the country today by President Wilson in a personal address to the senate."

"For the first time in more than a hundred years a president of the United States appeared in the senate chamber to discuss the nation's foreign relations after the manner of Washington, Adams and Madison. The effect was to leave congress, all official quarters and the foreign diplomats amazed and bewildered."

In his speech, Wilson addressed Congress on his vision to end the cycle of war. He declared that lasting peace in Europe would never result if one side was victorious and imposed its will on the other. Only a peace reached without victory could result in lasting peace. He spoke of the need to establish a global entity "to assure the world that no catastrophe of war shall overwhelm it again." And, he said the United States must participate in this organization, asking Congress to "formulate the conditions upon which it would feel justified in asking the American people for their formal and solemn adherence." The president's speech, was reversing nearly one hundred years of American foreign policy.

The reaction both domestically and abroad was harsh and emotional with most in Congress staunchly against involvement and Canada furious that a country that hadn't shed an ounce of blood in the conflict had the arrogance to propose solutions. Wilson, however, believed deeply in the need for a monumental shift in mankind, determined to stay the course.

\*\*

As the Mets returned from their week off, Vancouver had beaten Spokane and Spokane had beaten Portland. Seattle was still in first at 9-5, with Vancouver in second at 7-6, Spokane in third at 7-7, and Portland in last at 5-10. Portland had now lost twice as many games as it did all last season and was 3-6 under its new coach. Murmurs were beginning to creep into the Seattle media about winning the pennant and hosting the World Series. With ten games yet to play, it was just idle talk.

During the bye week, Mickey Ion had been asked to return as a referee with the stipulation he not officiate Portland games. The *Seattle Post-Intelligencer* said that if Ion agreed, "hockey fans all over the circuit will welcome his return, as he was the most popular official in the game. His work has been satisfactory at all times, and the action of the Portland club in protesting against his work is regarded as poor sportsmanship all the way around the circuit."

On Friday, the Mets traveled to Vancouver to play the suddenly hot Millionaires, having won three of their last four, for a marquee Saturday night contest. Mickey Ion accepted the invitation to return and went to Vancouver to referee the game though the big announcement on the day was that after five weeks, Cyclone Taylor was going to make his return for the Millionaires. For the Mets, Cully Wilson was still not 100 percent so Doc Kelton held him out of the game.

The largest crowd of the year came out to cheer on Cyclone's return and from the outset, it was two great teams playing their best hockey. Both goalies played superbly, repelling shot after shot before Vancouver executed "one of the best combination plays seen on local ice for some time" when Doc Roberts grabbed the puck and started a rush towards the goal. The entire forward line from Vancouver simultaneously followed suit, sending passes back and forth until Frank Patrick sent a beautiful pass to Stanley, who beat Hap to give the Millionaires a 1-0 lead. Jim Riley later snuck one past Hugh Lehman and the first period ended tied.

When the second period began, Frank Patrick grabbed a loose puck, sprinted up the ice and fired a crisp shot at Hap that looked like a sure goal. Hap made a brilliant save but Vancouver's Speedy Moynes was there to immediately skip the deflection back to Frank who this time buried the net to break the tie. Doc Roberts banged home a goal eight minutes later, and the Millionaires led 3-1.

The score remained the same until the beginning of the third when Bernie won the faceoff and flew up the ice, sending a perfect pass over to Jim Riley who scored his second goal of the night, but the Mets got no closer. The Millionaires had won a critical home game over the Metropolitans. The Vancouver Daily World wrote, "after one of the fastest games seen here for some time, and one of the most stubbornly fought, the Millionaires were returned victors by the close score of 3-2."

Cyclone Taylor had starred in his return. The Mets players told the *Post-Intelligencer* "the Cyclone was a wonder. He showed no signs of being disabled and was a prominent factor in the Vancouver victory." In the *Seattle Times*, one of the Seattle players joked that "an operation for appendicitis is a great thing for a hockey player" as Cyclone "played in better form than he showed early in the season" when he was the leading scorer in the league. With a healthy Cyclone Taylor, Vancouver was going to be tough to beat down the stretch.

After fifteen games, Bernie Morris was still leading the league in points with thirty-three, four more than Doc Roberts of Vancouver. Frank Foyston was fourth with twenty-five points. Jack Walker was just outside the top-10 with sixteen points, with Bobby Rowe and Jim Riley just behind him with eleven. Three of the Mets top-5 scorers were former Victoria players, the same team now in Spokane that was in last place in goals scored for the season.

Riley had really come on strong as of late. The *Seattle Times* reported "the surprise of the Seattle team just now, however, is youthful Jim Riley. Riley has played a slashing game ever since given a regular job. He is fast as a streak, goes crashing into his opponents no matter how big they are, follows the puck closely and is developing skill as a stick handler and goal shooter." He was on the cusp of becoming a star. The combination of Riley and Cully Wilson's nineteen points would have been good for eighth in the league, tied with Vancouver's Mickey MacKay and Spokane's Ran McDonald and Lester Patrick. When Cully was injured, he was tied with MacKay and McDonald for tenth in points, one spot in front of Lester Patrick. The Mets desperately missed Cully's heart and competitiveness but Riley had played so well that they hadn't lost a step in offensive production during his absence.

Seattle remained in first place at 9-6, with Vancouver, winners of three in a row and four of five, now just a half-game back at 8-6. Spokane was in third place at 7-7, just one-and-a-half games behind the Mets with Portland remaining in the cellar at 5-10. The Mets led the league in goals scored at seventy-one, one in front of Vancouver and led the league in least goals allowed at fifty-two, eight less than second-place Spokane. They were also the least penalized team. All in all, it was easy to see that they were the best-coached team in the league.

Despite the loss to Vancouver, the Mets still felt confident. They had Spokane coming to town early the next week while Vancouver had to travel down to Portland to face the Rosebuds. Both teams were getting healthy and ready for the sprint to the finish.

# CHAPTER 9 –THE PENNANT CHASE BEGINS, JANUARY 30-31, 1917

January 30 was the coldest day of the year in Seattle with a noon temperature of a mere twenty-four degrees. The Northern Bank & Trust Company, on Fourth and Pike, defaulted and was taken over by the State for liquidation. It was the first bank failure in Seattle in twenty-five years. The default caused a rush on the remaining banks in the city, though they all paid out that day. In Washington D.C., United States ambassador to Mexico; Henry P. Fletcher, had been ordered back to Mexico City as it had been decided in that day's cabinet meeting to officially resume diplomatic relations with Mexico.

The Spokane Canaries were in town that night on a mission to climb back into first place in the standings; the first of two games that week between the two teams. Win both and the Canaries would leapfrog the Mets in the standings, needing only one Vancouver loss against Portland to tie for first place. The *Seattle Times* wrote, "viewed from every angle a victory for the Canaries tonight spells disaster for Seattle, even though Vancouver should lose." Vancouver was playing at Portland, the toughest place to play on the road, and Frank Patrick had announced the previous day that Cyclone Taylor would not make the trip. He was exceptionally sore after the Mets game. Neither man thought he could handle the strain of traveling plus playing in the contest. He would remain in Vancouver and rest up for the Friday night rematch with the Rosebuds.

Like a boxer down late in a fight, Lester Patrick was looking for the knockout punch to catapult his Canaries back to the top of the standings. He knew the Mets were playing the best hockey in the league. He also knew he was one of the best players in the game and he wasn't going to leave any stone unturned. So, Lester changed the lineup that night, making the decision to play rover rather than his customary spot on defense. The move gave him more freedom to chase the puck anywhere on the ice and better defend the Morris-Walker-Foyston line that was beginning to rival Vancouver's as the best in the league.

When Seattle's starting lineup was announced, a familiar name was back at right wing. After five weeks, Cully Wilson had finally been cleared to start and the boys were thrilled to have his tenacity back on the ice. His impact was immediate. From the opening puck drop, the pace of play was fast. Lester Patrick was everywhere on the ice and Norm Fowler was again dominant for Spokane. The Mets broke through seven minutes into the game when Cully made a great rush on goal before dumping a sterling pass to Bernie Morris for the score. Muldoon soon subbed Jim Riley for Cully and shortly thereafter, Frank Foyston made a brilliant pass to Riley for the goal and a 2-0 lead. It was great to have both Wilson and Riley contributing with no selfishness towards staying on the ice. Each man on the Mets continued to play hard every moment to push the team to victory, another mark of a well-coached team.

A late Spokane goal made the score 2-1 to end the first. In the second period, Fowler stood tall in the cage. The Mets had plenty of chances early, bombarding the goal without success. Nearly four minutes into the period, Lester Patrick tied the score but before the Canaries could grab the momentum in the game, Jim Riley switched over on defense and shut Lester down. The *Seattle Times* wrote, "the comedy of the evening was provided by Patrick and Jim Riley. Riley does not care how big they are or how fast they come and he seemed to think his special mission last night was to stop Patrick. He succeeded in this for the most part and every time the two of them came together one of them – and sometimes both – went down on the ice." It was another step forward in Riley's development. He had already proven that he could score; now he was showing similar ability on defense.

As the puck dropped to begin the third, the defenses continued to shine until the Morris-Walker-Foyston trio once again stepped up midway through the period. First, Frank scored on a pass from Bernie at the ten-minute mark and then Bernie doubled the lead on an assist from Jack three minutes later. Hap played brilliantly in the third, keeping the Canaries off the scoreboard as the Mets won a hard-fought battle 4-2. In all, Hap shut out Spokane for the final thirty-six minutes of the game.

It had been a total team effort. The *Seattle Times* wrote, "picking individual stars from the Seattle team is difficult, for every man on the ice was in the game every minute. Holmes played a fine game inside the net and Carpenter showed his best form of the year. Bobby Rowe was the same old reliable Bobby and Jim Riley played with his usual aggressiveness. The Morris-Foyston-Walker combination was working well and figured in all of Seattle's scores." Even "Cully Wilson got in the game for his first real workout in several weeks. He favored his injured knee a little but proved that he is recovering rapidly and that his layoff has not softened his scrappy disposition."

As anticipated, Portland beat Vancouver to give the Mets a little breathing room in the standings. Seattle sat in first place at 10-6, a game-and-a-half up on Vancouver at 8-7. Spokane was two-and-a-half back at 7-8 and the defending champs from Portland remained in the cellar at 6-10, four games out of first place.

** 

The next day, they all awoke to roars of championship talk in the newspapers. The sub-headline in the *Seattle Star* read, "Victory Helps Mets In Fight For Big Title" while the *Seattle Post-Intelligencer* read, "Mets Skate Like Champs in Final Session and Win." In his game recap, Royal Brougham wrote "those roistering, rollicking Mets, not passing up any victories in their merry sprint toward the Pacific Coast hockey championship, speared another hard earned win" while the Times said, "it is quite a way yet to the Pacific Coast Hockey Association pennant and no team in the circuit has the flag clinched, but Pete Muldoon's battle scarred warriors last night fanned their pennant prospects into a cheerful glow by trouncing the Spokane Canaries."

It was official, the pennant race had started. With eight games left to play, it was earlier than any of them had hoped but the people of Seattle were excited about the prospects of a championship and so it had begun nonetheless. Everything was now going to be magnified if they let it. Every game, every goal, every call by the officials would have the added weight of knowing it could mean the championship if they let it. Muldoon needed to keep their attention away from the pressures and distractions that chasing a championship creates and keep them focused on just playing the game. If they could just keep it to a game, their talent and their chemistry, what got them to this point, should allow them to be there at the end. Great teams don't chase championships. They just play hockey.

** 

Later that day in Washington D.C., German ambassador to the United States; Johann von Bernstorff presented U.S. Secretary of State Robert Lansing "a note from the German government, replying to the president's world peace address before the Senate." "In the note, Germany serves notice on the United States that because of the Kaiser's failure to open peace negotiations with the Allies, he would open unrestricted warfare on the seas."

The 200-point headline in the *Seattle Post-Intelligencer* simply stated "WAR LOOMS" while The *Seattle Star*'s read "U.S. is Facing War." The *Seattle*

*Times* wrote, "It is impossible to overestimate the gravity of the crisis that has developed for the United States as a result of the German note handed to Secretary Lansing." "At this time, it looks very much as if this country would be forced into war, either through the preliminary step of a severance of diplomatic relations or as a direct action following the ignoring by Berlin of an American ultimatum. There is no question that the United States has not sought and does not want war with Germany. Our people, in point of fact, are distinctly averse to mixing up in European politics."

The last time Germany used unrestricted submarine warfare, it brought America to the brink of entering the great conflict. Germany was using its submarines as "a starvation blockade of England, the likes of which the world has never seen." They were going to prevent all shipments of food, supplies, and anything else heading to the island nation in an attempt to force England into negotiating a peace settlement to end the war. Germany was making the calculation that the U.S. military would not be prepared to fight before England starved and capitulated. The Allies hoped otherwise.

Regardless, knowing America had only narrowly eluded war when Germany previously used unrestricted submarine warfare, almost no one believed it was avoidable a second time. All feared it was now inevitable.

# CHAPTER 10 – FEBRUARY 1-7, 1917

February 2 was Frank Foyston's twenty-sixth birthday. The Mets were in Spokane that day ready to deliver the same knockout punch to the Canaries that they had given Portland two weeks prior. A second consecutive win for Seattle would move Spokane three-and-a-half games out; essentially eliminating the Canaries from the race. Spokane's attendance had been rapidly declining over the past month and less than one thousand fans were expected. Though it certainly wouldn't be an easy game for the Mets, the Canaries wouldn't have their typical home-ice advantage.

Overall, there had been thirty-one games played in the PCHA. The home team, at 23-8, had won nearly 75 percent. Vancouver led the charge at 6-1 with Seattle just behind them at 7-2. Portland was uncharacteristically only 5-3 at home, but 4-1 against Seattle and Vancouver; the sole loss being Seattle's lone Portland win in two seasons. Not counting that night's game, the Mets and Rosebuds each had eight games to play while Vancouver and Spokane had nine.

For the stretch run, Vancouver had the easiest remaining schedule and Seattle the most difficult. Only three home games remained for the Mets with five on the road. Seattle had the most road wins in the league with three against four losses, but still had one difficult contest at Vancouver and two left at Portland, including the last game of the season. Of Vancouver's remaining nine games, five were at home and two of their four road games were at Spokane.

Muldoon's task was going to be to keep the Mets focused on just the game at hand. Unfortunately, the last game of the season at Portland was most likely going to loom large and therefore would remain in the back of their minds. From here on out, it was safe to say that for the next month, all of them would be scoreboard watching the next day's newspaper.

That morning, they woke to the headline in the *Seattle Post-Intelligencer* of

90

"Kaiser's Threat Wins." Denmark, Norway, Holland and Sweden were cutting off shipments, and thus supplies, to England for fear of German submarines. This was the exact response hoped for in Berlin and the clock was now ticking. Someone was going to need to stop Germany soon or Great Britain was going to starve. The entire western world anxiously awaited the U.S. response.

At half past eight, Mickey Ion called the Mets and Canaries to center ice. Cully Wilson was still sore from his first extended playing time on Tuesday and remained in Seattle to rest for the game next week against Vancouver; Jim Riley once again started in his place. From the opening puck drop, the Canaries were out fast and matched the Mets pace. Both goalies were up for the challenge and it was scoreless until the seventeen-minute mark when Frank made a great pass to Bobby Rowe for the first goal of the night. From there, the offense began to hum. Bernie won the ensuing faceoff and quickly got the puck to Jim Riley who sprinted up the ice and beat Fowler. A mere thirty seconds later, it was 2-0 Mets. Bernie won the next face and sent it to Eddie Carpenter, 3-0. On the next drop, Bernie once again grabbed the puck and immediately found Frank, 4-0 Mets. Seattle had scored four goals in one minute, forty seconds to head to the first break with momentum on their side.

When the second period began, Eddie Carpenter quickly scored his second goal and the Mets offense was in high gear. The game's pace began to settle before Bernie tallied his first goal at the thirteen-minute mark, the fifth Seattle player to net a puck as Seattle led 6-0. The Mets were answering the first test of the pressure cooker known as the pennant race in convincing fashion, continuing their recent stretch of dominance on both sides of the ice.

As the puck dropped again, the Mets pushed the action and aggressively attacked the Canaries. After a few minutes, Bernie Morris grabbed a loose puck and shot up the ice. From his rover position, Bobby Genge desperately attempted to cut Bernie off but as Morris made a move to clear the defense, Genge whacked him hard in the knee with his stick, sending Bernie awkwardly tumbling to the ice. Bernie immediately grabbed for his knee, screaming in pain. In an instant, it was clear that the pain was not from the impact, but something far more serious. Doc Kelton rushed out on the ice and the Mets could tell from his reaction that something was drastically wrong with Bernie's knee. The already quiet arena was now deathly silent. The Mets just stared in disbelief as one of their stars, the top scorer in the league, was now seriously injured.

Muldoon screamed at Mickey Ion for not calling a penalty, but Ion felt Genge was going for the puck so let the play stand without an infraction. Bernie was carried to the dressing room so Doc could do a more thorough examination. As the Mets returned to the ice, Foyston was the first to snap back into the game. With fire in his eyes, he quickly called the boys over and with a few sharp words, brought the rest of the team out of their fog as well. They were all enraged that Bernie was hurt on such a cheap shot but would deal with his absence tomorrow. Tonight, they were going to bury the Canaries.

Roy Rickey entered on defense as Bobby Rowe slid over to play center in Bernie's absence. The Mets attacked from the ensuing faceoff and Bobby soon scored his second goal, moments before the whistle ended the period. Fuming, the Mets came out for the third period and took it right at Spokane. Foyston from Carpenter, then Rowe from Foyston, then Rowe, Walker from Riley, Foyston from Carpenter, Foyston from Walker, and finally Rickey from Riley. It was 14-0 Seattle and every man on the team had scored a goal.

Leo Cook snuck a shot past Hap in the closing seconds to prevent the shutout, but it was an annihilation. The Mets had shown that they had a different gear than other teams. Many teams lose their edge after a crippling injury and come back flat. The Mets on the other hand, had instead exposed their true heart. No matter what, they were not going to back down from a fight and, more importantly, they were going to let their play do the fighting.

After the game, Doc Kelton was fairly certain that Bernie had torn everything in his knee, fearful that it may be career-ending. The plan was to x-ray the knee in Seattle the next morning and reevaluate. The Mets left Spokane angry, and more than anything, fearful of what the coming days would bring. As bad as they had beaten Spokane, they knew the Canaries were not the Millionaires. It was going to be damn tough to beat Vancouver without Bernie Morris.

**

The following morning, they awoke to the news that the United States had officially broken off relations with Germany; the headline in the *Seattle Times* read "War Cloud Looms Darker." President Wilson had once again addressed Congress to announce "the complete severance of diplomatic relations." Although he had taken the drastic measure, he said, "I cannot bring myself to believe that they will destroy American ships and take the lives of American citizens in the willful prosecution of the ruthless naval program they have announced their intention to adopt. Only actual overt acts on their part can make me believe it even now." This time, however, sentiment was positive and supportive of the president's position as he was given an ovation in Congress and wired letters of support from many governors across the country, though many feared an overt act was on the horizon.

German ambassador Count von Bernstorff was handed his passport and scheduled to depart Washington, D.C. on February 13 while American ambassador, James Gerard was ordered home immediately from Berlin. Later that day, German submarines sunk the American steamer *Housatonic* off the coast of Great Britain although all twenty-five seamen were rescued.

The team arrived back in Seattle mid-morning and Doc Kelton immediately took Bernie to get his knee x-rayed. Pete felt confident that Bernie hadn't torn everything and was hopeful they might even get him back by the end of the month. Cully Wilson was finally healthy and cleared to play so Muldoon planned to start him at center and leave Jim Riley at wing. The line of Foyston-Wilson-Riley-Walker was still as talented as any in hockey and he was feeling better about their chances now that they all had some time to cool off. He was still adamant that Bobby Genge's play was dirty but it wasn't going to help them win games to fight that battle. He had spoken his piece.

The PCHA All-Star team was named that morning with Frank, Jack and Bernie on the team, joined by Norm Fowler and Lester Patrick of Spokane, Moose Johnson of Portland, and Mickey MacKay and Doc Roberts of Vancouver. MacKay bested Jack for the rover position so Walker, one of the league's top players, was named utility. Bernie joined Doc Roberts and Lester Patrick as the only unanimous selections. It was an incredible accomplishment, considering that Roberts and Patrick were hockey royalty while Bernie had been an outcast fighting for a job just a year-and-a-half before.

The league stats were also released that morning. Bernie was still leading the league with thirty-seven points, one in front of Doc Roberts. Dick Irvin was third and Frank fourth, with thirty-five and thirty-two points, respectively. Roberts led the league with twenty-eight goals while Bernie led the league in assists with fourteen. They were closing in on the all-time PCHA scoring record of forty-five points set by Cyclone Taylor in the Millionaires' 1915 Stanley Cup championship season though it now looked like a two-horse race. The Vancouver Daily World wrote, "With Bernie Morris out of the game for some time to come, it looks like a race between Roberts and Irvin for the honors."

On Sunday, the x-rays "showed that the bones and muscles were not damaged." Luckily, it appeared that it was indeed just a bad contusion from the force of Genge's stick hitting the knee so Doc was optimistic that Bernie might be able to return in a week or two.

The night before in Vancouver, the Millionaires held on to beat Portland in overtime to remain a game-and-a-half out in the standings. Seattle was in first place at 11-6, Vancouver in second at 9-7, Spokane now three-and-a-half back at 7-9 and Portland five back at 6-11. Seattle hosted Vancouver that coming Tuesday while Portland played at Spokane.

**

The morning of the game, "Bernie, disregarding the mandates of the club physician, came forth with the announcement that he intended to play if he had to skate around on one foot." Although the injury was not as grave as first feared, Doc Kelton knew he wasn't healthy enough to play. Bernie made the announcement without consulting Kelton or Muldoon. His plan was to force their hand to let him play. It had been the struggle of a lifetime full of crushing disappointments just get to this point, and he was not going to let his team down at this moment in the season. Both morning newspapers ran the starting lineups that Muldoon had given them the day before with Cully Wilson at center and Jim Riley at right wing.

Muldoon decided to oblige his star and the *Seattle Times* updated the starting lineups for the afternoon paper, with Morris back at center and Cully Wilson at right wing. He was, however, ready with contingency plans in case Bernie was just too injured to compete. Wilson knew to be ready to play center and Jim Riley at wing if Bernie couldn't "stand the pace." And, if Wilson wasn't healthy enough or needed a break, Bobby Rowe would move to center and Roy Rickey would enter on defense. Cyclone Taylor was back in the Vancouver lineup as the Millionaires were finally healthy and starting their best seven.

The entire front page of all three Seattle newspapers was dedicated solely to the conflict in Europe. German U-boats had sunk thirty-five vessels since resuming submarine warfare less than a week ago, including fourteen the prior day. The headline in the *Seattle Post-Intelligencer* read "Gerard Held as Hostage." Word coming from Berlin was that Ambassador Gerard would be prevented from departing Germany until Count von Bernstorff had safely returned.

President Wilson preached restraint as he did not want the country to move fast towards war. The president's prudence caused British Prime Minister David Lloyd George to explode, "And so he is not going to fight after all! He is awaiting another insult before he actually draws the sword." Entering foreign wars was simply not something the United States did, and Wilson was not going to be rushed. He wanted to be prepared if war was necessary, but nothing was going to hasten that decision. "To that end, German rights and property in the United States are to have full protection of law and the president wishes every American citizen to forbear from any thought or act which might lead his country nearer to war."

Another sold-out crowd was on hand at the arena to see the top two teams in the league go toe-to-toe. The Millionaires, who hadn't been in first place since Boxing Day, knew this was their week to make a move on the Mets. Seattle had to play at Portland on Friday and stood a reasonable chance to lose. If the Millionaires could win tonight and then at home this weekend against Spokane, they would find themselves alone in first place Sunday evening. Finally healthy and with their best seven on the ice against a beat-up Seattle team, they liked their chances for all of those scenarios to come to fruition.

From the opening puck drop, the Seattle defense took control of the game. Eddie Carpenter and Bobby Rowe immediately locked on Cyclone Taylor and "had him bottled up so that he couldn't get away with anything." It wasn't just Cyclone they bottled up, however, as they were completely in sync with each other and using a technique where one of them would funnel the Millionaires forward with the puck directly into the other man's check. Vancouver struggled to even get off a shot early in the game. Any shot they did take was effortlessly blocked by Hap and sent back up the ice. Four-and-a-half minutes into the opening period, an injured Bernie Morris grabbed a loose puck and emphatically buried the back of the net. 1-0 Mets. On the ensuing faceoff, Vancouver secured the puck before Jim Riley stole it and sprinted back up the ice. As the Millionaires defense closed on him, he slid a perfect pass out to Bernie who again slammed the puck into the goal. Just under six minutes into the game and Bernie, playing through excruciating pain, had staked the Mets to a 2-0 lead.

The second period began with the same score and the Mets defense playing brilliantly until Mickey MacKay finally broke through for Vancouver and made the score 2-1 six minutes into the period. As play resumed, MacKay once again beat Bernie at the puck drop and the Millionaires rushed Hap in the goal ready to tie the score until Eddie Carpenter came out of nowhere to hook-check the puck away and start a sprint of his own back up the ice. Corkscrewing through the Vancouver defense, he flipped a shot past Lehman to make it 3-1 Mets. In an instant, the Mets had once again responded to a potential momentum shift with a soul crushing play. As lost as Eddie Carpenter had looked earlier in the season, he was back to his old dominant self with Royal Brougham describing that goal as "one of the prettiest efforts of the game."

The contest quickly unfolded into a heavyweight prize fight with both teams going blow for blow. Barney Stanley soon scored for Vancouver. Two minutes later, Cully Wilson scored on a pass from Bernie, then Cyclone Taylor tallied for Vancouver. With just seconds remaining in the period, Frank scored on a beautiful pass from Cully to send the teams to the break with Seattle ahead 5-3.

The third period picked up right where the second ended, with Bernie scoring and Doc Roberts answering. From there, it was all Mets. Cully and Bernie doubled the lead, and Hap locked down the net to give the Mets an unbelievable, perhaps improbable, 8-4 victory over the Millionaires. Royal Brougham wrote "the Met goalie was at his best, saving many hard shots in the latter stages of the fray."

The next day, The *Seattle Star* wrote that the audience had been on "its feet throughout the major portion of the entertainment" asking readers, "were you one of the biggest crowd that bought a seat at the Arena to see last night's hockey clash between Vancouver and Seattle and then never used it? So were we!"

An injured Mets team had thoroughly dismantled the red-hot Millionaires in all phases of the game. Despite a severely hobbled knee, Bernie Morris was on the ice all sixty minutes, scoring four goals with an assist to lead his team to a crucial victory. Cully Wilson played half of each period and was getting stronger by the day, scoring his first two goals in six weeks and adding an assist. The Mets, red-hot themselves, had now won three straight, seven of eight and were 11-3 since their disastrous start.

In Spokane, the Canaries beat Portland in overtime to hang on to hopes of getting back into the race. Seattle remained in first at 12-6, two-and-a-half games up on Vancouver at 9-8. Spokane was in third at 8-9, three-and-a-half games back with Portland now 6-12 and six out with six to play.

It was going to be a tight turnaround this week as the Mets had to travel to Portland. They all hoped Bernie and Cully would recover quickly and play against the Rosebuds. A win at Portland would essentially clinch the pennant while a loss would bring the Millionaires right back to only a game-and-a-half back, leaving little margin for error.

# CHAPTER 11 – FEBRUARY 8-14, 1917

The 100-point headline in Thursday morning's *Post-Intelligencer*, read "First Overt Act." Until now, German U-boats had warned ships that they were about to be attacked and, in some cases, allowed the crew to deboard the vessel before the torpedo strike. The S.S. *California*, a British passenger liner, was torpedoed without warning off the Irish coast. The only American on board had been rescued but fifty-five passengers were still missing, "including two women and several children." That afternoon's *Seattle Times* reported that fifty-nine ships had now been sunk in the eight days since the "German blockade order took effect on February 1."

In the sports pages, the Seattle papers were close to anointing the Mets as the PCHA champions after their win over the Millionaires. The *Seattle Post-Intelligencer's* headline read "Mets Have Title Almost in Grasp" while the *Seattle Times* wrote the Mets had "first place in the Pacific Coast Hockey Association race almost cinched." Although they had won seven of their last eight, the positive and optimistic Muldoon knew there was still a long way to go. And, he knew the upcoming game against Portland was not going to be an easy win as "Seattle has always found Portland a hard team to beat on the Portland ice." Even though the Rosebuds were in last place, Muldoon still believed they had one of the most talented teams in hockey.

On Friday morning, the Mets took the train south. According to news accounts that day, ten more ships were sunk by German U-boats. Despite the incessant sinking of vessels by the Germans, President Wilson was not yet prepared to ask Congress for a declaration of war. He was instead ramping up efforts to "protect American seamen and people." He did not want to join the Allied nations, still hoping to protect American interests as a neutral country by addressing the submarine crisis rather than entering the war.

That evening, referee George Irvine and judge of play Jim Seaborn called both teams to center ice and dropped the puck. Instantly the

Rosebuds were off and playing like the defending champions, aggressive on both ends of the ice. Everything the Mets tried was met with physical play and they struggled to mount much of a threat. Nearly halfway through the period, the Rosebuds' Charlie Tobin notched the game's first goal on a Dick Irvin assist. Irvin then scored off a Tobin assist near the end of the period and the Rosebuds led 2-0. The only thing the dreadful Mets had accomplished was two penalties, one from Bernie Morris and the other from Bobby Rowe.

It was a typical rough Rosebuds game in Portland and the Mets were completely floundering. The Uncle Sams added another score in the second as the game soon digressed further out of control with four penalties in the period. Cully Wilson was sent to the box once for Seattle while Smokey Harris took two trips for Portland and was joined on one trip by Tommy Dunderdale, the league leader in penalty minutes on the season.

The third period was uglier than the second with Seattle receiving three more penalties including Bobby Rowe earning five minutes in the box and a five dollar fine for going after judge of play Seaborn while Eddie Carpenter and Moose Johnson were ejected for fighting. In total, there were eleven penalties handed out with the Mets receiving six of them. It was the exact game that Portland wanted and the Mets fell right into their trap. Cully Wilson scored to avoid a shutout, but the Rosebuds drubbed the Mets 5-1.

It was disappointing to lose an important game late in the season but more disappointing to lose the game in this manner. It was no secret in hockey that the way to beat Seattle was to play extremely physical and bait the Mets into abandoning their usual athletic style and draw them into a slugfest. Over the course of the last two seasons, the players had become more adept at staying disciplined and playing through roughness. Tonight, though, it had worked to perfection.

The next day, Muldoon admitted to the press that his "boys had an off night and the Portland men played a hard, rough game." He was "not disheartened, however, and still has the firm belief that his team is the class of the league." Excited for the game on Tuesday, he said, "I think they will turn the tide when they get the Portland men on the Seattle ice." Bernie Morris and Cully Wilson had recovered well from the game and would be at full strength on Tuesday though Eddie Carpenter needed a few hours to regain his senses after taking a blow to the head fighting Moose Johnson. Regardless, Pete was confident he would have a healthy team on Tuesday.

On Saturday, the Millionaires thrashed the Canaries 8-1. Mickey Mackay scored four goals while Barney Stanley added two and two assists. A healthy Cyclone Taylor had been all over the ice, notching two goals himself. Despite their two recent road losses, Vancouver had won five of their last seven and with Cyclone's return, were peaking at the right time.

Seattle's loss coupled with Vancouver's win had once again tightened the race to a game-and-a-half. The Mets remained in first place at 12-7, followed by Vancouver at 10-8, Spokane at 8-10 and Portland, who was five back but mathematically still alive in the pennant race at 7-12.

For the Sunday papers, the league released tentative dates for the World Series, to be played on the home ice of the PCHA champion. Game One was tentatively scheduled for March 17, Game Two on March 20 and Game Three on March 23. The league stats were also released with Bernie still leading the league with forty-two points, now just three off the PCHA record. His fifteen assists continued to top the list while his twenty-seven goals were third. Dick Irvin had climbed into second at forty points, leading the charge with thirty-one goals. Doc Roberts was third and Barney Stanley fourth; Frank Foyston rounded out the top-5.

The Sunday *Seattle Times* also ran a feature on the Hockeyettes. For the last several weeks, Pete Muldoon had been putting the women through the paces on Thursday nights and they were quickly rounding into form. The *Seattle Times* wrote "whoever it was that invented the game of hockey, he probably had no idea that it would ever become the favorite sport of the fair sex. Fans who have seen Big Moose Johnson, of the Portland club, come tearing down the ice to crash into Cully Wilson, of the Seattle team, probably agree that the originator of the pastime had the right idea when he planned the game as a sport for men. With characteristic disregard of tradition, however, women have proceeded to demonstrate that they can become adept at what undoubtably is the fastest and one of the most virile games in the world."

Muldoon didn't care about "tradition" and enjoyed coaching the team. He had twelve women on the squad and they were gearing up for a game soon against Frank Vance's group. Miss Phoebe Nell Tidmarsh, "well known in social circles as an accomplished athlete and dancer" was establishing herself as one of the team's stars. She was aggressive and in the "thick of the fight." Another "one of the stars of the team is Miss Jessie Foyston, sister of captain Frank Foyston of the Mets. Miss Foyston has followed hockey since she was a little girl and her performances on the ice demonstrate that Frank has no corner on the hockey playing ability of the Foyston family."

His last big name on the team was Mrs. Sarah Wilson, wife of Cully, who the *Seattle Times* said was "by instinct and by association with her illustrious husband, adept at the game and fully capable of maintaining the family reputation on the ice." They all eagerly awaited the first game.

Monday, February 12, would have been Abraham Lincoln's one hundred eighth birthday. The Lincoln Memorial in Washington D.C. was in its third year of construction, with work commencing on Lincoln's birthday in 1914. The foundation work was finished in May of 1915 and today marked the completion of the superstructure. Thirty-six columns of

Colorado marble, representing the thirty-six states during Lincoln's Presidency, rose forty-four feet in the air. Because the fill to raise the ground level around the structure had not yet been added, the pillars and entrance to the Memorial currently towered thirty feet above the ground.

That day's *Seattle Post-Intelligencer* quoted Lincoln in regard to the current global situation, "Let us have faith that right makes might, and in that faith, let us to the end, dare to do our duty as we understand it." The *Seattle Star* ran a cartoon of President Wilson looking at a portrait of Lincoln with the caption from the sixteenth president's famous second inaugural address: "Fondly do we hope – fondly do we pray – that this mighty scourge of war may speedily pass away."

In the European conflict, it was a day of big developments. First, U.S. ships were going to be permitted to arm themselves against German U-boats. Next, there were conflicting reports about the safety of Ambassador Gerard. Some had him safely in Switzerland while others believed he departed Germany Saturday evening though his arrival in Berne had not officially been corroborated. Either way, his momentary detention by the German government had been poorly received in Washington. Over the weekend, both Germany and Austria had made peace overtures to the United States. Austria was offering to allow American ships safe passage in the Mediterranean in the hopes of averting the severance of diplomatic relations between the two countries. The U.S. flatly refused the German overture until the Kaiser lived up to their old agreement and rescinded his policy of unrestricted submarine warfare. Ultimately, Germany blocked Austria's offer, further inflaming the situation.

It was another crucial week in the pennant race as Seattle prepared to host Portland on Tuesday while Vancouver was again at home against Spokane. On Saturday, the Mets would journey to Vancouver for a pivotal head-to-head matchup. It would be the Millionaires third consecutive home game. They were 8-1 at home and the *Post-Intelligencer* said the Millionaires were "playing a brand of hockey which might carry them through the rest of the season without losing a game."

Two wins for the Mets and the race would be over although two losses could also signal the end of the race in favor of Vancouver. With a split, the Mets would no longer control their own destiny, requiring the Millionaires to lose another game or the best they could do was tie. Despite the ease of getting lost in all of the scenarios remaining on the schedule, all that mattered was the next game. They needed to take care of Portland first. After a lapse last Friday, the plan was to get really aggressive on defense with Muldoon saying, "the boys will be camping close to every Portland player on the ice."

On Tuesday morning, they all woke to the news that Germany had taken seventy-two American seaman hostage on the orders of the Kaiser's war council. Five more vessels had been sunk by German U-boats, pushing the total to seventy-eight since February 1. The headline in the *Seattle Times* read "Spark of War May Flash at Any Moment" with the article stating, "While it was reiterated today that the president would not be rushed into war, it is plain that all officials realize that the much-feared event may come at any time." President Wilson canceled his daily round of golf that morning to remain in his study.

The lone positive item on the front page was a large picture of King Gustav of Sweden with his grandchildren and other members of the Royal family out for a game of hockey at The Stadium rink in Stockholm. The game, rapidly growing in popularity in Europe, was only three years away from making its Olympic debut in the 1920 Antwerp Games.

That night, a packed house greeted the Rosebuds and Metropolitans in a must win game for Seattle. Mickey Ion was still banished from Portland games so George Irvine and Jim Seaborn were back officiating the contest. From the opening drop, "the Uncle Sams set a furious pace" with an aggressive Portland team controlling the game. Luckily, Eddie Carpenter and Bobby Rowe were up for the challenge and thwarted every Rosebud rush that neared the goal.

Twelve minutes into the scoreless period, Jack was on the wing setting up the Mets offense when he sensed a brief hole in the Portland defense and attacked instead. The surprised Rosebuds panicked and collapsed on him. Bernie read the play perfectly and immediately hit the space left open by the vacated Portland defenders. Jack hit him in stride with a beautiful pass, 1-0 Mets. It was a spectacular play by Jack and great finish by Bernie as the Mets snuck an early lead despite being outplayed.

The lead didn't last, and after Dick Irvin tied the score, Portland carried momentum into the second period. Despite the Rosebuds controlling the flow, the game remained clean and without any penalties. Portland continued to be the aggressor as Moose Johnson and his cohorts pressured Hap and the Mets defense. Two minutes into the period, Bobby Rowe grabbed an errant shot and sprinted the puck up the ice, "stickhandling his way through the entire visiting team" and beat Murray in the goal with a brilliant shot, 2-1 Seattle. Again, despite being outplayed, another great individual effort put the Mets in front.

As play resumed, momentum slowly began to shift towards Seattle. Almost thirteen minutes into the period, the Mets secured the puck and started a mad dash back up the ice towards the Portland goal. When they crossed the center line, a loud whistle stopped everyone. As the players looked for the call, there was utter confusion on the faces of the officials as neither had blown the whistle. Immediately, Portland manager Frank Scott was out on the ice with a whistle in his mouth berating George Irvine that Seattle had too many men in the game.

Still completely shocked, Irvine quickly counted the Mets standing before him: Holmes, Rowe, Carpenter, Walker, Morris, Foyston, Wilson. There were seven, the legal amount. An incensed and incredulous Muldoon was quickly out on the ice screaming at Scott, Irvine and Seaborn. Confusion and chaos ensued as there was no specific rule governing what to do in this situation. It had never happened before and no one in their wildest dreams believed a coach would blow a whistle to stop play in the middle of the game. Irvine and Seaborn ultimately chose not to punish the Portland manager and decided to simply resume play at center ice, sending Muldoon and the Mets into further rage. Once again, Frank Scott had made a mockery of the game and was not being held accountable.

Immediately on the resumption of play, "Tobin scooped the puck and made a pretty shot from the right wing" tying the score at 2-2. The Mets were so frustrated with what transpired that they forgot to play hockey for a moment and the Rosebuds quickly made them pay. They instantly snapped back after the goal and held Portland scoreless for the remaining three minutes though the damage had unfortunately been done. The Mets needed to regroup at the intermission and figure out how to take control of the game.

They were being outplayed and felt cheated in a game that was absolutely critical for them to win. The pressure in the locker room must have been palpable sensing their championship hopes slipping away. For the boys, it was definitely a Walker-for-Walker moment. Someone needed to crack a joke or somehow diffuse the tension overwhelming the team. They also needed Muldoon to remind them that Portland was not the best-conditioned team in the league and that the Mets had skated away from them late in previous victories. They had a home crowd and had worked extremely hard over the course of the season to be the most-conditioned club in the circuit. It was time to trust all their hard work, stop playing down to the Rosebuds' tactics and simply play their game. If they could focus solely on themselves, getting tunnel vision on what they could control, their talent would take over and the chances were high that they would win this game.

As the third period began, a different Mets team was out on the ice. Portland, however, remained aggressive and continued to play physical hockey so the score remained 2-2 until six-and-a-half minutes into the period when the Morris-Foyston-Walker trio shifted into high gear. First, it was Morris from Foyston to give the Mets the lead and then Morris from Walker to extend the lead. The Seattle defense continued to hold the Rosebuds in check before Frank scored the final goal of the night and the Mets captured an incredible 5-2 victory.

Despite a rough start, unruly behavior by Portland, and a disastrous call by the officials, the Mets found a way to win a critical game and hold their lead in the standings. The Seattle forward line, as it had all season, stepped up to meet the challenge presented by another must win game as had Hap Holmes, with Royal Brougham writing, "both goalies were at their best last night."

Bernie's three goals gave him forty-five points on the season and tied him for the all-time PCHA record held by Cyclone Taylor. Cyclone had played less games than Bernie but 1915 was also arguably the weakest season in the league as Portland was a new team and Victoria had fallen apart, allowing an astonishing seven goals per game. Regardless, it was an incredible achievement for both men.

Vancouver beat Spokane, its sixth win in eight games, to keep the race tight. After twenty games, Seattle, winners of eight of ten themselves, remained in first place at 13-7, with Vancouver still just a game and a half back at 11-8. Spokane was now 8-11 and four-and-a-half back with four to play and Portland, at 7-13, was officially eliminated from the race.

Of Seattle's four remaining games, three were on the road, one against each league team, plus a home game against Spokane. It was a tough slate to say the least. Of Vancouver's five remaining games, four were at home against each league team, with two against Spokane, and a road game at Portland.

As both Vancouver and Seattle still had to travel to Portland, everyone wondered if the Rosebuds would throw in the towel now that they were eliminated or if they would continue to compete. Spokane had completely fallen apart, having lost six of their last eight, so the Mets-Millionaires matchup on Saturday as well as the games at Portland were most likely going to decide the league championship and determine who would host the World Series.

All the Mets could do was prepare for Vancouver on Saturday. The game with the Millionaires was now all that mattered.

# CHAPTER 12 – FEBRUARY 15-22, 1917

The third week of February saw German Ambassador Count von Bernstorff finally depart America for Berlin, sailing from New York Harbor aboard the Frederik VIII and safeguarded by a heavily armed flotilla. Just before leaving, he spoke to the media about the prospects for the United States averting war, saying "he considered it conditional upon Germany being able to bring the Entente to its knees before anything happens to involve the United States." He knew America was trying its best to stay out of the conflict, which helped grow Germany's confidence that their strategy was working and that it could soon force England to negotiate for peace. Last, "he was emphatic in declaring that the submarine campaign is bound to increase in intensity as the weather gets warmer."

In Washington, President Wilson took a moment to honor an American hero. "In the stress of the most serious international crisis in the history of the nation, President Wilson has found time to write a cordial birthday letter to Dr. Anna Howard Shaw, pioneer suffragist, who is celebrating her seventieth birthday." An ordained Methodist minister and medical doctor, Shaw would become the first woman to win a Distinguished Service Medal.

By Friday afternoon, the Vancouver-Seattle game was already sold out. The arena management boasted that the crowd would be the largest ever to attend a hockey game in Vancouver and encouraged fans to arrive early.

That evening, Spokane traveled to Portland to play the Rosebuds and were trounced 9-1; the loss eliminated the Canaries from the pennant race. Portland's eight-goal margin of victory definitively answered the question if the Rosebuds were going to pack it in after being eliminated themselves. They were desperately going to fight to rise out of the cellar, now only a half-game behind Spokane, losers of three straight and seven of nine.

It was announced that night that the Canaries were done playing in Spokane for the season due to lack of attendance. Their last three home games, one against the Mets and two against the Millionaires would be moved to Seattle and Vancouver, respectively. The Seattle Ice Arena was already booked on Tuesday, February 20, for the annual Fireman's Ball so the game was moved to Friday, February 23. The scheduled February 27 Millionaires-Canaries game was pushed one week to March 3.

**

By Saturday, hype for the Millionaires-Metropolitans matchup was through the roof. The Vancouver Daily World called it "the championship game," the *Seattle Times* said the game "may settle the pennant race" and the *Seattle Star* agreed, "the game tonight practically settles the Coast title." There was no escaping the implications of the contest.

"A victory tonight will cinch the pennant for the Mets" putting them two-and-a-half games up with three to play while a loss "may sound the death knell" and force Seattle to "win each of its remaining games to finish in first place." Vancouver had won six in a row at home and with a healthy Cyclone Taylor back in the lineup, "the Millionaires right now are harder to beat than at any time this season." Despite the challenge facing the Mets, a confident Frank Foyston told the *Seattle Post-Intelligencer*, "we've got a hard battle on our hands, but the boys are going out to win, just the same."

Six-thousand fans packed the arena that night to see the biggest game of the year. At 8:30 p.m., Mickey Ion called both teams to center ice and dropped the puck. The contest started at a blistering pace, with both teams healthy and energized by the raucous crowd. Four minutes into the opening period, Doc Roberts got the Millionaires on the board with the first goal of the night. Six minutes later, it was Doc again to make the score 2-0. Thirty-nine seconds later, Doc again and it was 3-0 Millionaires. Four minutes later, Doc scored his fourth goal of the period, with "three of them being from a difficult position on the wing." It was 4-0 before the shell-shocked Mets could even blink. Despite Hap's best efforts, Doc was just too good tonight to be stopped.

The capacity crowd was beside itself knowing the implications of a rout on the playoff chase. Despite the noise, the Mets refused to quit and finally broke through after Frank scored on a pass from Bernie. Bernie's assist gave him forty-six points on the season, breaking the PCHA scoring record. Newsy Lalonde, Didier Pitre, Doc Roberts, Cyclone Taylor and all the greatest names in hockey had played in the PCHA over the years. The name Bernie Morris now sat above them all atop the record book. Regardless if he maintained his lead through the end of the season, he had been the first to break the record. It was truly an astonishing accomplishment for an orphan from Brandon, Manitoba.

When the second period began, Vancouver dropped everyone back on defense. Without an ounce of quit, the Mets blistered shot after shot "but circus stops by Lehman spoiled whatever chances they had" to chip away at the lead. Hap played well too, blocking everything sent his way and kept the score 4-1 to give the Mets a chance to get back into the game.

Seven minutes into the third, Bernie scored on a pass from Bobby Rowe to make it 4-2 and bring the Mets back to within striking distance but that would be the last goal scored on the night. It was a crushing defeat. Dreams of winning the pennant tonight had now been replaced by the realization that for the first time in nearly a month, the Mets no longer controlled their own destiny. If both teams won out, they would be tied at the end of the season, requiring a playoff series to decide the champion. With the way Vancouver was currently playing, the Millionaires were going to be an exceedingly tough opponent to beat in a series.

After twenty-one games, Seattle remained in first place at 13-8, a mere half game up on Vancouver at 12-8. Spokane was still in third at 8-12 but Portland was just a half game behind them at 8-13.

Both Seattle and Vancouver were 7-3 in their last ten games, but Seattle had played two away games in their last three, losing both, while Vancouver had gone 3-0 at home in their last three.

After a rare poor home stretch for Portland in late January, the Rosebuds had won three straight in the Hippodrome by a combined score of 25-9. Seattle desperately needed Vancouver to lose one more game, but even a Millionaires loss at Portland would hardly be celebrated knowing the Mets had to make the same trip to the Rose City to end the season. The math certainly wasn't in their favor.

All the Mets could do was prepare for Spokane on Friday, the game against the Canaries was now all that mattered.

As the teams entered the home stretch, the Seattle papers continued to highlight the "Three Hockey Races" on in the coast league that were top of mind. First and foremost, like everyone else, the media had figured out every possible scenario that could play out in regard to the pennant. The *Seattle Times* wrote "entering the final stretch of one of the closest races in the history of Pacific Coast hockey, the Seattle Hockey Club today is facing a situation that will tax every ounce of its playing strength if it is to win out in the race for the 1917 pennant" and that "Vancouver, going at a pace that makes it almost invincible, is the septet that is threatening to dethrone the Mets from first place." The entire city was captivated by the prospects of a championship and hosting the World Series with the Times writing "not even a thrilling finish in a baseball pennant race has equaled the interest with which Seattle fans are watching the outcome of the hockey fight."

The second race was for the scoring title, with Bernie Morris still leading the league. Doc Roberts was close on his heels with Dick Irvin in third. Frank Foyston had climbed back into fourth while Barney Stanley and Mickey MacKay had begun to fall off the pace though remained in fifth and sixth, respectively. It would be tough for Dick Irvin to make up five points in three games, but the race between Doc and Bernie was going to be entertaining to watch.

The last race being discussed was the most valuable player award that each team's official scorers would select at the end of the season. Royal Brougham, who would cast the Seattle vote, had "five men being considered" with three of them from Seattle. "Captain Frank Foyston, Bernie Morris and Jack Walker are the Seattle stars who are being groomed for the honor. Dick Irvin, the Rosebud sensation, is Portland's entry, while Mickey MacKay is Vancouver's bet." The Vancouver media thought that Doc Roberts would have a say as well.

On Tuesday evening, the Mets were handed a gift. The Rosebuds beat Vancouver 6-4 in Portland. It was not shocking because Portland was now 4-0 at home against the Millionaires, but surprising nonetheless as Vancouver had been peaking. The Mets now controlled their own destiny again and would win the pennant by winning out. It was not going to be an easy task with two trap games coming up against Spokane and the daunting trip to Portland to end the season.

That same night, the hockeyettes, coached by Pete Muldoon, were set to play their first game as the headliner of the Fireman's Ball, a fundraiser to support the Seattle Fire Department. It would be the Sourdoughs with Phoebe Tidmarsh and Jessie Foyston versus the Down Easters and Mrs. Sarah Wilson.

The program began with a free skate for spectators serenaded by the thirty-two-piece Fireman's Band. Next, the puck would drop for the game, with speed-skating races featuring the six local amateur hockey teams scheduled for the first intermission and an ice dancing program, headlined by none other than Pete Muldoon scheduled for the second. As part of his program, Pete skated on stilts to thrill the crowd.

The *Seattle Times* deemed the night a smashing success, as "fancy skating took a prominent part in the evening's entertainment. Pete Muldoon and Miss La Mont probably bringing down the greatest show of enthusiasm from the big crowd which had gathered to demonstrate their love of sport and their friendship for the city's firefighters."

As well received as the ice dancing was, the game between the Down Easters and the Sourdoughs "proved the attraction" of the evening with the Sourdoughs winning 3-1 on two Sarah Wilson goals. According to the *Seattle Times*, the teams "demonstrated to the skeptical ones that women can play the ice game just as well as they can vote and do other things supposedly out of their sphere."

The night served as a welcome distraction from the pressures of the pennant race. The boys had Spokane coming to town on Friday and were ready to begin the sprint to the finish.

# CHAPTER 13 – FEBRUARY 23-28, 1917

Friday, February 23 was the worst day of the German submarine campaign since the first week, with twenty-eight thousand tons sunk and eleven more ships. Any hopes that the campaign would lose steam without action were clearly misguided as Germany had instead tightened its noose around Great Britain. It was a dangerous game of chicken, but the United States showed no intention of fighting without overt provocation.

The Mets hosted Spokane that night and it was a worrisome game for two reasons. First, the Canaries were fighting for their lives to stay out of the cellar and a loss tonight would put them in last place. Second, it was a classic trap game for the Mets. With Spokane having lost seven of nine, it was easy to look past them and begin to think about the game in Portland next week. What was worse, the Mets had two games against Spokane. Muldoon needed to keep the team focused on playing against the game rather than the opponent and keep their foot on the gas pedal.

From the opening puck drop, the Mets were in control. They weren't playing well but Spokane was playing worse and Seattle quickly jumped out to a 2-0 lead halfway through the period. The second ten minutes saw the Mets allow a Spokane goal before quickly scoring two more themselves to go up 4-1 with the opportunity to put the game away. Instead, they let the Canaries right back in the game, giving up two late goals to head to the first intermission only up one at 4-3.

The second period was all Seattle, with the Mets outscoring the Canaries 4-1 to take a commanding 8-4 lead. When the third period began, the Mets continued to control the action. Five minutes into the session, Cully Wilson scored his fifth goal to make it 9-4 but the team began to coast from there. Momentum slowly shifted to Spokane, and the Canaries quietly slipped two goals past a slackened Seattle defense. With just ninety-seconds remaining, the Canaries added a third score and what had been a walk in the park minutes before promptly mushroomed into panic; the Mets could feel the game slipping away. Luckily, they held on for dear life and limped to the locker room with a victory though the *Seattle Times* wrote, "had the game continued another ten minutes, the Canaries might have forged to the front and won."

It was a win, but from a mental standpoint, it was demoralizing and the type of game that kills the team's momentum. The *Seattle Times* reported that "neither Seattle nor Spokane played first-class hockey last night, and the game was not spectacular. Several of the Mets obviously were off their game and with two exceptions, the Canaries were not up to their top form" while Royal Brougham succinctly wrote "the local team didn't look like world's champions last night."

Thankfully, the Mets played Spokane again with a chance to right the ship and regain their momentum. Unfortunately, it wasn't going to get any easier with so much attention constantly shined on the Portland game. Even the *Seattle Times* recap that night mentioned it, noting that after Tuesday's contest versus Spokane, "the Mets must meet the Uncle Sams in Portland and this is certain to be a hard game for the Portland septet is a difficult bunch to beat on its own ice." Everywhere they turned, the focus was continuously placed on the final battle in the Hippodrome.

Afterwards, Muldoon said he was "thankful that his men got the game they played out of their systems" and was "confident that the team will be in form for the next two games." Vancouver was scheduled to host Portland the next night and while the Millionaires were currently 10-1 at home, there was always the chance that the Rosebuds would win the game and take the pressure off Seattle.

The guys now had three days to mentally grind on the upcoming game. If the two teams played like they had in the last ten minutes, the Canaries would win and deliver Seattle a crushing defeat. The Mets would be forced into a must-win game at Portland to merely tie Vancouver. Another ugly win would send Seattle into the lion's den disjointed and out of rhythm, making it a tall task to beat the Rosebuds. Luckily, Muldoon had those same three days to get them refocused and confident. He again needed to get them playing against the game rather than down to the level of their opponent. It was something that was easy to talk about and difficult to do.

On Saturday night, Vancouver came back from a 4-2 deficit to beat Portland 5-4. After twenty-two games, the Mets were still in first place at 14-8, one game up on Vancouver at 13-9. Portland, now 9-14, and in third place, was percentage points ahead of Spokane at 8-13. For the first time since early January, the Rosebuds were out of the cellar.

The Sunday papers provided another big day of news on the war front. Both reported the impending break of diplomatic relations between neutral Holland and Germany. The Germans sunk ten more ships on Friday, including seven Dutch vessels despite a safe-passage agreement between the two countries.

After an arduous journey out of Germany, Ambassador Gerard was now safely in Spain, readying to sail to America amid deep fears that his boat might be sunk by German submarines. Many advised him to remain on the European continent until it was safer to sail through the North Atlantic. Gerard, however, was anxious to debrief President Wilson in person. Both sides knew that if anything happened to Gerard's ship, it would be the overt act to draw the U.S. into war.

In sports, both newspapers previewed the week ahead for the Mets, saying "the race to date has been one of the most thrilling in hockey history." Neither considered the Tuesday game against Spokane a sure win after the Canaries' late surge but remained more concerned with the Portland trip. The *Seattle Times* wrote, "Instead of facing an easy contest at the close of the season, the Mets will face one of the most difficult games of the year" while the *Post-Intelligencer* said, "of the two contests the Portland struggle is the hardest one, but the Seattle aggregation realizes they have to beat Spokane first."

Always the optimist, Muldoon told the *Post-Intelligencer* that "the boys think nothing can stop them now. We realize that Spokane is still dangerous, and Portland more than dangerous, but the team is playing well, and I think we can finish in front." Pete had been through a lot with his team over the past two years and had tremendous confidence in them. While outsiders wanted to believe him, they knew the reality of the situation with Royal Brougham perfectly summarizing, "those who have seen the former games between Seattle and the Uncle Sams are not so cocky as to the result, as Portland has rubbed it into the local men rather severely on several occasions. However, if Seattle beats Spokane on Tuesday here, the hopes of the fans will be with Muldoon and his near champs when they invade the lair of the Moose Johnson crowd."

Bernie Morris still held a two-point advantage over Doc Roberts for the scoring title. Frank Foyston passed Dick Irvin and was now in third with Jack Walker in tenth. Notably, there were no Mets players in the top-5 for penalty minutes.

On Monday, the first reports of the RMS *Laconia's* sinking reached American newspapers. The 200-point headline in the afternoon *Seattle Times* simply stated "WAR MOVES" in bold, all caps. The *Laconia*, a Cunard line steamship, set sail from New York on February 18 bound for Liverpool. It was sunk, without warning, by German submarines at 10:50 p.m. Sunday night. Of the 335 souls on board, 278 survivors had already been rescued with differing reports on the number of casualties. Two Americans were already confirmed dead; a third would soon be added.

That afternoon, President Wilson found himself before Congress, this time to ask for a bill to arm merchant ships. The tone, however, was far different than the last time the president stood before Congress just three short weeks prior. "Today the thrills that accompanied the appearance of February 3, when relations with Germany were severed, were absent. The president came as a man doing a chore, with tired voice and with a less confident note in his declaration." Congress was vigorously opposed to granting the president his request.

As the Rosebuds passed through Seattle on their way home, they stopped to talk to the Seattle media. While they were in Vancouver, a prominent Millionaires fan offered to pay the Uncle Sams a bonus to beat the Mets on Friday. All three Seattle sports pages ran stories of the offer with the *Seattle Times* reporting, "to fan the flames of enmity some Vancouver hockey fan who is careless with his coin has offered the Rosebuds $200 if they can take Seattle down the line in that final game. Having no chance at the World's Series cash, the Uncle Sams will fight for that $200 with just as much desperation as the Allies fought for Verdun."

Frank Patrick issued a press release that day regarding a potential playoff series between Seattle and Vancouver. If the Mets and Millionaires were tied at the end of the season, a two-game playoff would be held to determine the champion. One game in Seattle; the second in Vancouver with aggregate goals deciding the winner. It was nice to open at home and establish some momentum though the advantage was clearly with Vancouver. The Millionaires would know the exact goal total needed to win the championship with their home crowd at their backs.

On Tuesday, tensions on the war front peaked as many Americans feared the sinking of the *Laconia* was the overt act to plummet the nation into war. The *Seattle Times* headline read, "Sinking of *Laconia* is Overt Act! Crisis Near." Whether it was or not, most of Europe now thought it a foregone conclusion that the U.S. would soon enter the conflict.

An article in the *Seattle Times* summed up the French news reports saying, "*The Figaro* thinks that President Wilson knows well that war is inevitable, but that he will not have it said that it was let loose by the United States" while "the *Petit Journal*, referring to the torpedoing of the *Laconia* believes that events are likely to force the president's hand."

While British and Canadian frustration mounted over America's cautious attitude thus far, former French Prime Minister Georges Clemenceau praised Wilson's prudence, writing, "a pacifist out and out, President Wilson does not stand for peace at any price. On the day when the dignity and sovereignty of the United States are menaced or attacked he will enter on another course. His first step was to exercise moral pressure on Germany. Such was the meaning of the rupture of diplomatic relations. As that failed, he has proclaimed armed neutrality and thus began to exercise material pressure. This pressure will be transformed into material action and that means war."

That evening, in response to the Vancouver fan's $200 offer to Portland, "Alexander Pantages, one of Seattle's most ardent hockey fans, has offered to wager $200 that the Mets will win the pennant and will give the money to the Seattle players if they turn the trick." Pantages, a prominent resident and vaudeville magnate, began his theater empire in Seattle. The original Pantages Theater, a simple three-story brick structure on Second Avenue between Seneca and University streets was built in 1904. Soon, Pantages Theaters were springing up all over the western United States and Canada as his wealth and influence increased. In 1915, a beautiful new palatial, white terra-cotta Seattle Pantages Theater was erected on the corner of Third and University, just two blocks from the Ice Arena.

Pantages sat in his customary seat that night in the front row, center ice, for the penultimate game of the 1917 season; the last home contest for the Mets. A capacity crowd was on hand to will the boys to victory over Spokane. From the opening puck drop, the real Mets were back and attacking the Canaries relentlessly. Eddie Carpenter scored first to give Seattle a 1-0 lead. From there, Frank Foyston, Bernie Morris, Jack Walker and the Mets forward line took over. At the fifteen-minute mark, Frank scored on a pass from Jack to make it 2-0.

Just over a minute into the second period, it was Morris from Walker, 3-0. Then Foyston from Cully Wilson, 4-0 Mets. Morris from Rowe, 5-0. Then Frank scored his third to make it 6-0. Finally, Bernie added his third as the Mets thoroughly dominated the Canaries 7-0. Hap recorded his second shutout, the only two PCHA shutouts to date. It was the exact game the Mets needed.

"The high-class display left a sweet taste in the mouths of the couple thousand fans who turned out to boost the locals in their dash towards the championship," Royal Brougham wrote. "Last night's affair was one-sided in score only. Despite Seattle's big lead, the contest was as interesting as any game staged on the local ice for some weeks." If the previous Spokane game had been perhaps the worst possible outcome for a win, this one had been the best. Spokane had given the Mets everything they had, and the team responded by simply dismantling the Canaries.

"Pete Muldoon's charges got one of the best games they have played this year out of their systems last night," the *Seattle Times* agreed. "Playing superb hockey at every stage of the game the Mets clearly outclassed the Canaries. The Spokane men were not outgamed, however, and were fighting the Mets every step of the way."

Frank Patrick, who attended the game, commented afterwards, "they look like champions and no mistake. If Portland does slip over a win, we will have a hard time beating a crowd like that." Royal Brougham didn't disagree, closing his game recap with, "But once in two years has Seattle been able to best the Rosebuds on their own ice, but local followers believe the Mets have an excellent chance to stow the old title away Friday if they play in last night's form."

The Mets had now clinched at least a tie for the championship "in the closest race in the history of the Pacific Coast Hockey Association." They were heading to the lion's den full of momentum and confidence, ready to win the title outright.

Finally, the Portland game was all that mattered.

# CHAPTER 14 – THE BIG GAME, MARCH 1-3, 1917

On Thursday, March 1, Americans awoke to news virtually guaranteeing war with Germany was imminent. It was no longer a question of if the United States would enter the war, it was now simply a matter of when. The headline in the Thursday morning *Post-Intelligencer* exclaimed, "WAR PLOT BARED," as President Wilson divulged to the country that Kaiser Wilhem II himself had nefariously plotted to induce "Mexico and Japan to make war on the United States" if America abandoned neutrality and joined the Allies.

"Damnable confirmations of Germany's infamous plotting and traitorous intriguing in this country is officially disclosed by the text of the Berlin note to the German minister in Mexico City," the *Post-Intelligencer* article continued. "Professing friendship and avowing a desire for amity, Germany has all along been ready to strike at this republic if opportunity offered. And, it has stealthily invited opportunity."

In January, British cryptographers intercepted and deciphered a telegram sent from German Foreign Minister Arthur Zimmermann to Ambassador Count von Bernstorff who passed the missive on to Heinrich von Eckhardt, the German Minister to Mexico. The telegram hatched a plan to return territory in the United States back to Mexico in exchange for the Mexican government aiding Germany against America. The telegram read:

*"On the first day of February we intend to begin submarine warfare unrestricted. In spite of this, it is our intention to endeavor to keep neutral the United States of America.*

*If this attempt is not successful, we propose an alliance on the following basis with Mexico:*

*That we shall make war together and together make peace. We shall give general financial support, and it is understood that Mexico is to reconquer lost territory in New Mexico, Texas and Arizona. The details are left to you for settlement.*

114

*You are instructed to inform the president of Mexico of the above in the greatest confidence as soon as it is certain that there will be an outbreak of war with the United States, and suggest that the president of Mexico, on his own initiative, should communicate with Japan, suggesting adherence at once to this plan; at the same time, offer to mediate between Germany and Japan.*

*Please call to the attention of the president of Mexico that the employment of ruthless submarine warfare now promises to compel England to make peace in a few months."*

The entire country was immediately aghast. The *Post-Intelligencer* article concluded, "if anything were needed to cement this Union, inspire a robust, virile Americanism, silence the blind pacifists, put an end to small partisanship at Washington and solidify the country behind the government and the flag, surely this astounding disclosure will serve that goodly purpose and make true Americans of us all!"

Public opinion was beginning to sway towards a new foreign policy to act against Germany with examples pouring in from across the country, including when "ninety-eight members of the faculty of Stanford University signed a telegram to President Wilson declaring the 'time has come when the highest interests of humanity require that all means at the command of the United States be employed to defeat the purposes of the nation that sunk the *Lusitania* and the *Laconia*.'" Americans were cautiously coming to terms with the notion of entering the conflict.

\*\*

In preparation for the big game, it was announced that a special car would be added to the *Shasta Limited* train to take fans to Portland to cheer on the Mets. The train was scheduled to depart Saturday at 9:30 a.m. with a roundtrip ticket costing fans seven dollars and fifty cents.

After hearing the pundits talk non-stop for two weeks about this game, the guys knew every relevant stat about their prospects: Seattle was 1-6 all-time in Portland while the Rosebuds were 6-1 at home this season against the league's best, the Mets and Millionaires. Additionally, Portland had won four straight in the Rose City while outscoring their opponents 31-13. The Mets knew the experts thought their prospects slim. They simply didn't care. Muldoon told the Times he was confident "his charges will bring back the pennant when they return home."

While the Mets played in Portland on Saturday, Vancouver hosted Spokane with championship scenarios abound. According to the *Seattle Times*, "never in the history of the Pacific Coast Hockey Association has a team been forced to fight for the pennant in a final game." It had been the greatest race in the history of the league and the Mets were now just sixty short minutes away from their first coast championship.

A packed train of fans accompanied the Mets south and joined four thousand raucous Rosebud partisans in the Hippodrome, ready to cheer on the two immense rivals in the year's biggest game. After shocking the Millionaires a week-and-a-half ago, the Rosebuds hoped to once again be the "crushers of championship hopes" and devastate the Mets.

Although the gamblers listed Portland as favorites, the Mets had their own plans with Royal Brougham crowing, "Muldoon and his men are planning on upsetting the dope and giving the southerners a beating in their own town." Muldoon told the *Seattle Times*, "we are in the best shape possible for the game and will have no alibis." Wired communication connections were established between the two arenas to send periodic score updates. Management in both Portland and Vancouver knew everyone would be anxiously awaiting scores throughout the evening.

With the sound waves of the largest crowd of the year reverberating off the ice and shaking the players to their core, George Irvine called both teams in for the faceoff. From the opening minutes of the contest, it was one of the best games of the year. Both teams flew across the ice, relentlessly attacking the opposing goal but the two best defenses in the league prevented any pucks from finding the net. Portland finally struck first with less than two minutes left in the opening period, scoring on a Stan Marples goal and sending four thousand fans into "pandemonium." The sound so loud it was deafening in the arena. The Mets continued attacking to no avail and the first period ended with Portland up 1-0.

With the teams in their locker rooms for the intermission, the score from Vancouver was announced at the Hippodrome. At the end of the first period, the Millionaires were up 2-1. While the Mets were hoping for a miracle, no one was shocked to hear Vancouver was on top.

The second period in Portland picked up where the first ended, with both teams playing in championship form. Nearly four minutes into the period, Seattle broke through at last and evened the score when Bernie Morris scored on a pass from Frank Foyston. The Mets excitement, however, was short lived as Portland immediately responded one minute fifteen seconds later to pull ahead on a Tommy Dunderdale goal, 2-1 Rosebuds.

Seattle continued to attack but could not get a shot past Tommy Murray. Ten minutes into the period, the score remained 2-1. Fifteen minutes in, still 2-1 and the pressure was beginning to mount. A little over a minute later, Frank snagged a loose puck and raced up the ice, sprinting past Rosebuds defenders. As he closed on Murray, he made a great move to get the goalie out of position and buried the back of the net to once again tie the score. It was a confident play and brought the Seattle fans in the arena to their feet, knotting the score at two. After the ensuing faceoff, both goalies continued to play brilliant hockey for the remaining four minutes of the period and the teams went to the break tied.

The score from Vancouver was announced as the teams entered the locker room. Vancouver dominated the second period to take a commanding 8-3 lead over the Canaries. It was apparent that it wouldn't be like last year when the Mets lost the last game at Portland but finished in second place because Lester Patrick's squad knocked off the Millionaires. This year, it was all up to them. They now had twenty short minutes to notch a goal and win the first PCHA championship in Metropolitan history.

In the previous games that Seattle beat Portland, the Mets outskated the Rosebuds in the third period and pulled away late. There was, however, no tomorrow for Portland and the Mets knew they were going to get everything the Uncle Sams had in the last period, and then some.

As the teams took the ice to start the third, the volume of sound was overwhelming. From the opening minutes, it was obvious that it was a different third-period Portland team than in previous matchups as the Rosebuds still had more than enough left in the tank. The pace of play was lightning-fast and both Murray and Hap repelled great shot, after great shot, after great shot. Finally, nearly five minutes into the period, Cully Wilson grabbed the puck out on the wing and attacked the Rosebud goal. Moose Johnson quickly collapsed on him as Murray sprang out to block Cully's shot. Instead, Wilson floated a perfect pass to Frank who had anticipated the entire sequence and was alone in space next to the goal. 3-2 Mets.

The players celebrated the goal wildly, joined by the ecstatic Seattle fans scattered around the arena. It was now fifteen minutes to glory. When play resumed, an already frantic pace intensified as both teams continued their onslaught of the goal. Irvin, then Morris, then Smokey Harris, Cully, Frank, and Jack Walker pelted the goalies with shots, but Murray and Hap were too good tonight and nothing broke through. The clock passed the ten-minute mark as the tension in the arena ratcheted up with every second ticked off the clock.

At the eleven-minute mark, Dick Irvin grabbed a loose puck with only Eddie Carpenter and Hap between the Rosebuds star and a tie game. As Irvin closed, Eddie aggressively skated over to block his path. Instead, Dick made an incredible move, quickly changing directions against Eddie's momentum and using him as a shield to block Hap's view of the play. In an instant, the puck was in the net. It was an extraordinary individual effort by Irvin and a crushing goal, bringing the crowd back to life. Portland had once again fought back to tie the score at 3-3.

After fifty-one minutes of play, the teams were right back where they started. There were nine minutes left to determine who walked out of the Hippodrome on top of the world. Frank huddled the team before the faceoff. Immediately, he could tell by the look in their eyes that nothing had changed. They were going to continue to relentlessly attack the goal and not take a single second off out on the ice. If they were going to lose,

Portland was going to have to beat them tonight. Muldoon subbed Roy Rickey for Eddie and the boys prepared for the faceoff.

With the arena rocking to its foundation, George Irvine dropped the puck once more and the title fight continued. Again, the Rosebuds stars traded shots with the Mets forward line, both sides trying frantically to break through and take the lead but Hap and Murray blocked everything as the clock continued to tick, passing the fifteen-minute mark in the period. Dick Irvin once again secured the puck and made a brilliant move to shake loose from the Mets front line and close on the goal. The entire Rosebuds forward line sensed the opportunity and attacked their lanes ready for a pass. Just as Dick was about to make his move, Jack Walker came out of nowhere to hook-check the puck straight to Roy Rickey who had the puck going back the other direction immediately.

Bernie read Jack perfectly and was already sprinting back up the ice himself with only Moose Johnson and Tommy Murray back on defense. Moose aggressively closed on Rickey hoping to rattle the younger player and force a mistake. Roy, however, calmly drove the puck straight at the larger man, showing no fear and the instant Moose launched a check to separate him from the puck, Roy slipped a beautiful pass out of Moose's reach and hit Bernie perfectly in stride. Tommy Murray tried everything he could to block the shot but could only watch as the puck "glanced off his skate into the net" immediately silencing the four thousand Rosebuds fans rocking the arena only moments before; 4-3 Mets with four minutes to play.

Bernie had done it again. Frank and the team were instantly on top of him celebrating as they could now smell victory. From the bench, Muldoon subbed Eddie Carpenter back into the game and paced back and forth, encouraging his boys to finish strong. Irvine soon dropped the puck and both teams were back at it, the pressure continuing to rise as the seconds ticked off the clock. Portland sent everyone forward and gave it everything they had. Moose took a shot, blocked. Irvin rushed the net, hook-checked by Jack. Three minutes to play. Irvin to Marples, blocked. Two minutes to play as the Mets grabbed the puck and tried to mount a rush of their own. Murray was again up for the challenge. One minute to play.

The pressure on both sides was palpable as each team frantically flew across the ice, fighting for every possession. Thirty-seconds to play as Muldoon continued to stalk the sidelines screaming out encouragement. Ten seconds on the clock as both teams scrambled for a loose puck. Five seconds left. The Mets won the puck just as George Irvine blew his whistle to end the game. An eruption of pure joy overwhelmed the boys as they piled on each other in a thrilling release of emotion, realizing what they had just accomplished. They had done the impossible, stepping right into the lion's den and taking everything that the defending champs could throw at them. It was indeed a heavyweight title fight of epic proportions and the

Mets had won. Pete Muldoon had his first PCHA championship and Seattle was soon to host its first World Series.

Bernie Morris, as he had done in the Metropolitans' inaugural game, scored the game winning goal. That one had immediately endeared the team to Seattle. This one, however, was the franchise's biggest goal in its most important game. It had given the Mets the title in the tightest race in the history of the Pacific Coast Hockey Association. Bernie was now officially a star.

The final was soon announced from Vancouver with the Millionaires winning 11-5 as Doc Roberts had a big night, adding three goals and two assists to bring his total to fifty-three points. Immediately after the Seattle game became final, Frank Patrick canceled the remaining meaningless game between the Millionaires and Canaries. Bernie's two goals tonight gave him a record fifty-four points on the season and the scoring title, a record that would never be broken. Frank Foyston finished the season in third at forty-eight points.

"It's all over but the shouting," Royal Brougham crowed. "Showing all kinds of dash and pep, the Seattle Mets won the 1916-17 championship of the Pacific Coast Hockey Association by trimming the Portland Uncle Sams four goals to three. The winning marker was sagged in the last five minutes of play by Bernie Morris."

"Victor in the most thrilling pennant fight in the history of the league," the *Seattle Times* concurred. "The Seattle Metropolitans today are undisputed monarchs of the Pacific Coast Hockey Association."

The Mets won the championship at 16-8, with Vancouver in second at 14-9, Portland in third at 9-15 and Spokane in the cellar at 8-15. Vancouver led the league in goals at one hundred thirty-one, with Seattle close behind in second at one hundred twenty-five, Portland in third at one hundred fourteen and Spokane last with eighty-nine. Seattle, however, led the league in assists with eighty, eight more than Vancouver and twenty more than the third-place Canaries. In goals against, Hap and the Mets ran away with the title, allowing a paltry eighty goals on the season. The next closest team was Portland at one hundred twelve goals allowed with Vancouver and Spokane far behind.

After beginning the season with the worst offense and worst defense in the league, the team had responded in a dominant manner. Since their disastrous 1-3 start, the Mets led the league in most goals scored and least goals allowed. It was a testament to Pete Muldoon. He stuck by his guys and pulled them through their struggles.

**

The next day, Germany confirmed the authenticity of the intercepted Zimmermann telegram. "Foreign Secretary Zimmermann's instructions to the German minister to Mexico, as published in the United States, are admitted in Berlin to have been correctly quoted." In addition, Germany attempted to rationalize the action, proclaiming, "After the decision had been taken to begin unrestricted submarine warfare on February 1, we had to reckon, in view of the previous attitude of the American government, with the possibility of conflict with the United States. That this calculation was right is proved by the fact that the American government severed diplomatic relations with Germany soon after the proclamation of a barred zone and asked other neutrals to follow her example." What the Germans didn't know, however, was that the United States already possessed the intercepted cable before Germany notified Secretary of State Lansing on January 31.

**

The same morning, twenty thousand workers were locked out of the Putilov Mill in St. Petersburg in a dispute over wages. Tensions in Russia were beginning to boil.

# CHAPTER 15 – MARCH 4-15, 1917

The return trip to Seattle, with a euphoric third rail car of Mets fans, arrived in the city Saturday morning. They were greeted at Union Station by members of the media as excitement in the city was at an all-time high with Frank telling the *Post-Intelligencer* "it was the hardest struggle he has ever been through." "The Rosebuds never let up a minute," he said. "And we simply had to give everything we had to hold them even. Bernie Morris scored the winning point on a pass from Rickey. Morris played a great game, as did Walker and Holmes, while all the rest of the boys were in winning form." Curtis Lester, president of the Metropolitans and Seattle Ice Arena stepped in to "add that Captain Foyston was a tower of strength himself, and besides getting two goals and an assist, he played an excellent all-around game."

The Mets were still awaiting their opponent. The NHA split their season into halves, with the winners playing a two-game series to determine the league's World Series representative. The defending Stanley Cup champion Montreal Canadiens won the first half and the Ottawa Senators were currently leading the second half, with the playoffs set for March 7 and 10. Neither team would be an easy opponent; most in the east thought Ottawa was best team, but only marginally better than the champs.

The silver anniversary of Lord Stanley of Preston's donation, this was to be the twenty-fifth year that a champion would be crowned but only the third World Series staged between the two leagues for "the coveted Stanley Cup." At a cost of $48.67 in 1892, the Dominion Hockey Challenge Cup was awarded to the top amateur hockey team in Canada, first given to the Montreal Amateur Athletic Association in 1893. In 1906, the trustees of the Stanley Cup first allowed professional teams to win the Cup and in 1915, allowed the PCHA and NHA champions to play for the Cup with the West's lone winner being Frank Patrick's 1915 Millionaires squad. What first began as a Dominion Cup for amateurs was now the most sought-after championship trophy in North America.

In Vancouver, "the Millionaires were bitterly disappointed when the Mets won the championship by beating Portland Friday night. The Vancouver players did not think Seattle would win and were confident that the regular season would end in a tie." They were sure they were the better team and thought certain they would beat the Mets in the playoff, thus earning the right to host the World Series. In the *Seattle Post-Intelligencer*, Royal Brougham reported, "Although beaten fairly, the Vancouver aggregation believes that the Mets are fluke champions, and that the Millionaires are the best players in the league."

Not content with simply being frustrated, Vancouver wanted to put their discontent to action. It was normal for the team competing in the World Series to play exhibition games to remain sharp and the Millionaires were determined to use those games as a means to prove their superiority. And, the media willingly obliged. "Convinced that it is the better team despite the fact that Seattle won the championship by fighting back the strongest attack of every team in the league, the Vancouver septet has issued a challenge to meet the Mets in a special two-game series." To sweeten the deal and in the hopes of incentivizing Seattle to play their best, Henry Birk & Son, a prominent Vancouver jeweler offered gold medallions to the winners, confident his team would win. Not to be outdone, Alexander Pantages stepped up and agreed to contribute gold medals as well, winner take all.

The Mets agreed to play in the games, as Portland had done the year before, with Frank adding that the Mets "could defeat the Millionaires any day they started for money, marbles or rusty nails." The games were scheduled for Tuesday, March 6 in Seattle and Friday, March 9 in Vancouver with the teams using NHA rules of six-man hockey for half of each game.

The *Seattle Times* closed the article with "the Millionaires are unquestionably a great hockey team. Had Cyclone Taylor been in the lineup all season, the pennant race might have ended differently." But, "had Cully Wilson not been out of the Mets lineup for a half dozen games or more, Seattle also might have made an even better showing. The Mets won the pennant despite the handicap, however, and are ready to defend it against Vancouver or any other team." Both teams had suffered major injuries to key players, the Mets, however, were simply a deeper team and handled it better. The reality was that Seattle went 2-2 in the most hostile venue, Portland, while Vancouver went 0-4.

**

As a somber nation's capital prepared for President Wilson's second inauguration on Monday, Congress officially killed his request to arm merchant ships at 3:30 Sunday morning. Nearly eighty Democrat and Republican senators signed a letter into the senate record, "designed to inform the country just who was responsible for failure of the measures."

A small group of senators had employed the use of a filibuster as a means to block the vote from reaching the floor before their Congressional session adjourned. The term for the 64th Congress of the United States was set to expire at noon on Sunday, March 4 with the swearing in of the newly elected Congress. They were simply just going to run out the clock.

In the view of most Americans, Washington was broken by partisan politics and stunts like this just served to further those frustrations. The majority of senators wanted to rightfully place the wrath of the American public squarely on their obstinate brethren as only twelve senators had refused to sign the manifesto. An overwhelming majority were for the bill and it would have certainly passed.

The Manifesto read:

*"The undersigned United States senators favor the passage of senate bill 8322 to authorize the president of the United States to arm American merchant vessels. A similar bill already has passed the house of representatives by a vote of 403 to 13. Under the rules of the senate allowing unlimited debate it now appears to be impossible to obtain a vote prior to noon, March 4, 1917, when the session of congress expires.*

*We desire the statement entered in the record to establish the fact that the senate favors the legislation and would pass it if a vote could be obtained."*

The next day, the nation's twenty-eighth president, Woodrow Wilson, took the oath of office for the second time. At 12:30 p.m., he stood at the dais and addressed the nation. Rather than rehash his administration's previous accomplishments or paint a vivid picture of its future, Wilson's address was steeped solely in the present. Declaring that "we are provincials no longer," Wilson proclaimed that the last thirty months "have made us citizens of the world. There can be no turning back."

The first southern-born president elected since Reconstruction, Wilson's views on race were abhorrent. Despite this great flaw, many of his domestic policies as well as his leadership and vision globally set America on its current course. After more than two thousand years of the sword settling conquests and wars, he knew it was time for diplomacy to become the weapon of choice for the modern world. It was time for power struggles and oppression to end, time for each country to govern itself.

His vision was a world in peace, a world where leaders were servants of their people, a world where countries large and small were treated equitably and with dignity. He saw a time where a soldier was regarded as a person rather than a pawn, a time when the military existed for prevention rather than provocation and a time when a global entity existed to hold the balance of power.

Wilson knew that America was born of a set of ideals, a set of principles that governed its way of life and he knew it was time for all the modern world to adopt those ideals as well. Terms such as freedom and equality, transparency and self-determination were concepts that transcended borders.

In 1917, forays into international affairs were not American notions or norms and it had been a tall order to sway public opinion. These were complicated times with a nation deeply divided though a nation fortuitously led by a complicated man with the vision to alter the modern world.

America was not yet a super power. More the younger brother that had unhitched himself from a bullying older brother, simply desiring to be left alone. That young sibling, however, had now grown into the richest and strongest and was needed to restore order. Not conquests as its brothers had endeavored in the past but a beacon for what was right and just in the world. Wilson knew it was time for America to shed its blanket of isolation and help lead the new world order.

**

That same afternoon, in the midst of planning for the upcoming playoffs, C. W. Lester and Pete Muldoon made the announcement that ticket prices from the regular season would remain intact for the World's Series. "Hockey fans who have been anticipating pawning the family cook stove to raise the price of admission to the World Series," the *Seattle Times* quipped, "will be pleased to learn that such a sacrifice will not be necessary."

Muldoon explained to the *Times* that the team had tremendous gratitude to the fans who had come out and supported them all season long and that they simply wanted to show their appreciation by keeping the prices unchanged. It was a bold gesture, because the players split the gate receipts from the first three games of the World Series as their playoff bonus, the same as in Major League Baseball, but they were willing to take less as a thank-you to those that supported them most. Frank Patrick had always taught Pete that hockey was for the common man, not merely the elite and the Mets were putting that sentiment to action.

In the NHA, Ottawa won the second half and would soon square off against Montreal to determine the Mets' opponent. The Seattle players who had previously played in the eastern league were certain that Ottawa would beat the Canadiens, thinking the Senators just too athletic for Montreal. They were a similar team to Seattle, young and fast. The Senators against the Mets would be a brilliant matchup for the fans. Montreal, on the other hand, was as skilled as Vancouver but played tough, physical hockey like Portland. They were going to be a tough matchup for the Mets.

The next morning, it was announced that Frank Foyston was the 1916-17 Pacific Coast Hockey Association Most Valuable Player. He was chosen first by Royal Brougham of Seattle and Lou Kennedy of Portland and second by A.P. Garvey of Vancouver, who placed Mickey MacKay first. J.S. Bain of Spokane chose Bernie Morris first and Mickey MacKay second. Jack Walker and Doc Roberts received the remaining two second-place votes. It had indeed been a special season for Frank, finishing third in the league in scoring. He was considered by many to be an elite defensive player and was arguably the best leader in hockey. Frank possessed the rare ability to make everyone around him better without diminishing his own level of play. There might be more individually talented players in hockey but there was not a more all-around player and there certainly wasn't a greater champion than Frank Foyston.

As Seattle and Vancouver prepared for their upcoming exhibition game, its importance began to surpass reality. For the Mets, it was truly nothing more than an opportunity to stay in shape and work on six-man hockey. However, the Millionaires petty rhetoric had transformed the contest into validation of West Coast supremacy with the *Seattle Times* writing, "a victory for the Millionaires would be regarded by the Mets as a reflection on their championship record and Muldoon's men want no smudge cast upon their title" adding that if Vancouver won, they would say, "well, Seattle is in there fighting for the championship, but we know who ought to be playing for it." At the end of the day, the Millionaires had twenty-four games to win the league, the same as the Mets, and, Pete needed to remind his boys of that. Vancouver could say or think anything they wanted, the Mets on the other hand had a Cup to win.

That night, Vancouver beat Seattle 6-4 as the Mets struggled mightily the thirty minutes they played without the rover. Royal Brougham wrote, "the Mets didn't work well together at the six-man style" while the *Seattle Times* added, "combination play and team work has been the long suit of the Mets all season and was the biggest factor in bringing the pennant to Seattle. Vancouver, with several men who are stars at individual playing was able to outclass the Mets in the time the six-man rule was in effect." From Muldoon's point of view, it was a great learning experience as they were going to have to play at least one game of six-man hockey in the World Series.

One positive from the night was that those outside the Metropolitans locker room seemed to gain perspective on the series as the *Times* closed its game recap with, "Vancouver doubtless derived a proportionate satisfaction from victory greater than the grief felt by Seattle over the loss of the conflict." It was a meaningless game for Seattle and the most important outcome was that all nine men remained healthy and ready for the World Series.

Before Friday's second game, any perceived importance to the series had vanished. "The Mets are going out to win but will not take needless chances of injuring themselves with a world's series yet to be played." It was one thing to get caught up in banter a few days beforehand but an exhibition contest was not worth losing the Stanley Cup and every Mets player knew it. They wanted to get their work in and practice the six-man game, everything else was just noise. Muldoon had been practicing the team in the eastern style all week and was anxious to see their improvement.

That evening in Vancouver, the Millionaires again won, this time outscoring the Mets 5-3. Reports from Vancouver said, "although the session was only billed as an exhibition it was one of the fastest and most exciting played here this season." Pete Muldoon told the *Seattle Times*, "the game was one of the fastest I ever saw. It was anybody's battle right up to the last minute. I used several substitutes and made a number of switches in my lineup, and despite their defeat all the Seattle boys played good hockey. The boys took no chances, however, on injuring themselves before the World's Series and did not fight for the game as they would have if more had been at stake." The Mets still weren't as accomplished without the rover as the *Vancouver Daily World* made note that the seven-man style was more exciting than the six-man, but Pete now knew specifically where the team needed to improve and they had more than a full week of practice to get there.

There was always the fear that the early drama of the series coupled with two losses could hurt the momentum of the team. It was worth the risk, however, because the Mets had played a fast Game Two, and they were able to practice sixty-minutes of six-man hockey against one of the best teams in the world, something they could have never recreated in practice. While the rivalry with Portland was contentious, a strong rivalry based on respect and intense competition had sprung up between Seattle and Vancouver and the exhibition series had been a success for the Mets.

The NHA initially wanted to push back the World Series by a few days but finally relented and agreed to come west sooner, beginning the World Series on the previously agreed upon date of Saturday, March 17. Game Two was scheduled for March 20 with Game Three on Friday, March 23. The two if necessary games were scheduled for Monday, March 26 and Wednesday, March 28. The Pacific Coast Hockey Association released another All-PCHA team, this one complied by Vancouver's official scorer, A.P. Garvey with Hap Holmes, Bernie Morris and Frank Foyston named to the squad.

**\*\***

On Monday, cryptic reports from Russia had filtered out through Sweden to the rest of the world. "Serious food riots coupled with peace demonstrations have occurred in both Petrograd and Moscow. Cossacks charged a wild mob that formed in the Russian capital Thursday night. For more than an hour the mob was in control of large sections of the city. The rioters stopped the tramway service, smashed shops and paraded the streets, shouting alternately: 'Give us food' and 'Give us peace.' " It had taken four days for the news to reach the west as the newspapers had been suppressed. The military issued "a proclamation warning the people that the troops will shoot to kill if orders to move are not obeyed." Russia was truly falling apart.

That same day, reports reached Seattle that Montreal had narrowly edged Ottawa Saturday night by a goal to win their playoff series. Within two hours of the final whistle, "the famed French-Canadian band of hockey stars" were on a private rail car heading for the West Coast. Muldoon was ecstatic, telling Royal Brougham "he would rather have a squad with the reputation of the Montreal men against his men than a poor team because the honor will be greater" while Jack Walker said "he did not care much which team won although he admitted that the Canadiens were a hard lot to beat because of their long experience in the game."

It was a lengthy train ride from Quebec to Seattle and there were questions as to the Canadiens' ability to stay in top shape over the course of their journey. Royal Brougham wrote that "the Montreal squad will keep in condition and train by the usual methods employed by football teams. At every station the men will pile out and jog up and down the platform until the conductor calls 'All aboard.' " Muldoon added that the team had trainers on board. There was no question that they would be in great shape when they arrived saying "they take excellent care of themselves and will run no chances of getting out of condition." Montreal planned to stop for an exhibition game in Bernie Morris' hometown of Brandon, Manitoba and would practice in Vancouver as well. The Canadiens were expected to arrive in Seattle early Thursday. They planned to practice that day and the next to be in peak condition for Saturday's Game One.

On Friday, the first news reports in a week escaped Russia throwing the world into shock. The unthinkable had occurred. Czar Nicholas II, head of the Romanov dynasty, abdicated his throne. His younger brother, Grand Duke Michael was named regent. The new foreign minister, Professor Paul Milukoff told reporters, "the anger of the people was such that the Russian revolution was almost the shortest and most bloodless in history." The next Russian revolution, eight short months later, would not be so bloodless.

# CHAPTER 16 – THE WORLD SERIES PREVIEW

At the outset of the Civil War in 1861, Seattle had a robust population of 188. In 1880, before the Klondike gold rush began, Seattle's population was 3,533, just slightly smaller than New York City's population of 1.2 million. On the eve of the World Series, after a decade-and-a-half of explosive growth and intense desire to be a great city, Seattle was ready to step on to the big stage. In his *Post-Intelligencer* article previewing the series, Royal Brougham wrote "Seattle will shake the dust of small-town sport from her feet and bust into big league company this coming week when a championship of the world will be fought and decided right in our back yard."

The week started ominously at practice Tuesday when Bobby Rowe badly injured his shoulder in a nasty collision with Cully Wilson. An x-ray showed no broken bones but Rowe had to be "carried from the rink and put under the care of a nurse." Doc Kelton ruled him out for Game One and every effort was being "made to get him in condition to play in the second game." It was a tremendous blow as the Metropolitans were a different team without Bobby on the ice. A disappointed Pete Muldoon announced that Roy Rickey would start the opening contest.

During the Vancouver exhibition series, Muldoon and C.W. Lester made the decision to have a week of festivities around the World Series with the junior Mets team winning the city championship on Saturday and a second Fireman's Band benefit scheduled at the arena Tuesday evening. The program once again featured music from the band and a full schedule of ice events headlined once more by the Hockeyettes. The Sourdoughs and Down Easterners, sans Jessie Foyston who had already returned to Minesing, were excited to be part of the activities. In addition, Pete Muldoon was set to ice dance with Miss Venita Engle and an encore provided by the firemen themselves, participating in a "burlesque hockey game between the north and south sections of the firemen, which will be played with a football and brooms. None of the men who will compete have ever been on skates before and an amusing time is expected when they skate out onto the ice for the contest." It would be a fun evening to kick off the week.

Ticket packages for the first three World Series games went on sale Wednesday morning and sold out almost immediately. Fans "lined up in front of the box office an hour before the seat sale opened" to buy their one dollar per game tickets. Interest in the series was so high that a second ticket window had to be opened to handle demand and the decision was made to allow for Standing Room Only tickets. Wednesday's *Seattle Times* reported "indications are that the largest crowd that ever entered The Arena will be on hand for the opening game Saturday night and a record attendance for the series is anticipated."

In addition to ticket sales, interest was sky-high among journalists. A second media box was added to the arena, one for locals and one for visiting press. Arrangements were made for direct wires to carry the "story of the games from Seattle to newspapers in Eastern Canada."

When the Ottawa Senators traveled west to face Vancouver in 1915, they brought the Stanley Cup with them. When they lost the series, they left the Cup with the Millionaires. Last March, Portland took the Cup back to Montreal for their series and left it with the victorious Canadiens.

When the Flying Frenchmen left Montreal last week, they left the trophy at home. They were more than confident there was no need to bring it to the States.

For the first time, the Stanley Cup would be contested on American ice. With the Mets as hosts, PCHA rules were to be enforced in Games One, Three and Five. They would play seven to a side with forward passing allowed between the blue lines. Games Two and Four would be played under NHA rules, six to a side without forward passing and goaltenders were not allowed to pass more than ten feet in front of the net.

Few in Seattle had ever seen the Flying Frenchmen in person and excitement was high to see the famed bunch. For those who had seen them, none thought Seattle stood a chance. George Irvine, the judge of play for the series, had seen them back east. Irvine "thinks the Mets will have their hands full downing the Montreal seven," Royal Brougham reported. "They are a wonderful combination and that Seattle will be up against the strongest bunch of puck chasers in the world."

"The big series will be fought between a squad of heavy veteran players and a much smaller, but faster team which has a big advantage in speed," Brougham continued. "The Montreal men are said to be physically the largest team in hockey, the players averaging close to one hundred eighty pounds. When it is remembered that Muldoon's lads tip the beam at an average of about one hundred fifty pounds it can be seen that there is a world of difference in weight."

Muldoon had faced substantial weight disadvantages before in his boxing career. What he loved about hockey, was that skill and speed could still beat size and strength.

Montreal not only drastically outweighed Seattle, they were significantly more experienced. The forward line for the Canadiens had a whopping forty-four seasons of professional experience between the four men. Seattle's front line had a meager fifteen. Montreal's starting seven averaged eight-and-a half years as professionals while the Mets' starting seven averaged slightly more than four.

In addition to being physically imposing and experienced, talent was perhaps the Canadiens most apt attribute as they were "a team composed of some of the greatest individual stars in the game."

The *Seattle Post-Intelligencer* printed bios of each of the Canadiens' stars. Goalie, Georges Vezina was "regarded as the most brilliant performer in the game. His eye is so sure that he uses his stick like a baseball bat to wing on long drives. He is a phenomenon at close range." Defenseman Harry Mummery "is the heaviest man playing the professional game, tipping the beam at 235 pounds. Mummery naturally uses his weight to best advantage and is a punishing body checker. He is not fast but packs a terrific shot."

"Bert Corbeau, defense, is also a heavyweight, scaling 200 pounds. Not only is he a hard checker, but he is very fast and a clever stick handler."

Superstar Newsy Lalonde, "Canada's most famous athlete, a wonderful hockey and lacrosse player, is edging towards forty but this year has been his best season. Lalonde is a great ice general and a keen strategist. He is probably the trickiest player in the game and packs a deadly shot that he can drive from any angle. He is a willing mixer. Lalonde does not look for trouble, but as most of his opponents can testify, he is quite capable of defending himself." In reality, Lalonde was six months shy of his thirtieth birthday. He had been dominant for so long that it must have felt like he was forty.

For a time, Muldoon and the Mets thought Lalonde might not make the trip. He had been ejected for hitting an opponent with his stick early in the season and had done it again in the first playoff game against Ottawa. League rules stipulated that two major infractions of this sort resulted in suspension for the remainder of the year. Lalonde had missed Game Two of the Ottawa series, but NHA president Frank Robinson said the rule only pertained to NHA games and lifted the suspension. None of the Mets were surprised.

Right wing Didier Pitre "is credited with packing the hardest shot in the game, a cannonball drive that is the terror of the goal tenders. Pitre drew a professional hockey record salary in 1910, when he got $3,000 for the season." The Canadiens played sixteen games that season, meaning Pitre's per game salary of $187.50 was more than three times the salary of Major League Baseball's top earner, Ty Cobb, whose $9,000 earned him $59.50 each ballgame.

"Jack LaViolette, who will play wing, is another veteran. He is a lacrosse player, motor cyclist and driver of race cars. LaViolette is very fast and a valuable back checker."

The final starter for Montreal was Tommy Smith. "Three years ago he was the leading goal getter of the league and helped Quebec to win two championships. He faded after that but showed a remarkable comeback this year. Smith is not fast, but is a dangerous shot close to the nets. It was his tricky plays which enabled the Canadiens to win the title from Ottawa."

Despite all the superlatives heaped on the Canadiens, there were indeed those that thought the Metropolitans stood a chance to win. Four of the Seattle players had won the Cup with Toronto, and the Mets had taken down both Portland and Vancouver this year to develop the reputation as one of the most athletic teams in hockey.

On Thursday, it was announced the Bobby Rowe would play in Game One. He was sore but recovering well and insistent that he would not miss any of the World Series action. The Canadiens were scheduled to arrive that day but word had been received that the Frenchmen now wouldn't arrive until Friday evening. They stopped in Winnipeg for a workout so were behind schedule. News also broke that Spokane Canaries center, Sibby Nichols, had enlisted in an overseas regiment and was scheduled to leave for the front next week during the series. He planned to return to hockey after the war.

The Canadiens reached Vancouver on Friday afternoon and decided to practice, pushing their arrival in Seattle back to Saturday morning. At the arena, Montreal manager George Kennedy bluntly told reporters that "the Canadiens will win without much effort." Newsy Lalonde chimed in to remind the journalists not to "lose sight of the fact that we played against the majority of those Mets for two seasons in the East and there is nothing they can show us about hockey."

It was true, the core of the Mets had played against the Canadiens when they first broke into professional hockey. However, that was before they spent two years training with Pete Muldoon.

And, more importantly, the Canadiens had never before seen one Bernard Patrick Morris.

# ACT III

The 1917 Seattle Metropolitans

Photo Credit: Hockey Hall of Fame

# CHAPTER 17 – GAME ONE

The Montreal Canadiens finally arrived in Seattle the morning of Saturday, March 17. They found fair skies with a high of fifty-three degrees. The Canadiens stopped for pictures at the ferry terminal before making their way to the twelve-story Savoy Hotel on Second Avenue to rest before the game.

Manager George Kennedy took a few minutes to talk to reporters at the terminal, "I do not expect my men to have their feet tonight because of the long trip they have just finished," he acknowledged. "They will be in fighting form by Tuesday, however, and we have not the slightest doubt of the outcome of the series. Seattle may win tonight, but after that I shall be greatly surprised if my men do not make a clean sweep of the remaining games."

Seats to Game One were officially sold out and fans were buying standing room only tickets. "Hockey followers from all over the Northwest are flocking to Seattle for tonight's contest," claimed Royal Brougham. "From as far north as Alaska, as far south as Los Angeles and as far east as Nelson B.C. have reservations been made for seats, and every nook in the University Street Arena will be filled when the play starts."

The gamblers gave the Game One advantage to the Mets, but were offering even money for the series, mostly because they had never seen the Canadiens play in person.

The lineups in the game program were sponsored by Butch's Billiard and Pool Parlors on Third and Union. Muldoon was going to start his regulars, even the injured Bobby Rowe on defense. With the addition of the seventh player, Kennedy was going to pull Tommy Smith off the bench to play center and move Newsy Lalonde to rover. The words "kindly refrain from smoking during the game" were written in large bold text below the Mets lineup. There was fear that the large crowd coupled with tobacco smoke might excessively warm the arena and soften the playing surface.

Alexander Pantages sat excitedly at center ice, eagerly waiting for the game to begin. Seattle was ready. The World Series was set to begin at 8:30 p.m. with Mickey Ion as referee and George Irvine, his judge of play.

**

Before he addressed the team, Muldoon sat in his office, dressed in his favorite suit and famous high collar. Breathing slowly and deeply, he quietly reflected on his life to this point and all that he had sacrificed to get here. Leaving home. Leaving college. Changing his name. The nomadic lifestyle. At nearly thirty-years old, his peers were married and raising families. He, on the other hand, remained single. He thought of the punches he had absorbed boxing. He thought of his journey to finally manage a team. He knew the only thing preventing greatness was opportunity, which had finally arrived. Last, he thought about what winning the Cup would mean to him and the validation it would bring.

It was 8:15 p.m. and he could hear the crowd intensify as the Canadiens took the ice. He now had five minutes before the Mets, too, would take the ice. He went over the lineup one last time. Taking a deep breath, he stood up and slowly walked to the dressing room. The players were scattered around the room, milling with nervous energy as he entered. They immediately grabbed seats; the time had finally come. Muldoon took one last breath, looked each man in the eyes and delivered the speech of his life. They were playing at home. They were playing by western rules. And, they were the better team. By the end, the intensity in the room was at a fever pitch, matched only by the overflow crowd that was causing the arena to shake.

The players rose to their feet and exited the dressing room; pure, unbridled intensity flowing between them. Morris nodded to Foyston as he began the walk out to the ice. His gait was slow and methodical, his chest full of air. As he neared the door, he again looked himself in the mirror. His head high, shoulders cocked back, with eyes glaring into their mirror image and projecting confidence. Bernie still needed that reassurance before every game.

As the team took the ice and skated to warm up, the atmosphere was like nothing Muldoon had ever experienced. Looking around, he saw a sea of humanity jammed into every corner of the arena. Schoolkids had climbed the roof and were peering through the transoms. Three feet away, he couldn't hear Mickey Ion's pre-game instructions. Ion's mouth was moving but the words were consumed by the low hum of crowd noise dominating the arena. Muldoon had fought many prizefights where the intensity had produced an almost electric feeling. And, he'd coached many hockey games where the noise was deafening. This, however, was the extreme of both at once. It was so overwhelming that it almost dulled his senses.

He took a deep breath, scanned the crowd one last time and thought again about what winning the Cup would mean to him and the throngs of people in the arena. He then looked at his players and thought about the hours spent on the ice, the sacrifices each one of them had made to the team and to themselves to get here and what winning the Cup would mean to them. And, he thought about what this would mean for his adopted hometown. He soaked it all in and wanted to deliver for all of them.

As Mickey Ion called both teams to center ice for the faceoff, the intensity emanating from the rafters became suffocating. The boys soaked it in as their hearts pounded in their chests. Bernie Morris slowly glided to the center, eyes down, getting his mind ready for the battle about to begin. The Canadiens' Tommy Smith postured at center ice waiting for him, hands on his knees, back straight with his head cocked up, eyes glaring at Morris' every move. Confidence in every fiber of his body.

At 8:32 p.m., Ion dropped the puck and play began. Morris controlled the faceoff and passed to Cully Wilson on the right wing. Cully immediately rushed the net and fired the first shot of the series. Wide right. Pitre controlled the loose puck and zigzagged around the Mets' defense back up the ice. The Canadiens did not look like a team that had spent the past week on a train, nor did they look overwhelmed by their surroundings. They were fast and physical and taking the game right at the Mets. After nearly two minutes of controlling the puck, Pitre found himself near center ice with a look at the goal. Didier fired. 1-0 Canadiens. Pitre's shot was like nothing any of them had ever seen before. Royal Brougham exclaimed, "the puck was shot for fifty straight feet into the net" while the *Seattle Times* added, "it was straight out of a canon, moving a mile-a-minute." The Mets were quickly seeing how great the Canadiens were.

From the bench, Muldoon knew the first few minutes were going to be fast and frenetic and urged his team to play their game. He knew one goal would not beat them. He hoped they could control the faceoff and net an equalizer to keep the crowd in the game.

With two minutes twenty-two seconds off the clock, the puck dropped a second time. Smith and Morris again battled for control with Smith winning and flipping a quick pass to Pitre in almost the same spot. He fired again and buried the back of the net in the blink of an eye. The Mets were stunned. In the wild Canadiens celebration that ensued, Mickey Ion came crashing through and waved off the goal calling Pitre offside. Muldoon, the team and the entire crowd exhaled collectively as an instant catastrophe had been averted.

When play resumed, both teams traded fierce rushes without a goal. The game began to stabilize into a consistent flow as the seconds ticked off the clock. With a little less than fourteen minutes remaining in the period, Morris secured the puck on a rebound near the goal. With a slight movement of his head, Morris got Georges Vezina to lean left and he flung a well-placed shot into the top right corner of the net. The crowd erupted like nothing the boys had ever heard. The score was now tied 1-1. As they celebrated and began the slow skate back for the faceoff, they felt the relief of being back in the game and a renewed sense of confidence.

As the Mets arrived at center ice, the Canadiens were waiting, unfazed. Smith was in his familiar position, hands on his knees, back straight with his head cocked up, eyes glaring at Morris' every move. Morris slowly skated in and the puck dropped a third time. Smith got his stick in first and flipped the puck to his left to a moving Jack Laviolette who controlled it in stride and sped past the first line of Mets defenders with ease. Cully Wilson dropped back frantically, but Laviolette made one move and was instantly past him. With a quick shake of the wrists, the puck was in the air. Hap was completely off-guard, and the shot sailed past him and into the back of the net. Twenty-two seconds later, it was 2-1 Canadiens.

In an instant, the life was sucked out of the building and, as Muldoon looked around the ice, his team as well. He couldn't believe how quickly excitement had turned to despair. As play began again, the Mets started to press and looked out of rhythm. Seconds later, Lalonde slammed viciously into Morris and got three minutes in the penalty box. After the hit, rather than attack the undermanned Canadiens, the Mets pulled back. The offensive flow became non-existent and for the next seven minutes an ugly, slow hockey game unfolded that greatly favored the Canadiens. As the clock neared the fifteen-minute mark, Laviolette controlled the puck and passed to a wide-open Didier Pitre at center ice. Another rocket left his stick in a flash. 3-1 Canadiens.

The first period closed without any more scoring but the damage was done. Lalonde received three more minutes for another vicious hit and the Mets were in a daze. Two goals allowed from close to center ice and a sloppy goal twenty-two seconds after the Mets lone score had them reeling. Muldoon quickly gathered the boys between periods and reminded them that a new period brought new hope and that a goal would bring them right back into the game.

When the teams took the ice to begin the second period, a better flow to the game developed and the Mets looked more comfortable with their surroundings. Solid passing, attacking rushes and a coordinated defense entertained the fans and kept the score intact. Nearly five minutes into the period, Morris skated the length of the ice, put a move on Corbeau and took a clean shot on goal. Vezina swatted it away as if it was an amateur's shot rather than that of the leading scorer in the PCHA.

Lalonde secured the loose puck, turned it up the ice and sprinted towards the goal.   As he rushed up the ice, the defense collapsed on him and he dropped the puck to Corbeau on the move.  Wilson and Rowe quickly snuffed out the rush causing Corbeau to flick a harmless shot at Holmes from near center ice.  As the players turned to head back up the ice, they saw the shot glance awkwardly off Hap and slowly continue its journey through his legs into the net.  Hap frantically lunged back for the puck but was too late.  4-1 Canadiens.

It was a shot that Hap blocked a hundred times out of a hundred.  A shot he could stop in his sleep.  How had this one found the net?  The Mets were stunned.  How had this game gone so wrong?  This was not the game the guys had been dreaming about their entire lives.  The players knew Montreal was a great team.  The Canadiens were the defending champions after all, though they didn't expect themselves to hand the game to the Canadiens.  The game started like every other this season but had quickly disintegrated into a place where they lost their confidence and the trust of their athleticism behind it.

The remainder of the second period was sloppy with the Mets appearing lost out on the ice.  With a minute-and-a-half left on the clock, Newsy Lalonde hammered the puck past Hap for another Montreal score.  The rout was on.  The Mets disconsolately entered the locker room for the final intermission down 5-1.

The third period started with two quick goals by Morris and Foyston and a renewed vigor brought the Mets back within striking distance.  The pace of play soon picked up and began to favor Seattle.  The Canadiens countered by playing physical as Mummery, and then Laviolette, were sent to the penalty box.  The next two minutes saw the Mets intensely push the short-handed Canadiens but they just couldn't get anything past Vezina.  Three minutes later, Pitre sent another missile past Hap.  6-3 Canadiens.  The Seattle players were numb.  Whatever the Mets did, the Canadiens had an answer.

Morris scored again two minutes later on a Cully Wilson pass, but Montreal answered with goals from Pitre and Corbeau to make the final score 8-4.  It was a resounding victory for Montreal.

When Brougham finished tallying the final stats, the Mets had taken five times more shots than the Canadiens.  Most were the harmless volleys of an out-of-sync offense but even those that weren't were effortlessly swatted away by Vezina.  Pitre had knocked in four goals for the Canadiens, Morris had tallied three for the Mets.  They had been out-played, out-hustled and dominated in every facet of the game.

When the final whistle had mercifully signaled the end, Muldoon went straight back to his office to collect his thoughts in disbelief.  Shell-shocked, he shut the door, leaned back against it and was nauseous.  How had this gone so wrong?  What did he need to do to fix it?  He began to pace his office, thoughts swirling inside his head. Were they not prepared? Were they not good enough? Had the exhibition games against the Millionaires affected their confidence?

No, they were prepared. They were good enough. He'd made this game more important than it needed to be. The moment itself was big enough. He thought about his pregame speech. He'd underestimated the intensity in the arena and had pushed the boys right up to the limit as they took the ice. Then, the game itself had pushed them beyond a competitive point. They were completely overwhelmed by the moment. He needed to change that and get them comfortable in this environment.

As he sat on the corner of his desk, he thought about his own pregame thoughts. He'd made it too big for himself too. He thought about the sacrifices he'd made to get to this point and realized that none of them had been sacrifices. He hadn't given up anything. He'd only chased the things in life he loved most. It wasn't about validation. It wasn't about achieving greatness. It wasn't about him. It was about being part of something great. It was about hockey. He loved hockey. It made sense to him. It inspired him.

The athleticism. The precision. The creativity. It was him, wrapped in a game. He loved the teamwork. He loved the guys. And, he was ready to get them refocused on what they needed to do to play their best. He needed them to play the game they loved, not try to win a championship. The game was the same whether on the frozen ponds of their hometowns or played for the Cup in front of the world. If they played their game, he liked their chances. If they played their game, he'd be satisfied regardless of the outcome.

He knew the course. He inhaled deeply, filling his lungs. As he exhaled, he stood up and walked out to address the team. The players' heads were bowed, breathing shallow and bodies slumped throughout the room. Their heads rose as he entered only to betray eyes of disbelief. He knew they were having the same thoughts he had just had. And, he knew they'd be fine. He looked at Frank Foyston and he knew they had the best player on the ice. He looked at Hap Holmes and knew they could lock down the Canadiens' offense. He looked at seven other faces in that locker room and saw the most talented group of players he had ever seen assembled. Athletic. Intelligent. Unselfish. This team could beat you so many ways that you couldn't defend it. This team had depth. This team had scorers. This team had defenders. His breathing began to intensify as seeing the boys reinforced their greatness to him.

He talked to them about the moment. They got beat, it happens. They played poorly, it happens. They let the moment get too big for them. They had taken a punch and it hurt. He'd taken a punch in every fight he'd ever fought. It hadn't knocked him out then and it wouldn't knock them out now. As he talked, his eyes met the gaze of each and every player in that room. Slowly, their breathing became deeper and their posture stronger. One game didn't define a series and one game doesn't define a team. They were going to be fine. They were going to be great. He talked to them about the game they had played as boys. These games were no different. Slowly, the confidence in their eyes returned. It was still hockey and they were great at it. One last scan of the room showed him they were back. He knew they were ready to reconnect to their childhood game. He called a practice for ten o'clock the next morning and told them to leave their sticks at home. With that, he looked each one of them in the eyes one last time and exited the room.

# CHAPTER 18 – THE DAY AFTER

The sun rose on March 18 as it had every day before. It was just a game. And, it was just one of five.

It was a gorgeous late winter morning in Seattle. The Sunday forecast called for mid-60s with a light easterly wind. Muldoon awoke with a sense of vigor and excitement for the day ahead. He scanned the morning papers to read the game coverage.

"For the first couple of periods the locals played like a lot of school boys. The defense resembled the breaking up of a hard winter," Royal Brougham penned. "The goal keeper leaked like a fork. Then the Mets began to realize that the invaders were only human, after all, and they started to show their real speed. But the biscuits had been burned." Muldoon smiled at Royal's prose, knowing it was an apt description, and continued reading.

"The victory of the visitors scrambles the dope and makes the wise ones who were predicting Seattle to win look foolish. Saturday night's fracas was expected to be the Mets' best chance to stop the Montreal crowd as everything was in their favor. Seven-man hockey bothered the Frenchmen not at all and if they play in last night's style and if Seattle isn't over its stage fright by Tuesday the home pets are in for another drubbing."

Muldoon dressed and wanted to go for a walk to collect his thoughts before the boys arrived for practice. As he exited the arena, his surroundings took his breath away as they did every day before. The morning sun glistened off the waters of Elliott Bay, projecting a beautiful pink hue over the majestic Olympic Mountains standing guard in the background. To his left, there it stood. Mt. Rainier's imposing presence dominated the landscape serving as the foundation to Seattle's identity. Its stunning beauty and soft gentle slopes betrayed the fierceness brewing inside. Immediately to the right of Rainier, the Smith Tower stood tall over the city. Muldoon was once again awestruck by the sight. He exhaled deeply, turned around and walked north down Fifth Avenue towards Pike Street. When he arrived at the corner of Fifth and Pike, he saw the sparkling white terra cotta façade and concave entrance to the stunning new Coliseum Theater. A new photoplay, *Sapho*, was showing for fifteen cents. The matinee began at eleven o'clock that day.

At Pike, he turned left and walked one block west towards the water, stopping to admire Westlake Avenue's apex as it terminated into the juncture of Pike Street and Fourth Avenue. Arne Sunde's watch store was in the first floor of the Seaboard Building to his right, a beautiful clock outside the shop told time to pedestrians walking the busy sidewalks. The triangular Plaza Hotel wedged ever so carefully between Fourth and Westlake on his left. It was a busy intersection with people and automobiles and trolleys converging from every conceivable angle, but it was that busy intersection that served as the beating heart of a bustling city. There had been many intersections in Muldoon's life. As he reflected, the most chaotic and stressful intersections had led to the most memorable moments. The memories of those intersections that had been easy had long since faded from his mind.

As he continued west three blocks, he found himself standing across the street from the market at the corner of First and Pike. Walking the cobblestone streets, Muldoon saw the lighthearted smiles and laughs of people out for a walk or on their way to Sunday services. Some were perhaps in the arena the night before yelling and cheering their voices hoarse. Their lives had not been impacted by his team's loss. The sun had truly risen on a new day. Feeling inspired and with a clear mind, he began the short walk back to the arena to prepare for the boys' arrival.

**\*\***

As he walked onto the ice of the dark arena, the stark contrast to the night before struck him. Standing in almost the same spot as he had the night before, he could now hear every sound in the arena including the low racket of the ice machine below. As the lights flickered on, the sound of the boys entering the dressing room to lace up their skates overtook the arena. Muldoon knew the moment would soon be here and slowly walked to the dressing room.

As he entered the locker room, the dim light cast a calm tone. The boys were again slowly milling around and grabbed their seats. Their mood was better than he had anticipated. Their eyes shown frustration rather than defeat. They expected a lot of themselves and they hadn't played to their standard. Muldoon began the talk by reminding them that teams don't win championships by trying to win championships. Teams win championships by playing their game. They had to compete against themselves and the game itself rather than against the Canadiens or for the Stanley Cup. Their eyes softened and stayed focused on him. He could tell the message was hitting the right note.

To do that, they had to connect to the game they had played as kids. They could not think their way back to playing great. They had to feel it. They were going to have to let go of their rational brains and trust their athleticism to take over. Pete told them the story of a blind golfer he had met in Vancouver. The man had played golf as a child but had lost his eyesight in the war. He refused to let his disability affect his life and would not give up the game he loved. He learned to play by touch and with his ears, consistently shooting in the 90s. Muldoon implored the boys to not let the adversity of the night before affect their lives. He implored them to let go and play by feel. The look in their eyes was of wonderment and respect for the golfer, and of understanding for their task at hand.

Muldoon led the team out of the dressing room and gathered them at center ice under the bright arena lights. He talked to them about the flow of the game. There was a flow, or pace, to every game played. Players could not play any faster than the flow, or likewise, any slower. The best players get into the flow quicker and the best teams learn to harness that flow to play at a pace unnerving to their opponents. As a team, they needed to recognize that flow. They could think of the flow like a symphony.

The foundation or heartbeat of a symphony is the bass drum. It's constant thumping signals the beat for the rest of the instruments to follow. A symphony increases or decreases its tempo to the drumming thud emanating from that beating heart in the rear. For the Mets, Frank Foyston was that heartbeat. His tempo would dictate the pace for everyone else. Foyston had a sixth sense for the flow of the game and for exploiting the opportunities presenting themselves all over the ice. His sixth sense gave the rest of them confidence to just play their games. In an orchestra, no one instrument on its own can carry the breadth of the tune. And, in hockey, no one player can win a game. No one needed to put the team on his shoulders and bear that burden. If they all just played their games, the opportunities that all of them created in unison were indefensible. The opponents would have to choose between the lesser of multiple evils and Pete knew they could win that situation every time.

As Muldoon scanned their eyes, he could clearly see the comprehension and excitement in the boys. They had understood his message and they were ready to reconnect to the ice. He told them they had the remaining twenty minutes to just skate. As the team broke and started to skate, the bass drum from the Fireman's band started to beat. First faintly, slowly increasing in intensity until it's sound overwhelmed the arena. Soon, the rest of the thirty-two-piece band joined in and created the most beautiful music for the team. Muldoon knew the effect the music would have on them from the many hours he'd spent ice dancing. He hid a smile watching them just skate the ice as if they were teenagers out with their friends. He was grateful the firemen were such passionate hockey fans to come in on a Sunday morning and play for his guys.

At the end of practice, Muldoon knew his boys were back and in the right mindset to finish the series. He dismissed the team and told them to go out and enjoy the rest of a gorgeous Sunday afternoon.

**

As Muldoon prepared for bed that night, he saw the afternoon *Seattle Times* sitting on the table. In it, he read "The game outclassed for speed and spectacular playing anything seen since Seattle first was introduced to the great ice game. Somebody passed the word around that the Canadiens were big and powerful but slow. Whoever said the Canadiens were snails never saw them play, for they skimmed over the ice like feathers floating down an airshaft instead of robust athletes on shining steel blades."

Muldoon reflected on this paragraph and smiled once again. He did not want to beat a lesser team to win the Cup. The Mets had entered the lion's den in Portland and beaten the Rosebuds against all odds to fend off the intense chase of the Millionaires. He wanted to compete against the biggest, fastest, strongest team playing its best when it mattered most. He wanted his best against their best. He wanted to test his boys against the greatest and he wanted to test himself. In the end, it wasn't going to be the Canadiens that the Mets were going to have to overcome, it was solely themselves. There were a million factors outside of their control that would ultimately lead to who hoisted the Cup. While that was important, it wasn't the prize. Muldoon simply wanted to see his boys play great hockey. He wanted to see nine individuals collectively push the limits of their capabilities and trust all the hard work and dedication a lifetime of preparing for this moment had produced. He wanted to win the Cup, sure, but more than anything, he wanted to see his boys be great. He laid down to sleep, awaiting the rising sun of the coming two days.

# CHAPTER 19 – GAME TWO

March 20 finally arrived. Muldoon and the team awoke to a cold, driving rain with temperatures reaching a peak of forty-six degrees that afternoon. Bookkeepers had the Canadiens as a ten-to-six favorite to win and take a commanding lead in the series.

Despite the Mets' poor showing in Game One, advance ticket sales for Game Two pointed to an even larger crowd. All seats were sold and fans were continuing to purchase standing room only tickets.

A confident Pete Muldoon implored the fans to come back with the same gusto as in Game One. "We aren't predicting a win," Muldoon pleaded in *Seattle Post-Intelligencer*, "but all that we ask is that the fans who turned out Saturday come out tonight and see the boys play. They want to redeem themselves and, unless I am due for the surprise of my life, they are going to give the Montreal skaters a beating Tuesday."

In the *Seattle Times'* sports section, the headline read "Seattle Hockey Team is Facing Crucial Contest." Going down 2-0 to the defending champions would make it nearly impossible for the Mets to win the Cup though Muldoon was more concerned with just getting his guys to play their best. And, he was certain they would, calmly explaining, "My team got all the bad hockey out of its system Saturday night. The boys know they did not play their best in the opening game and the thought of their showing then has not improved their dispositions. They are at a fighting pitch and eager for a chance to show the fans that they are a better team than the Canadiens."

Hap Holmes was especially excited to get back on the ice and put Game One behind him. He'd had a few bad games over the course of the season but had responded each time in convincing fashion and the newspaper scribes felt confident he would do it again. "One of the most determined players of the Seattle team is Harry Holmes, the valiant guardian of the goal," claimed the *Seattle Times* in its Game Two preview. "Holmes will be out tonight to stop every shot that comes his way and he expects to show up the hard-shooting Pitre, the clever Laviolette, the tricky Lalonde and the dashing Corbeau."

Game time was again set for half past eight with Mickey Ion as referee and George Irvine his judge of play.

**

The clock ticked past eight o'clock. Muldoon sat in his office chair going over the lineup for the game. To solve the six-man problem, he decided to sit Cully Wilson and move Jack Walker to right wing thus keeping his best line of Foyston – Morris – Walker on the ice. Bobby Rowe's injured shoulder was worsening so Muldoon planned to sit him in favor of Roy Rickey. Rowe would dress but only play if necessary. It was a devastating blow as Bobby was the Mets' de facto ancillary captain. The Metropolitans had not typically played well without him, whether through injury or penalty. Despite the loss, Muldoon did as he had done all season and did not lament the situation. He trusted Roy Rickey and he trusted his team to overcome.

As was his routine, he stood up at precisely 8:15 to walk to the locker room and address the team. Nervous energy pulsated throughout his body, though he was feeling confident that his guys were ready to play their game. He simply needed to see it on the ice to feel at ease. Taking a few deep breaths, he opened his office door and walked out to meet the team. The crowd was every bit as frenetic as Saturday night, their sounds audibly penetrating the arena's brick bowels.

When Muldoon entered the locker room, the team was already gathered around the chalk board talking through their assignments for six-man hockey. Frank had gathered the team a few minutes early to ensure that everyone was on the same page. Jack Walker noticed a weakness in the Canadiens stickhandling in Game One and was showing the team when to attack the puck. When he was done, Hap, calm as always, chimed in, "Just give me a chance to play percentage, boys. I'll stop half of them when they get inside. You fellows just don't let too many get in there."

Muldoon was sure they could suffocate the Canadiens offense, even without one of their defensive stars. He had built this team on depth. His two bench players, Roy Rickey and Jim Riley, were every bit as talented as the starters. They were merely the youngest players on the team.

Muldoon went over the six-man assignments with the team one last time. He then reminded the team of the blind golfer. They needed to let go of the pressures of the World Series and play the game with feel. They needed to let go of their rational thoughts and just enjoy the night. It was not about try. It was not about do. It was just about playing the game they had always played. He called for the team to get a break and walked out to the ice.

The players rose to their feet and began exiting the dressing room. Excitement and nervous energy pumping through their veins. Cully Wilson exited first, a wry smile on his face. Hap, calm as always, exited next. As Bernie stood, he found Frank's eyes and read the calm in his friend's demeanor. He took a deep breath and filled his chest with air, feelings of apprehension swirling in his head. He just needed to take the ice. They all just needed to take the ice and start playing. As he neared the door, he again looked himself in the mirror on his way out. His head again high, eyes staring into their reflection and projecting confidence. He exited the door and entered a wall of noise as he took the ice. It was finally time to just play.

**

At half past eight, Mickey Ion slowly slid into position for the faceoff. Four-thousand raucous fans, standing on their feet, had overfilled the arena. It was so loud on the ice that all communication had long since ceased. Newsy Lalonde took over center duties for the Frenchmen as Tommy Smith was on the bench for the six-man game. Newsy did not do any of the posturing that Smith did. He let his aggressive game do the talking. At 5'9", he stood two inches taller than Morris and outweighed Bernie by more than twenty pounds. With coarse dark hair, a thick neck and big brown eyes, Lalonde was used to his presence intimidating his opponents. Bernie showed no awareness of Newsy and took his place, awaiting the puck.

At last, it was time to play. Bernie won the faceoff and flipped the puck to Frank. The Mets were out fast, attacking the goal before a hard hit from Lalonde separated Frank from the puck. Laviolette grabbed it and the Canadiens mounted their attack. As they rushed up the ice, Roy Rickey flew over and delivered a clean hit, knocking Laviolette off his skates and sending the puck careening down the ice. The players loved it. Rickey had met the Canadiens' aggressiveness head on. The Mets would not back down today.

The game quickly settled in to the fastest hockey game that any of them had ever played. Both teams fought for every advantage and the checking was physical and on-point. Walker's hook-check strategy was working to perfection and the Canadiens' frustration mounted.

Nearly halfway through the period, Montreal spread out to set their offense. Just as Pitre received a pass ready to fire a rocket, Jack Walker slid in on a knee and hook-checked the puck straight to Frank in center ice before Didier could raise his stick to shoot. Without looking up, Foyston pushed the puck to the far side of the ice where it met a sprinting Bernie Morris in stride. Bernie had too much speed and outraced the Canadiens' defenders. Closing on the goal, he gave Vezina a shoulder fake causing the

Canadiens' goalie to lung to his right. Bernie effortlessly flipped the puck into the vacated corner of the net. 1-0 Mets. As in Game One, the capacity crowd erupted like nothing any of them had previously experienced. It was deafening.

When Mickey Ion pulled both teams in for the faceoff, the Canadiens were clearly frustrated. This was a different Mets team that had shown up tonight. The puck dropped a second time with Bernie once again winning and flipping it to Frank, who quickly passed it to Jack on the wing. Lalonde smashed into Frank a split-second after the puck left his stick, catapulting him across the ice. Frank popped up immediately and put Lalonde on his back, touching off a small skirmish. Mickey Ion raced in and separated the participants, sending Lalonde and Foyston to the penalty box for three minutes each. Muldoon subbed in Cully Wilson while George Kennedy sent in Laviolette, returning from a three-minute penalty.

As play resumed, the Canadiens immediately attacked the Mets goal only to once again be stymied by a hook-check. Flying up the ice, Pitre sent a perfect pass over to Laviolette looking to tie the score. Instantly, Roy Rickey pounced, stealing the puck and sending it over to Jack Walker. Zigzagging up the ice, Jack saw Cully Wilson sprinting up the left side, blowing past defenders with fresh legs. Closing on the goal, he sucked the defenders in and slid a perfect pass over to Cully in stride. The Mets' sparkplug blasted a shot past Vezina. One minute forty-three seconds later, 2-0 Mets.

Seattle controlled the pace for the remainder of the period while Hap was perhaps playing his best game of the year. He directed the defense brilliantly and repeatedly swatted away the Canadiens' shots. The first session ended with the Mets up 2-0.

As the puck dropped to begin the second period, the pace of play did not diminish. Both teams flew across the ice, smashing into each other on almost every possession. The Mets were taking it right at the Canadiens offensively, peppering Vezina with shots. On defense, Jack Walker was everywhere, blanketing the Canadiens as the lauded Montreal offense struggled mightily. Newsy Lalonde was so frustrated that he chirped at Mickey Ion non-stop up and down the ice.

Five-and-a-half minutes into the period, Bernie grabbed a loose puck and rushed up the ice with Mummery and Corbeau back on defense. Skating at full speed, he got Corbeau leaning outside and then flipped the puck back in, shooting past him in a heartbeat with Mummery closing fast. Bernie quickly pushed the puck out wide to avoid a vicious hit from Mummery and slapped a shot past Vezina. 3-0 Mets. The crowd erupted as Bernie had just beaten a one-on-three.

When play resumed, the Mets were in control of the game's flow and began to ratchet up the tempo. The Canadiens respond by playing more physical, with both Mummery and Lalonde earning trips to the penalty box, but the Mets maintained their composure and continued to outskate the famed Frenchmen.

Soon, Muldoon re-entered Cully Wilson's fresh legs into the game hoping to keep the Mets' foot firmly pressed on the gas pedal. Eleven and a half minutes into the period, Seattle settled into an offensive set. Eddie Carpenter passed the puck over to Cully on the left wing. He immediately attacked the Canadiens defense, with Tommy Smith and Corbeau quickly collapsing to stop the rush. Cully used his strength, powering through the larger men towards the goal and forcing Coutu to help from the backside, leaving a hole on defense to Vezina's left. Frank immediately attacked the hole and Cully slid a perfect pass to the Mets' streaking captain who wristed a shot into the back of the net. Textbook Muldoon combination play. 4-0 Mets. Pete hid a smile on the bench as they were playing their style of hockey.

The remainder of the period was played without a goal. The Seattle crowd was into the game, cheering loudly for the Mets and jeering every time a Canadiens player was sent to the penalty box. Montreal had amassed six penalties to the Metropolitans' one. The defense played superbly, constantly frustrating the Canadiens offense.

As dejected as the Mets looked in Game One, the Canadiens looked equally frustrated tonight. Newsy Lalonde chewed on Ion incessantly as the teams settled in for the faceoff. The puck was dropped and both teams fought hard for possession. As rough as the Canadiens had played in the first two periods, the third period began rougher with both Mummery and Lalonde sent off the ice in the first minute. Newsy once again berated Ion, receiving a ten dollar fine in addition to his three-minute penalty.

A few minutes later, Coutu took a cheap shot at Roy Rickey and an all-out brawl erupted. Rickey quickly popped up and the pair scuffled as both teams rapidly converged. Hal Mummery leapt from the penalty box and joined the fight. It took several minutes for Ion and George Irvine to separate the teams and restore order. Mummery, Coutu and Rickey each received ten-minute penalties and Mummery was slapped with a five-dollar fine.

When play finally resumed, the Mets looked unfazed by the Canadiens style of play. They pressed the Canadiens on offense and continued to stymie them on defense as the entire team used the hook-check to perfection. Halfway through the period, Frank took a pass from Bernie and scored. 5-0 Mets. There was very little celebration this time as the Mets were now determined to bury the Canadiens for their rough style of play.

A minute-and-a-half later, the same combination connected again. Morris flipped a perfect pass to a flashing Foyston, a half-step in front of Newsy Lalonde. Back corner of the net. 6-0 Mets. At center ice, a fight broke out between Jack Laviolette and Cully Wilson. Both teams rushed the scrum as Mickey Ion and George Irvine tried to restore order. With frustration boiling inside him, Newsy Lalonde slammed the butt end of his stick into Irvine and sent him sprawling across the ice. Irvine needed to be carried off and remained out for the final minutes of the game. Wilson, Laviolette, and Lalonde were ejected; Lalonde was fined twenty-five dollars.

When the final whistle blew, the Mets had dismantled Montreal 6-1. The Canadiens' Tommy Smith snuck a goal past Hap with ten seconds remaining to prevent the shutout; it had regardless been the Mets' most dominating performance of the season. "Didn't I tell you we would skate away from 'em," an ecstatic Pete Muldoon crowed to Royal Brougham. "My boys can best that team any time they start. Watch them Friday night."

George Kennedy, on the other hand, chalked it up to over-confidence, "Too many parties. We are going to cut out all the pleasure and get down to hard work from now on. We'll win the championship yet."

"Customers who left The Arena last night unsatisfied either were deaf and blind or unfortunate enough to have wagered their kopers on the Flying Frenchmen," the *Seattle Times* remarked. "Spectators who were not up on their feet during most of the contest must have been brought to the battles in wheeled chairs or hobbled to the rink on crutches. Altogether it was one of the most tumultuous occasions staged for the benefit of Seattle fans since Mr. Puget excavated the Sound."

The contrast in playing style was evident. The Mets were pure speed and athleticism while the Canadiens were rough and physical. Through two games, the Canadiens had spent seventy-four minutes in the penalty box on twenty trips while the Mets had been just four times. Bernie Morris was leading all scorers with seven points on five goals and two assists, while Frank Foyston and Didier Pitre were tied for second with four goals.

There was talk of suspending Lalonde for the remainder of the series for his hit on Irvine. President Frank Patrick ultimately ruled that the current rules did not allow for the punitive suspension of future contests and allowed Newsy to continue playing in the series.

The Mets eagerly awaited Game Three on Friday.

# CHAPTER 20 – WILSON ADVOCATES FOR WAR

The world had changed in the four days since the series began. The first domino fell the same day as Game One. On Saturday, March 17 at 2:30 p.m., Archduke Michael, at the behest of the people, declined the Russian throne. After more than three hundred years, the Romanov dynasty was no more; the great eastern empire was now a republic.

"Autocracy has received, in Russia, the severest blow dealt it since the French Revolution. Every throne in Europe is rocking today," the *Seattle Times* declared. "Just as they rocked when the people of France proved that the 'divine right of the people to rule themselves' was more potent than 'the divine right of kings.' Tomorrow, it may be the Kaiser or his companion autocrat, the Austrian Emperor, who will be thrust from his unsteady throne."

The Romanovs were the first European monarchy to fall during the Great War. They would not be the last.

** 

On the day of Game Two, the second domino fell. On Tuesday, March 20, President Wilson and his cabinet met in the White House to discuss the increasing aggression coming from Berlin. The previous Sunday, three U.S. ships had been sunk in "quick succession with loss of American lives." The total number of Americans killed from Germany's submarine campaign had now surpassed two hundred. "The president and all his advisers have recognized that a state of war existed" without a single dissenting vote. The cabinet was "more thoroughly united than it has been on any other question that has come before it." They all knew the next move.

The 65th Congress was scheduled to convene on April 16. After the cabinet meeting, President Wilson "called Congress to assemble in extraordinary session on April 2 to deal with the situation." The legislators were summoned "to receive a communication concerning grave matters of national policy which should be taken immediately under consideration." It was to be the fifth time in the early months of 1917 that the president would address Congress.

This time, it was to ask for a declaration of war.

# CHAPTER 21 – GAME THREE

As the world was falling apart around them, seventeen men in Seattle were focused only on a critical Game Three. March 23rd was a Friday. Temperatures that day reached a peak of forty-six degrees, with moderate winds from the Southwest bringing rain.

"The boys realize that the game is most important," Pete Muldoon told the *Seattle Times*. "We feel confident that Friday will see the Mets in the lead, but I am expecting a hard battle. This game won't be any walk-away, and the team that is in the best shape and gets the breaks will win. The beating the Canadiens handed us Saturday shows that they certainly know how to play that seven-man style, and we won't have as easy as a time as we did Tuesday in winning."

George Kennedy responded that, "We beat the Seattle team before at seven-man hockey, and I think we can duplicate the win Friday. Everybody is feeling fine and ready for a hard game."

The Canadiens had an intense practice on Thursday. The Mets, on the other hand, had a light skate to get their blood moving.

By ten o'clock Friday morning, every seat in the house was sold. For the third game in a row, the largest crowd to ever see a hockey game in Seattle was expected at the Ice Arena. The gamblers had the game at even money and Royal Brougham wrote, "The last two battles between these two great aggregations of puck chasers have not been any pink teas, but the wise ones are predicting the keenest struggle of the series tonight."

Mickey Ion was set to drop the puck once again at 8:30 p.m. with George Irvine back as his judge of play.

**

At eight o'clock, Pete Muldoon sat in his office chair reviewing the lineup in the midst of his pregame routine. They were playing seven-man hockey so Jack Walker would move back to rover and Cully Wilson would again start at right wing. Bobby Rowe's injured shoulder was much improved though still not 100 percent. Muldoon planned to start Roy Rickey though he would use Rowe regularly in this game.

Muldoon felt much better pregame than he had in Games One and Two, but the nervous energy was still there. Whichever team won this game would take a commanding lead in the series and stand a good chance to win the Cup. It was the playing style his team was more comfortable with, although it was tough to keep the doubts out after their Game One performance. More skaters on the ice also lessened the impact of pure speed, greatly favoring the Canadiens though the PCHA rules benefitted the Mets. Regardless, he was confident in his front line of Foyston – Morris – Wilson – Walker. He knew that if they were playing in unison, they would be tough to beat. If the team could control the game flow early, he felt good about their chances.

At 8:15 p.m., he exhaled, fixed his collar and stood up go address the team. When he entered the locker room, he saw a relaxed atmosphere. Hap was quietly relaxing at his locker, visualizing the Canadiens offense and the shots he'd be seeing that night. An amped Cully Wilson stalking the area between lockers, unaware of everyone around him. Foyston and Walker were talking through their game plan with Bernie Morris and Jim Riley listening intently. Bobby Rowe, Eddie Carpenter, and Roy Rickey were on the far end of the locker room going over their assignments and their plan to snuff out the Canadiens' offense.

He calmly called them to attention and began to speak. They had to continue to play their game and not get caught up in the physical play or cheap shots of the Flying Frenchmen. The team that controlled itself best would win. Today was a day to go out and play hard, play fast, and be able to handle more adversity than their opponents. The team that needed things to be perfect was going to lose. The team that could play through anything: opponents, referees, crowd noise, or injury would stand victorious at the end.

He called for the team to get a break and left for the bench. As the team broke, Cully Wilson and Roy Rickey were the first to exit. They planned to match the physical play of the Canadiens as they had in Game Two and were excited to get on the ice. Hap calmly followed, eyes focused, gait slow, looking ready to play another fantastic game. Bernie stood up alongside Frank and took a deep breath. He could feel the nervous energy dissipating as game time neared. Frank, on the other hand, was a pillar of confidence, he was ready to go. Both men exited the locker room together with Bernie again looking himself in the mirror, projecting confidence. The Mets were ready to play.

**

The atmosphere inside the arena was electric as another capacity crowd was rocking the arena to its foundation. The players could feel the sound waves bouncing off the ice. Tommy Smith was back in his familiar position at center, posturing to intimidate Morris. His hands were on his knees, back straight with his head cocked up, eyes glaring at Morris' every move. Bernie was unfazed as he slowly skated in for the faceoff.

Mickey Ion dropped the puck and play began. Smith won the faceoff and immediately sprinted towards Hap in goal. Suddenly, Jack Walker had the puck going the other direction and quickly hit Frank Foyston with a pass before Montreal could react. Frank fired a shot past Vezina and the already buzzing crowd erupted with the Mets wildly celebrating a quick 1-0 lead. It was just the start Muldoon was hoping to see.

In the celebration, George Irvine was blowing his whistle at full throat, waving off the goal. Irvine ruled that Foyston was a step in front of Walker and therefore offsides. No goal. Cheers quickly changed to boos and insults rained down on Ion and Irvine from nearly every seat in the house. As Frank started to react to the call, Muldoon immediately shouted at the boys to keep playing. He was not going to let the referees affect them tonight. Frank put his skates in the ice to stop, shut his mouth and immediately went to the faceoff. He was ready for the next play. Muldoon did not think Frank was offsides. He was frustrated that an obvious goal was waved off but trusted this team to not need every break tonight. They needed to keep competing. Great teams did not need everything to break perfectly.

Ion gathered the teams and dropped the puck again. The pace was faster and more physical than in Game Two. The Seattle forwards controlled the action and continuously fired rockets at Vezina. On defense, the Mets had locked down the Canadiens' offense. Jack Walker made Pitre a non-factor while Roy Rickey and Eddie Carpenter were playing physical hockey and not letting the Canadiens set their offense. Through eight minutes, the Mets had set the pace of play but were unable to capitalize on their opportunities. The score remained 0-0.

Ten minutes in, Jack had the puck on the point and attacked the goal. As Lalonde and Mummery collapsed to stop him, Jack fed a slashing Foyston in stride. Frank started to shoot but noticed a wide-open Bernie Morris to his left and quickly redirected the puck instead. As Vezina lunged to block Frank's shot, the puck was already in the air from Bernie's stick and into the vacated space. 1-0 Mets. The crowd erupted as the Mets let out a collective sigh of relief. They had finally broken through.

Mickey Ion called the teams to center ice and dropped the puck a third time. The Canadiens won the faceoff and began to attack the Mets goal when Eddie Carpenter slammed into Tommy Smith and was sent to the bench with the first penalty of the game.

After the penalty, the Canadiens immediately attacked the shorthanded Mets. Newsy Lalonde had the puck on the wing and rushed the goal. As Jack Walker and Roy Rickey collapsed to stop the puck, Lalonde slid a pass to a streaking Corbeau in stride. Foyston lunged at the puck as it skidded past but was a fraction of a second late. Corbeau blasted a shot. Blocked. Hap miraculously deflected it over the goal and into the corner. As well as Holmes had played in Game Two, he was playing better tonight.

For the fans, it was the best hockey they had ever seen. Fast skating, precision passing and rockets fired from every imaginable angle. With just minutes to play in the first period, Coutu smashed into Roy Rickey and a fight ensued. Roy had stepped in to fill the shoes of an extremely popular Bobby Rowe and played magnificently. He had not shied away from contact and had ultimately set the tone for the Mets response to the Canadiens physical play. Both Rickey and Coutu received five-minute penalties for the fracas. After order was restored, play continued at the same pace until the first session ended with the Mets up 1-0.

Seattle had dominated every facet of the game but only scratched out one goal. The mood in the locker room between periods was light but there was a sense of not wanting to let the Canadiens remain in the game too long. Muldoon implored his boys to keep playing hard.

When the whistle blew to begin the second period. Four thousand people remained on their feet and the atmosphere inside the arena was intense. Sound was ricocheting off every surface, redirecting to the ice. The two teams traded fierce rushes up the ice for the first ten minutes but neither could score.

Finally, Frank grabbed the puck and fed Bernie Morris in stride on a full sprint towards the goal. One quick move and he shot past a Montreal defenseman near center ice with too much speed for anyone else to catch him. Vezina stayed in the box awaiting the rush and then lunged out at the last second as Bernie took his shot. The shot bounced off Vezina's leg and slid back over the line into the goal before he could stop it. The crowd let out an immediate roar of relief as the Mets had added some critical separation. The team celebrated, feeling the uneasy tension of the close game leave them.

Amid the celebration, George Irvine's whistle again broke through the noise. After a quick conference with Mickey Ion, the referees concluded that the shot went past Vezina but did not cross the goal line and was therefore not a goal. The stunned crowd went silent. The boys were shocked; it was an obvious goal. The stress of dominating play without pulling ahead on the scoreboard was growing heavy on the team. Morris and Cully Wilson went after the referees only to hear Pete Muldoon shouting from the bench to keep playing. He was not feeling the stress and knew they would break through. They just needed to keep playing and trust that their efforts would be rewarded. Only teams that panic lose these games. He was not going to panic.

When play resumed, Coutu body checked Rickey and a second fight broke out between the pair. Fists flew from every direction and it took both teams to break it up. Coutu received a twenty-minute penalty and Rickey ten. The Canadiens could sense the Mets frustration and began to play even more physical knowing that Seattle could be baited. It had certainly worked in Game One as Montreal had unquestionably caused the Mets to abandon their game plan. They knew they had a golden opportunity to do it again.

Moments later, Jack Laviolette slammed into Bernie Morris and received three minutes for roughing. The crowd was feeding off the Canadiens dirty play and was enraged. Muldoon screamed incessantly at the team to maintain composure but it was getting tougher by the moment. Frank could sense things spinning out of control and called the team together, imploring them to keep competing. This was an obvious tactic by the Canadiens and the Mets needed to let it go and attack the now undermanned Canadiens' defense.

With just under a minute to play, Bernie Morris stole a pass from Lalonde and started a rush up the ice. Mummery was the only Canadiens player back on defense, retreating as fast as he could. With a fake to the outside, Morris pushed the puck back in and flew past Mummery who could only use his stick to hit Morris in the chest and knock him off his skates. Both teams and referees flew in to separate the players as the crowd booed mercilessly. When ordered was restored, Mummery was sent to the box for ten minutes, joining Coutu and Laviolette.

The Mets had dominated the first two periods but led only 1-0. After playing cleanly in the first period, the Canadiens had filled the penalty box in the second with four infractions for thirty-six minutes.

At intermission, Muldoon furiously stormed to the locker room though he quickly calmed down before entering. He gathered the team around and praised their play. They had played faster, they had player more aggressively and Hap had been brilliant in goal. He loved the way they were handling adversity and continuing to compete.

Looking each one of them in the eyes, he scanned the room. Great teams did not need everything to break for them. Great teams relentlessly competed despite their surroundings. He could sense the Canadiens beginning to wear down and implored the team to keep pushing the pace. His cadence was rapid, rhythmic and confident. He was not about to get caught up in the pressures of the moment. Their ability to play hard throughout the second period had given him confidence in their toughness and he knew they would shortly break through.

Two minutes in to the final period, Jack Walker knocked the puck away from Pitre. It went directly to Eddie Carpenter who corkscrewed past the Canadiens defenders, quickly closing on Vezina. A quick fake drew Vezina out of the cage before Eddie flicked a beautiful shot to the open corner of the goal. Wide right. Still 1-0 Mets.

Lalonde quickly controlled the puck and sprinted up the ice. Reaching the mid-line, he flipped a pass out to Smith on the wing. Eddie Carpenter, showing incredible hustle, raced back from his near-miss, intercepted the pass, and skated back toward Vezina. This time, he shot as he head-faked; a surprised Vezina could only watch the puck fly past. Off the iron and into the corner.

Walker beat Lalonde and Pitre to the corner and retrieved the puck, hitting Wilson on the point who quickly passed it over to Foyston on the opposite wing before the Canadiens could set their defense. Frank immediately attacked the goal as Bernie timed a simultaneous rush from the right. Vezina stayed in the cage, unsure where the puck was coming from and was on his heels when Frank fired a shot across his body and into the back of the net. Five-and-a-half minutes into the third period, it was finally 2-0 Mets. To score on a hustle play after two consecutive point-blank misses once again showed the championship heart beating within the Mets. George Irvine's whistle remained dangling around his neck, this score would count.

As the teams met again, Mickey Ion dropped the puck to a chanting home crowd. The Canadiens won the faceoff but couldn't get anything going before Seattle gained possession. Wilson passed to Foyston, back to Wilson and over to Morris who sensed a weakness in the Canadiens defense and attacked. Before the gassed defenders could rotate over, Morris had the puck in the air and past Vezina. 3-0 Mets. One minute and forty seconds later, Bernie had given the Mets even more breathing room.

The crowd was going crazy, louder than at any point in the contest. The physical exhaustion of the Canadiens players was evident. Their breathing was rapid and shallow with their posture erect, desperately trying to open their lungs to get oxygen. The puck dropped again with Morris and Tommy Smith fighting for control. As both teams converged on the loose puck, Bernie emerged from the scrum sprinting straight at Vezina in goal. One slight hesitation move and the puck was again in the back of the net. Sixteen seconds off the clock and it was now 4-0 Mets, pandemonium ensued. Spectators were jumping over themselves in the stands as the Mets celebrated on the ice. Muldoon flashed a huge smile as his boys had stayed the course, never once getting flustered and had turned this game into a rout.

With twelve-and-a-half minutes to play, Seattle settled in to play defense and run out the clock. The pace of the game dramatically slowed but the exhausted Canadiens could not take advantage. Tommy Smith, for the second straight game, snuck a late goal past Hap to break up the shutout, but the Mets triumphed 4-1 and took a two games to one lead for the Cup.

Royal Brougham's column in the *Seattle Post-Intelligencer* effused praise on the Mets. "Every member of the team, from reliable old "Happy" Holmes to foxy Jack Walker, covered himself with glory," Brougham gushed. "As in Tuesday's contest, whirlwind speed and never-say-die aggressiveness won for the home club." The Mets passing had been outstanding, with Royal writing, "the local forwards slipped the puck through the legs of the visitors, passed it in front of 'em and in back of 'em, and the Frenchmen couldn't fathom the puzzling style of the Mets."

George Kennedy quickly blamed the officiating for his team's loss with Brougham addressing the claim in his recap. "Irvine banished several of the Frenchmen for rough work in the second period, and Kennedy thought the judge of play was laying it on too thick," Royal acknowledged. However, "the spectators can testify that the invaders played the rougher game."

**

Muldoon awoke the next morning to a knock at his door. It was Frank Patrick. George Kennedy had filed an official protest, asking for the game result to be thrown out. Kennedy claimed that the officials had incorrectly forced Coutu and Mummery to serve their penalties simultaneously because the Canadiens did not have another player to substitute. Frank told Muldoon that he had wired NHA President Frank Robinson to ask his opinion. Patrick would not rule until he received a reply.

"I do not believe that Kennedy's protest has any just foundation," said Muldoon in the *Seattle Times*, "and I cannot conceive of the president of the league allowing the game to be thrown out. If Kennedy had asserted his rights at the time the alleged error was made, the officials no doubt would have adjusted the matter."

"Manager Pete Muldoon believes Kennedy's action is comedy," Royal Brougham wrote. "Muldoon denies that the visitors got any the worst of the officiating, and points to the two goals which everyone thought were clean goals, but which were ruled off by the referee as proof his lads got nothing they didn't deserve."

# CHAPTER 22 – GAME FOUR

March 26 was a typical gray, rainy Seattle day though even the drizzle couldn't dampen the city's excitement for the game that evening. Late the night before, President Frank Patrick had overruled the Canadiens protest, giving the Mets a two games to one lead over the Canadiens. Anticipation in the city was peaking for a world championship. A sign with three simple words, Standing Room Only, was again placed at the box office window at ten o'clock that morning. Every seat in the house had long been sold although not one would be used. For the fourth straight game, the largest crowd to ever see a hockey game in Seattle would jam-pack the Ice Arena.

**

Sitting in his office, Muldoon felt a combination of nervous energy and excitement, yet clarity for what the team needed to do to play its best. Tonight was about enjoying the moment and trusting the years of hard work that had brought them all to this point. As he often liked to say, this game was on ice. The only thing left to do was play it.

He looked himself in the mirror, adjusted his collar, took a deep breath and walked into the dressing room to address the team. He was struck by the normalcy of the atmosphere inside. It could have been the locker room for a Tuesday game in the middle of any season he'd ever coached. Guys were walking around, going about their business preparing for this game like it was any other. Green, red and white barber pole sweaters hung stoically at their lockers. Some players were putting the finishing touches of tape to their bodies while others were lacing up their skates. Hap looked like he was asleep on his stool, leaning against his locker.

As Muldoon called them to attention, he took another deep breath and addressed the team. His pace was rapid and rhythmic, enunciating each syllable, yet he spoke with a soothing tone. He wanted to set their flow then and there. He wanted the game to be slow to them yet look blazing-fast to the Canadiens and the throngs of fans in the arena. They needed to appreciate the moment. They needed to enjoy the moment. It was the one they had spent countless hours dreaming about. But, they didn't need to do anything more in this moment.

They had succeeded. They had failed. But, they were there. And, they were champions because they were there. Tonight was about playing their game. Tonight was about trust. Trusting their preparation. Trusting their teammates. And, most importantly, trusting themselves and simply playing the game like they had every other day in their lives. Tonight was about leaving no regrets. Play fast. Play hard. And, be alright with the outcome so long as they can look themselves in the mirror sixty minutes from now knowing they had done both.

He scanned their eyes as he let that last message sink in. They were ready. The intensity in their eyes looked like every other game. They had heard his message. With that, he exhaled one last time and told them to take the ice.

The players rose to their feet, pulled on their sweaters and began to exit the dressing room, intensity and focus flowing between them. Bernie nodded to Frank as he did before every game and began the walk out to the ice. His gait was slow and methodical, his chest full of air. His head high, shoulders cocked back and nostrils flaring with each deep breath. This time, however, his chin was tilted down ever so slightly towards his chest so that he was almost glaring straight ahead from the tops of his eyes. It was not the look of someone projecting confidence. It was the look of pure confidence. Frank had never seen that look before. As he neared the door, Bernie didn't look himself in the mirror on his way out. He walked straight past and out the door. Today, there was no need. Ball game.

Muldoon entered the arena last. An eerie calm enveloped him. He looked up at the thousands of people around him in the stands. He could see their hands waving and mouths moving but there was no sound. He looked at the boys on the ice, they skated with one heartbeat as if they were skating to the same song in their head.

His eyes gazed to his left, he saw the puck in Mickey Ion's hand. He realized it was about that puck and the thirty-six hundred moments to come in the next sixty minutes. If he could keep the boys focused on just the moment at hand, they would play their best.

As his eyes went back to the team, Bernie Morris skated by and Muldoon saw a different look in his eye. A look he had never before seen. It was the look when the most talented player on the ice finally realized he was the best player on the ice. Muldoon knew then that they were about to see something miraculous. He took his seat on the bench. His boys were ready.

**

Game Four began with a rush. Morris beat Tommy Smith to the puck and kicked it out to Frank who took it up the ice. After a few short passes, the Canadiens stole the puck and zigzagged the other way. When the puck found Pitre ready to shoot, Jack Walker was in his back pocket and poked the puck to Frank before the Canadiens' star could mount a threat.

Foyston quickly turned the puck up the ice, sprinting past defenders. Three Canadiens were left to defend him with Bernie Morris trailing. He didn't have numbers and thought of pulling up. Instead, he sensed a weakness in the Canadiens spacing and attacked. As he reached center ice, he made a subtle hesitation move to get the defenders on their heels and then hit the hole. Two panicked Canadiens stopped him rather than one and Foyston dropped a beautiful pass to Bernie flying up the ice. Mummery, the third defender, rushed Bernie to deliver a vicious hit but Bernie's stick handling was too good. With one move, Morris pushed the puck forward and rolled off the hit as Mummery launched into what he thought was the "S" on Bernie's chest. The glancing blow shot Mummery past and Bernie maintained his speed towards the goal, puck perfectly in front of him. He closed like a freight train and fired a shot past Vezina from five feet away. 1-0. Vintage Mets. Foyston was the only guy on the ice that could have created that opportunity and Morris showed why he had set the league scoring record by beating two of the best in Mummery and Vezina.

Both men immediately stuck their skates in the ice to stop and slowly pushed back towards center ice. Today was not a day to celebrate early victories. Today was a day to put their foot on the Canadiens' throat and not let up. From the bench, Muldoon scanned his guys. Each one of them had the same look as they converged on center ice. Facial muscles relaxed and bouncing in unison to each push of the skate. Eyes focused on their spots at center ice. Everything else vacant from their consciousness.

One minute and fifty-six seconds into the game, Ion approached center ice for the second faceoff. Tommy Smith was in his familiar posture, hands on his knees, back straight with his head cocked up. The Canadiens once again looked unfazed. They were not going to let one goal beat them tonight. As Morris slowly slid into position for the faceoff, the noise was deafening. The arena was so loud the boys could feel the sound waves of the standing room only crowd reverberating through their chests.

Ion dropped the puck again and play resumed. The wear and tear of three lightning-fast contests was beginning to show and the game's flow was slower than the previous games. Both offenses settled in and traded unsuccessful rushes on goal. Halfway through the period, Pitre secured the puck and zigzagged his way near center ice with a clear shot on goal. Didier launched another blazing rocket. Holmes calmly swatted it away.

Jack Walker grabbed the deflection and turned it up the ice but slipped near the blue line and lost the puck. Sore legs and fast ice were causing both teams to fall frequently. Lalonde grabbed the puck and instantly raced towards the goal before the Mets could get back on defense. As Roy Rickey frantically rushed over to stop him, Lalonde effortlessly dropped it to a waiting Pitre. He fired another missile. Holmes again calmly swatted it away. Disaster averted. On the bench, Muldoon let out a deep breath. His boys were playing their game. The first period soon ended without a penalty and with the Mets in the lead 1-0.

As Muldoon entered the locker room during the break, he was again struck by the normalcy. The players were talking through Montreal's offensive sets as well as their opportunities to exploit the Canadiens' defense. The atmosphere looked more like a regular season game in December than a team forty minutes away from their first championship. Muldoon chimed in with what he was seeing and sent the team back out on the ice. Nothing more needed to be said.

When the second period began, the Mets took the action right at the fatigued Frenchmen and both teams soon settled in to another quintessential title fight. Seattle continued to attack as they outshot the Canadiens five-to-one to open the period but couldn't push anything across. The pace remained slower than the previous games but neither side gave an inch.

Eight minutes into the period, the Mets finally broke through when Frank grabbed the puck near center ice, Bernie crashing up the right wing behind him. Frank attacked with such precision and aggression that he passed the lone Montreal defender in a heartbeat, forcing Vezina out of the net to block Frank's angle. Foyston sensed the perfect moment and slid the puck to Bernie. 2-0 Mets.

Both men shot small smiles to each other as they turned to head back up the ice. They were in the zone, completely unaware of the wall of noise cascading down on them from every conceivable space in the arena. Their teammates knew it and went straight back to center ice, eager to see what was coming next. The only people in the arena that couldn't see it were the Canadiens. They were defending champions and they were not about to lose this game or the Cup to an American team. The fight was still in their eyes.

The Canadiens won the faceoff and spread out to set their offense. There were no holes. As well as the Mets were playing offensively, their defense was better. After a few harmless passes, Walker poked the puck away from Pitre. Frank had anticipated Jack's move and was already breaking towards the goal. Jack led him perfectly as Frank shot past the other men on the ice in the blink of an eye leaving only Vezina. Foyston flicked a quick wrist shot to the corner of the goal. No contest. 3-0 Mets and pandemonium ensued.

For the first time in the game, the boys celebrated. It was a move they had practiced countless times and it was executed to perfection. To them, the game was moving in slow motion while their speed was overwhelming the hapless Canadiens. They were anticipating and seeing plays happen well in advance. The Mets were playing a different game than Montreal.

The contest was only half over but they could smell the finish line. As the game progressed, the Mets continued to relentlessly attack Vezina and the Canadiens goal on offense and suffocate the Frenchmen on defense, playing perfectly according to script. As the clock ticked under one minute to play in the period, Roy Rickey stole a pass and shot up the ice. As the defense collapsed on him, he dropped a perfect pass to Morris a few feet from the net. 4-0 Mets.

For the remaining twenty seconds of the period and the entire intermission, the crowd noise dwarfed the intimidating sounds they heard in Game One. This was truly something none of them had previously experienced. They were twenty minutes away from claiming the first Stanley Cup won by an America team. Twenty minutes from delivering the first world championship to Seattle. They were not going to let up.

Mickey Ion soon called the teams to center ice to begin the final period. The crowd was deafening. As the puck dropped, the Canadiens took control and set their offense. Lalonde to Mummery, back to Lalonde, over to Corbeau looking for a crack in the Mets defense. The Mets were still playing fast and shut off every hole, every gap. As Corbeau sent the puck back to Lalonde, Jack cut it off and rushed back up the ice. Pulling in Mummery to stop the attack, he dumped the puck to Bernie Morris sprinting up the right side. Bernie skated the remainder of the ice alone. 5-0 Mets. One minute and twenty seconds into the third period, the celebration had officially begun.

It was now evident the fight had left the Canadiens. Utterly exhausted from chasing the smaller, faster Mets around the ice for four games, their pace continued to slow. The Mets, in great physical condition, playing at home and buoyed by the crowd maintained their pace. Four minutes and twenty seconds later it was Morris again on a beautiful pass from Bobby Rowe. 6-0 Mets, 14:20 left on the clock. Eighteen seconds later, Foyston found the back of the net off another beautiful Bobby Rowe pass. 7-0 Mets, 14:02 to play. On the bench, Muldoon was struggling to hide the grin forming. His boys had executed the last three games to perfection. The world was witnessing the best team playing its best game.

The Canadiens finally broke through when Pitre snuck a shot past Hap with 12:05 to play. But two minutes later, Jack Walker weaved through the Canadiens defense and beat Vezina. 8-1 Mets, 9:52 left. Finally, as the clock ticked down near the seven-minute mark, the final goal was scored. Bernie Morris took another beautiful pass from Bobby Rowe and blasted a short range shot past Vezina. 9-1 Mets. Greatness.

The already raucous crowd reached another gear that shook the Ice Arena to its foundation. The final seven minutes ticked away harmlessly until the clock struck zero. As the final whistle sounded, the celebration on the ice was one for the ages. The ups and downs of a season of struggles was over and in its place was the Cup. The words "Seattle World's Champions defeated Canadians – 1917" would be forever etched on the lowest of the tiered rings.

Muldoon's pride burst onto the next day's *Seattle Post-Intelligencer.* "They all played like champions," an excited Pete rejoiced. "The boys went at top speed all the way and nobody could have stopped them." The sportswriters' pride beamed as well, with Royal Brougham penning, "The Seattle Metropolitans are monarchs of the hockey world" and the *Seattle Times* adding, "for the next twelve months, the Seattle team will demand and receive recognition as the highest power in hockey."

For Morris, the tragedies, failures, and disappointments of twenty-six often difficult years left him. He'd scored six goals tonight. Fourteen in the series to go with two assists, scoring more goals than the entire Canadiens team. For Foyston, it was another great game in another great season in a career full of both. He'd banged in seven goals for the series to go with two assists.

Not yet thirty years old, Pete Muldoon had achieved the pinnacle of his profession. Since paid players began competing for the Stanley Cup in 1906, a quartet of younger player-coaches had won the Cup, but, at twenty-nine years and nine months, Pete Muldoon is still the youngest coach to hoist the vaunted Stanley Cup as champion. His boys held off the 1915 Stanley Cup champion Vancouver Millionaires to win the PCHA and dominated the 1916 champion Montreal Canadiens in every phase of the game to claim Seattle's first professional sports championship.

The Metropolitans won this series with offense. They won it with defense. They won it with depth. And, they won it with teamwork. Muldoon had built a perfect roster and had managed them to perfection. Many coaches only see what a player cannot do, Muldoon, on the other hand, focused solely on what they could do. He saw the talent in every person and created an atmosphere allowing each to thrive.

As time marches on and memories fade, the lasting thoughts of greatness are often only of the final celebration. Greatness is not made in those moments, however, it is made in the countless successes and failures leading up to that moment. Through a disappointing start, injuries, and intense pressure and competition, Frank Foyston, Bernie Morris and the rest of the Metropolitans had played their best when it mattered most. They overcame the strongest teams on both coasts, and, they overcame themselves. As the first American team to claim the Stanley Cup, they not only achieved greatness, they achieved immortality.

# Epilogue

Frank Foyston with his 1917 MVP Trophy

Photo Credit: Barbara Daniels

# WAR

Six days later, on April 2, President Wilson addressed a joint session of Congress. The Monroe Doctrine's policy of isolationism had been pushed beyond its breaking point. "The present German submarine warfare against commerce is a warfare against mankind," bellowed the president. "There has been no discrimination. The challenge is to all mankind. Each nation must decide for itself how it will meet it." The concept of armed neutrality, it was now understood, would not work. It would only postpone the inevitable, the United States fighting alongside the allies to defeat Germany.

Wilson made clear that the fight was not against the German people, but against only the German government. "Our motive will not be revenge or the victorious assertion of the physical might of the nation, but only the vindication of right, of human right, of which we are only a single champion," he declared. "We have no quarrel with the German people. We have no feeling towards them but one of sympathy and friendship. It was not upon their impulse that their Government acted in entering this war. It was not with their previous knowledge or approval. It was a war determined upon as wars used to be determined upon in the old, unhappy days when peoples were nowhere consulted by their rulers and wars were provoked and waged in the interest of dynasties or of little groups of ambitious men who were accustomed to use their fellow men as pawns and tools."

Condemning the secret, nefarious plots of autocratic nations, he proclaimed that "self-governed nations do not fill their neighbor states with spies or set the course of intrigue to bring about some critical posture of affairs which will give them an opportunity to strike and make conquest. Such designs," he asserted, "can be worked out only under cover and where no one has the right to ask questions ... they can be worked out and kept from the light only within the privacy of courts or behind the carefully guarded confidences of a narrow and privileged class. They are happily impossible where public opinion commands and insists upon full information concerning all the nation's affairs."

Thundering on, the president advocated for an international body, contending that "peace can never be maintained except by a partnership of democratic nations. It must be a league of honor, a partnership of opinion. Only free peoples can hold their purpose and their honor steady to a common end and prefer the interests of mankind to any narrow interest of their own."

Finally, he asked for a declaration of war. "It is a fearful thing to lead this great peaceful people into war, into the most terrible and disastrous of all wars, civilization itself seeming to be in the balance," he acknowledged. "But the right is more precious than peace, and we shall fight for the things which we have always carried nearest our hearts – for democracy, for the right of those who submit to authority to have a voice in their own governments, for the rights and liberties of small nations, for a universal dominion of right by such a concert of free peoples as shall bring peace and safety to all nations and make the world itself at last free. To such a task we can dedicate our lives and our fortunes, everything that we are and everything that we have, with the pride of those who know that the day has come when America is privileged to spend her blood and her might for the principles that gave her birth and happiness and the peace which she has treasured."

**

On April 4, the Senate voted 82-6 in support of entering the war. In the early hours of April 6, the measure passed the House 373-50 and the United States formally declared war on Germany. It was not the war to end all wars. Like the second act in a three-act play, World War I set the stage for a lasting peace and new world order. Monarchies and autocratic rule gave way to self-determination and new democratic nations. Despite the objections of President Wilson, however, old scores were indeed settled during the Paris Peace Conference; winners and losers were thus declared. Those petty scores would set the stage for a second World War, a mere twenty-one years later. Only then would Wilson's vision of a League of Nations, a United Nations, ultimately be realized.

**

Eddie Carpenter, Frank Foyston, Roy Rickey, and Jim Riley would serve in the Canadian military though Riley was the lone Metropolitan to fight on the front lines of the Great War. Carpenter would miss the 1918 and 1919 seasons while Riley would miss the Metropolitans' 1919 season and doomed World Series.

Sadly, Bernie Morris would lose a year of his life to the war. Through a treaty signed by the United States and Canada, all Canadian citizens residing in America were subject to the U.S. military draft and vice versa. Bernie would be drafted into the U.S. Army six days before the Armistice was signed. Though he properly reported his Canadian residency to authorities, he was arrested on a technicality and sent to Fort Lewis to stand trial for draft evasion. Later convicted, he was sentenced to two years hard labor at the U.S. Military Prison – Alcatraz, missing the 1919 World Series and 1920 season. PCHA and Seattle officials continued to fight the conviction vigorously until he was finally released. Serving only one year in prison, he was granted full military benefits and an Honorable Discharge.

# METS

The Metropolitans competed for the Stanley Cup twice more. In 1919, Seattle again hosted Montreal but this time without an incarcerated Bernie Morris. A Spanish Flu outbreak struck late in the series, hospitalizing five Canadiens and killing Montreal's Joe Hall. The Canadiens offered to forfeit but Pete Muldoon and Frank Patrick declined, declaring the series a tie, the only year a champion was not crowned.

In 1920, the Metropolitans lost to the Ottawa Senators in five games. The Mets remained a team until 1924 when the Ice Arena was converted into the new Fairmont Hotel's parking garage.

# PROFESSIONAL HOCKEY

Infighting further deteriorated the NHA. On November 26, 1917, a new league formed at the Windsor Hotel in Montreal; the National Hockey League. Frank Calder was named president and a new Toronto franchise created, sans Eddie Livingstone. Toronto, starring Hap Holmes, won the inaugural NHL championship and defeated Vancouver for the Stanley Cup.

The PCHA operated as a three-team league in 1918 though the newly renamed Victoria Cougars reemerged after the war. The league ceased operations following the 1924-25 season. Vancouver disbanded, the Rosebuds moved to Chicago, becoming the Blackhawks and the Cougars moved to Detroit, soon renamed Red Wings.

# WORLD WAR I

On April 6, 1917, the U.S. declared war on Germany. Eight months later, a second declaration was made, this time against Austria-Hungary.

The conflicted ended on November 11, 1918 with the signing of an armistice. Europe was redrawn, replacing the German, Russian, Ottoman, and Austro-Hungarian Empires with Republics and adding new independent, self-determined countries across the continent. Headquartered in Geneva, the League of Nations was formed to prevent another such war. First proposed by President Wilson, the United States was never a member.

## SUFFRAGETTE

On May 21, 1919, the House of Representatives passed an amendment granting women the vote, followed shortly by the Senate. The 19th Amendment was formally ratified on August 26, 1920. Montana Congresswoman Jeannette Rankin, elected in 1916, became "the only woman who ever voted to give women the right to vote."

## ICE ARENA

In December of 1917, the Seattle Ice Arena hosted the Seattle Girls War Relief Bazaar, transforming the arena surface to depict the trench warfare experienced by soldiers. Over 10,000 citizens per day attended, raising more than $120,000 for the Seattle Chapter of the Red Cross.

The arena continued to host popular events and packed Metropolitans' games until its closure in 1924 to become the new Fairmont Hotel's parking garage. The structure was demolished in 1963 for the IBM building's construction, still standing on the site today.

**Pete Muldoon**     **Died:** March 13, 1929 (41 years old)

Asked to coach Portland in 1918, Pete could not defend the Mets championship. Returning in 1919, he coached the Mets until their demise in 1924. In his eight seasons in Seattle, the Metropolitans won four PCHA titles with three second-place finishes, playing in three World Series.

Named the Chicago Blackhawks first head coach, he left after one tumultuous season. Pete returned to Seattle where he built the Mercer Arena, home to his new minor league team, the Seahawks. He married in 1924 and had two sons, remaining a legendary figure in Seattle long after his death.

**Frank Foyston**     **Died:** January 19, 1966 (74 years old)

Frank played all nine Metropolitans' seasons. Considered among the greatest players of his generation, he won three Stanley Cups. He served in the Royal Air Service after the 1918 season though he remained in Canada and played the 1919 season.

Frank played his final two years in Detroit. He returned to Seattle and a turkey ranch next to Bernie Morris, coaching the minor league Seahawks to great success and was as beloved as his mentor. Frank remained lifelong friends with his Metropolitans teammates, often traveling on recruiting trips with his chief rival and close friend, Bobby Rowe. **Hockey Hall of Fame: 1958.**

**Bernie Morris**     **Died:** May 16, 1963 (72 years old)

In Bernie's seven seasons in Seattle, he was named an All-PCHA All-Star five-times and twice to the second-team. Although successful in hockey, his life remained marred by tragedy. Bernie divorced Minnie in 1919 citing desertion. His draft evasion arrest occurred two weeks later, on the day the PCHA playoffs began. On his release one year later, he traveled straight to Ottawa for the 1920 World Series.

Bernie played six games for the expansion Boston Bruins in 1924 and remained in hockey as a coach or referee until his 40s. He lived next-door to his close friend Frank Foyston until a falling out late in life. With his second marriage also ending in divorce, Bernie passed away alone and in obscurity at a military hospital in Bremerton, Washington. Despite still being occasionally mentioned in news reports, his obituary was the only Mets player not covered. **Hockey Hall of Fame: Still Awaiting Induction.**

**Harry "Hap" Holmes**     **Died:** June 27, 1941 (53 years old)

Holmes played eight seasons in Seattle and sixteen total, including his last two with the Detroit Cougars and won four Stanley Cups. Upon his retirement, he began coaching minor league hockey in Cleveland, Ohio and spent the offseason on his fruit farm in Florida. Since 1948, the Hap Holmes Memorial Award is given to the goalie with the lowest goals-against average in the American Hockey League. The first Mets player to pass away, Hap remained lifelong friends with his teammates until his death. **Hockey Hall of Fame: 1972.**

**Jack Walker**     **Died:** February 16, 1950 (62 years old)

Walker played all nine Metropolitans' seasons. The inventor of the hook check, Jack played his final two seasons for Detroit before moving back to Seattle. He won three Stanley Cups, all with Frank Foyston and Hap Holmes. Jack continued to stay in hockey, refereeing periodically while he worked at the Rainier Brewery until his death. While sick in the hospital, Jack received notes or visits from Frank Foyston, Bernie Morris, Cully Wilson, Roy Rickey. Jim Riley and Mickey Ion. **Hockey Hall of Fame: 1960.**

**Bobby Rowe**    **Died:** September 21, 1947 (62 years old)

Rowe played nine seasons in Seattle. Alongside Bernie Morris, he played four games for the expansion Boston Bruins before returning to the Northwest as a highly successful minor-league coach in Portland. In addition to hockey, Rowe became the Rose City's biggest sports promoter, bringing Auto Racing, tennis, football and more. Prior to his death, he remained friends with Frank Foyston and his Metropolitans teammates.

**Cully Wilson**    **Died:** July 6, 1962 (70 years old)

Cully played four seasons in Seattle before his banishment from the PCHA for a vicious hit on Mickey MacKay, later one of Wilson's closest friends. After his expulsion, he played five seasons in the NHL including his last with Pete Muldoon and the Blackhawks. By retirement, he had amassed more than eighty stitches in his face and one hundred total. Returning to Seattle, he was an embarking checker at the Port of Seattle. Deeply respected for his competitive fire, Seventy-three-year-old Newsy Lalonde picked his "all-time meanest, toughest team" in 1961 and named Cully Wilson as the center on his second line.

**Eddie Carpenter**  **Died:** April 30, 1963 (72 years old)

Carpenter played only two seasons in Seattle, leaving after the 1917 championship to return to Port Arthur before serving in the military. After the war, he played two seasons in the NHL before a successful coaching career, leading the 1924-25 and 1925-26 Port Arthur senior teams to Allan Cup championships. In 1941, he served on the Port Arthur city council.

**Roy Rickey**    **Died:** September 6, 1959 (66 years old)

Rickey played seven seasons in Seattle, retiring after the 1922-23 season when he was one of the top defensemen. Newsy Lalonde twice tried unsuccessfully to sign him in the mid-20s. Rickey briefly managed minor league hockey before returning to the Pacific Northwest. He fought in World War II, stationed as a gunner in England in 1941.

**Jim Riley**    **Died:** May 25, 1969 (74 years old)

Riley played seven seasons in Seattle, becoming a four-time All-Star. A two-sport star, he played hockey and baseball. Riley made his Major League debut with the St. Louis Browns before a short stint with the Washington Senators. Riley later played for Pete Muldoon's Blackhawks, making him the only person to play in the NHL and Major League Baseball. A scratch golfer, he later traveled the country with his custom-made golf cart. Riley remained close with Frank Foyston and his Metropolitans teammates.

**Royal Brougham   Died:** October 30, 1978 (84 years old)

Brougham became one of the longest tenured employees of a U.S. newspaper, working for 68-years at the *Seattle Post-Intelligencer*, primarily as sports editor. The patriarch of Seattle sports, he passed away after suffering a heart attack in the Kingdome press box during a Seahawks game. Today, the street between the Mariners' and Seahawks' stadiums is named Royal Brougham Way.

**Mickey Ion        Died:** October 26, 1964 (78 years old)

Ion remained in Seattle and continued as a top official, later becoming Referee in Chief for the NHL. Mickey lost both legs late in life to phlebitis. Frank Foyston took a wheelchair bound Ion to Toronto for his Hall of Fame induction. **Hockey Hall of Fame: 1961.**

# APPENDIX A – PRESIDENT WOODROW WILSON'S PEACE WITHOUT VICTORY SPEECH

*Gentlemen of the Senate:*

*On the 18th of December last, I addressed an identical note to the governments of the nations now at war requesting them to state, more definitely than they had yet been stated by either group of belligerents, the terms upon which they would deem it possible to make peace. I spoke on behalf of humanity and of the rights of all neutral nations like our own, many of whose most vital interests the war puts in constant jeopardy.*

*The Central Powers united in a reply which stated merely that they were ready to meet their antagonists in conference to discuss terms of peace. The Entente Powers have replied much more definitely and have stated, in general terms, indeed, but with sufficient definiteness to imply details, the arrangements, guarantees, and acts of reparation which they deem to be indispensable conditions of a satisfactory settlement. We are that much nearer a definite discussion of the peace which shall end the present war. We are that much nearer the discussion of the international concert which must thereafter hold the world at peace.*

*In every discussion of the peace that must end this war, it is taken for granted that that peace must be followed by some definite concert of power which will make it virtually impossible that any such catastrophe should ever overwhelm us again. Every lover of mankind, every sane and thoughtful man must take that for granted.*

*I have sought this opportunity to address you because I thought that I owed it to you, as the council associated with me in the final determination of our international obligations, to disclose to you without reserve the thought and purpose that have been taking form in my mind in regard to the duty of our government in the days to come, when it will be necessary to lay afresh and upon a new plan the foundations of peace among the nations.*

*It is inconceivable that the people of the United States should play no part in that great enterprise. To take part in such a service will be the opportunity for which they have sought to prepare themselves by the very principles and purposes of their polity and the*

179

*approved practices of their government ever since the days when they set up a new nation in the high and honorable hope that it might, in all that it was and did, show mankind the way to liberty.*

*They cannot in honor withhold the service to which they are now about to be challenged. They do not wish to withhold it. But they owe it to themselves and to the other nations of the world to state the conditions under which they will feel free to render it.*

*That service is nothing less than this, to add their authority and their power to the authority and force of other nations to guarantee peace and justice throughout the world. Such a settlement cannot now be long postponed. It is right that before it comes, this government should frankly formulate the conditions upon which it would feel justified in asking our people to approve its formal and solemn adherence to a League for Peace. I am here to attempt to state those conditions.*

*The present war must first be ended; but we owe it to candor and to a just regard for the opinion of mankind to say that, so far as our participation in guarantees of future peace is concerned, it makes a great deal of difference in what way and upon what terms it is ended. The treaties and agreements which bring it to an end must embody terms which will create a peace that is worth guaranteeing and preserving, a peace that will win the approval of mankind, not merely a peace that will serve the several interests and immediate aims of the nations engaged. We shall have no voice in determining what those terms shall be, but we shall, I feel sure, have a voice in determining whether they shall be made lasting or not by the guarantees of a universal covenant; and our judgment upon what is fundamental and essential as a condition precedent to permanency should be spoken now, not afterwards when it may be too late.*

*No covenant of cooperative peace that does not include the peoples of the New World can suffice to keep the future safe against war; and yet there is only one sort of peace that the peoples of America could join in guaranteeing. The elements of that peace must be elements that engage the confidence and satisfy the principles of the American governments, elements consistent with their political faith and with the practical convictions which the peoples of America have once for all embraced and undertaken to defend.*

*I do not mean to say that any American government would throw any obstacle in the way of any terms of peace the governments now at war might agree upon or seek to upset them when made, whatever they might be. I only take it for granted that mere terms of peace between the belligerents will not satisfy even the belligerents themselves. Mere agreements may not make peace secure. It will be absolutely necessary that a force be created as a guarantor of the permanency of the settlement so much greater than the force of any nation now engaged, or any alliance hitherto formed or projected, that no nation, no probable combination of nations, could face or withstand it. If the peace presently to be made is to endure, it must be a peace made secure by the organized major force of mankind.*

*The terms of the immediate peace agreed upon will determine whether it is a peace for which such a guarantee can be secured. The question upon which the whole future peace and policy of the world depends is this: Is the present war a struggle for a just and secure peace, or only for a new balance of power? If it be only a struggle for a new balance of power, who will guarantee, who can guarantee the stable equilibrium of the new arrangement? Only a tranquil Europe can be a stable Europe. There must be, not a balance of power but a community power; not organized rivalries but a organized, common peace.*

*Fortunately we have received very explicit assurances on this point. The statesmen of both of the groups of nations now arrayed against one another have said, in terms that could not be misinterpreted, that it was no part of the purpose they had in mind to crush their antagonists. But the implications of these assurances may not be equally to all--may not be the same on both sides of the water. I think it will be serviceable if I attempt to set forth what we understand them to be.*

*They imply, first of all, that it must be a peace without victory. It is not pleasant to say this. I beg that I may be permitted to put my own interpretation upon it and that it may be understood that no other interpretation was in my thought. I am seeking only to face realities and to face them without soft concealments. Victory would mean peace forced upon the loser, a victor's terms imposed upon the vanquished. It would be accepted in humiliation, under duress, at an intolerable sacrifice, and would leave a sting, a resentment, a bitter memory upon which terms of peace would rest, not permanently but only as upon quicksand. Only a peace between equals can last. Only a peace the very principle of which is equality and a common participation in a common benefit. The right state of mind, the right feeling between nations, is as necessary for a lasting peace as is the just settlement of vexed questions of territory or of racial and national allegiance.*

*The equality of nations upon which peace must be founded if it is to last must be an equality of rights; the guarantees exchanged must neither recognize nor imply a difference between big nations and small, between those that are powerful and those that are weak. Right must be based upon the common strength, not upon the individual strength, of the nations upon whose concert peace will depend. Equality of territory or of resources there of course cannot be; nor any other sort of equality not gained in the ordinary peaceful and legitimate development of the peoples themselves. But no one asks or expects anything more than an equality of rights. Mankind is looking now for freedom of life, not for equipoise of power.*

*And there is a deeper thing involved than even equality of right among organized nations. No peace can last, or ought to last, which does not recognize and accept the principle that governments derive all their just powers from the consent of the governed, and that no right anywhere exists to hand peoples about from sovereignty to sovereignty as if they were property. I take it for granted, for instance, if I may venture upon a single example, that statesmen everywhere are agreed that there should be a united, independent, and autonomous Poland, and that, henceforth, inviolable security of life, of worship, and of industrial and social development should be guaranteed to all peoples who have lived hitherto under the power of governments devoted to a faith and purpose hostile to their own.*

*I speak of this, not because of any desire to exalt an abstract political principle which has always been held very dear by those who have sought to build up liberty in America but for the same reason that I have spoken of the other conditions of peace which seem to me clearly indispensable because I wish frankly to uncover realities. Any peace which does not recognize and accept this principle will inevitably be upset. It will not rest upon the affections or the convictions of mankind. The ferment of spirit of whole populations will fight subtly and constantly against it, and all the world will sympathize. The world can be at peace only if its life is stable, and there can be no stability where the will is in rebellion, where there is not tranquility of spirit and a sense of justice, of freedom, and of right.*

*So far as practicable, moreover, every great people now struggling toward a full development of its resources and of its powers should be assured a direct outlet to the great highways of the sea. Where this cannot be done by the cession of territory, it can no doubt be done by the neutralization of direct rights of way under the general guarantee which will assure the peace itself. With a right comity of arrangement, no nation need be shut away from free access to the open paths of the world's commerce.*

*And the paths of the sea must alike in law and in fact be free. The freedom of the seas is the sine qua non of peace, equality, and cooperation. No doubt a somewhat radical reconsideration of many of the rules of international practice hitherto thought to be established may be necessary in order to make the seas indeed free and common in practically all circumstances for the use of mankind, but the motive for such changes is convincing and compelling. There can be no trust or intimacy between the peoples of the world without them. The free, constant, unthreatened intercourse of nations is an essential part of the process of peace and of development. It need not be difficult either to define or to secure the freedom of the seas if the governments of the world sincerely desire to come to an agreement concerning it.*

*It is a problem closely connected with the limitation of naval armaments and the cooperation of the navies of the world in keeping the seas at once free and safe. And the question of limiting naval armaments opens the wider and perhaps more difficult question of the limitation of armies and of all programs of military preparation. Difficult and delicate as these questions are, they must be faced with the utmost candor and decided in a spirit of real accommodation if peace is to come with healing in its wings, and come to stay.*

*Peace cannot be had without concession and sacrifice. There can be no sense of safety and equality among the nations if great preponderating armaments are henceforth to continue here and there to be built up and maintained. The statesmen of the world must plan for peace, and nations must adjust and accommodate their policy to it as they have planned for war and made ready for pitiless contest and rivalry. The question of armaments, whether on land or sea, is the most immediately and intensely practical question connected with the future fortunes of nations and of mankind.*

*I have spoken upon these great matters without reserve and with the utmost explicitness because it has seemed to me to be necessary if the world's yearning desire for peace was anywhere to find free voice and utterance. Perhaps I am the only person in high authority among all the peoples of the world who is at liberty to speak and hold nothing back. I am speaking as an individual, and yet I am speaking also, of course, as the responsible head of a great government, and I feel confident that I have said what the people of the United States would wish me to say.*

*May I not add that I hope and believe that I am in effect speaking for liberals and friends of humanity in every nation and of every program of liberty? I would fain believe that I am speaking for the silent mass of mankind everywhere who have as yet had no place or opportunity to speak their real hearts out concerning the death and ruin they see to have come already upon the persons and the homes they hold most dear.*

*And in holding out the expectation that the people and government of the United States will join the other civilized nations of the world in guaranteeing the permanence of peace upon such terms as I have named I speak with the greater boldness and confidence because it is clear to every man who can think that there is in this promise no breach in either our traditions or our policy as a nation, but a fulfillment, rather, of all that we have professed or striven for.*

*I am proposing, as it were, that the nations should with one accord adopt the doctrine of President Monroe as the doctrine of the world: that no nation should seek to extend its polity over any other nation or people, but that every people should be left free to determine its own polity, its own way of development--unhindered, unthreatened, unafraid, the little along with the great and powerful.*

*I am proposing that all nations henceforth avoid entangling alliances which would draw them into competitions of power, catch them in a net of intrigue and selfish rivalry, and disturb their own affairs with influences intruded from without. There is no entangling alliance in a concert of power. When all unite to act in the same sense and with the same purpose, all act in the common interest and are free to live their own lives under a common protection.*

*I am proposing government by the consent of the governed; that freedom of the seas which in international conference after conference representatives of the United States have urged with the eloquence of those who are the convinced disciples of liberty; and that moderation of armaments which makes of armies and navies a power for order merely, not an instrument of aggression or of selfish violence.*

*These are American principles, American policies. We could stand for no others. And they are also the principles and policies of forward-looking men and women everywhere, of every modern nation, of every enlightened community. They are the principles of mankind and must prevail.*

# APPENDIX B – PRESIDENT WOODROW WILSON'S SECOND INAUGURAL ADDRESS

*My Fellow Citizens:*

*The four years which have elapsed since last I stood in this place have been crowded with counsel and action of the most vital interest and consequence. Perhaps no equal period in our history has been so fruitful of important reforms in our economic and industrial life or so full of significant changes in the spirit and purpose of our political action. We have sought very thoughtfully to set our house in order, correct the grosser errors and abuses of our industrial life, liberate and quicken the processes of our national genius and energy, and lift our politics to a broader view of the people's essential interests.*

*It is a record of singular variety and singular distinction. But I shall not attempt to review it. It speaks for itself and will be of increasing influence as the years go by. This is not the time for retrospect. It is time rather to speak our thoughts and purposes concerning the present and the immediate future.*

*Although we have centered counsel and action with such unusual concentration and success upon the great problems of domestic legislation to which we addressed ourselves four years ago, other matters have more and more forced themselves upon our attention-- matters lying outside our own life as a nation and over which we had no control, but which, despite our wish to keep free of them, have drawn us more and more irresistibly into their own current and influence.*

*It has been impossible to avoid them. They have affected the life of the whole world. They have shaken men everywhere with a passion and an apprehension they never knew before. It has been hard to preserve calm counsel while the thought of our own people swayed this way and that under their influence. We are a composite and cosmopolitan people. We are of the blood of all the nations that are at war. The currents of our thoughts as well as the currents of our trade run quick at all seasons back and forth between us and them. The war inevitably set its mark from the first alike upon our minds, our industries, our commerce, our politics and our social action. To be indifferent to it, or independent of it, was out of the question.*

*And yet all the while we have been conscious that we were not part of it. In that consciousness, despite many divisions, we have drawn closer together. We have been deeply wronged upon the seas, but we have not wished to wrong or injure in return; have retained throughout the consciousness of standing in some sort apart, intent upon an interest that transcended the immediate issues of the war itself.*

*As some of the injuries done us have become intolerable we have still been clear that we wished nothing for ourselves that we were not ready to demand for all mankind--fair dealing, justice, the freedom to live and to be at ease against organized wrong.*

*It is in this spirit and with this thought that we have grown more and more aware, more and more certain that the part we wished to play was the part of those who mean to vindicate and fortify peace. We have been obliged to arm ourselves to make good our claim to a certain minimum of right and of freedom of action. We stand firm in armed neutrality since it seems that in no other way we can demonstrate what it is we insist upon and cannot forget. We may even be drawn on, by circumstances, not by our own purpose or desire, to a more active assertion of our rights as we see them and a more immediate association with the great struggle itself. But nothing will alter our thought or our purpose. They are too clear to be obscured. They are too deeply rooted in the principles of our national life to be altered. We desire neither conquest nor advantage. We wish nothing that can be had only at the cost of another people. We always professed unselfish purpose and we covet the opportunity to prove our professions are sincere.*

*There are many things still to be done at home, to clarify our own politics and add new vitality to the industrial processes of our own life, and we shall do them as time and opportunity serve, but we realize that the greatest things that remain to be done must be done with the whole world for stage and in cooperation with the wide and universal forces of mankind, and we are making our spirits ready for those things.*

*We are provincials no longer. The tragic events of the thirty months of vital turmoil through which we have just passed have made us citizens of the world. There can be no turning back. Our own fortunes as a nation are involved whether we would have it so or not.*

*And yet we are not the less Americans on that account. We shall be the more American if we but remain true to the principles in which we have been bred. They are not the principles of a province or of a single continent. We have known and boasted all along that they were the principles of a liberated mankind. These, therefore, are the things we shall stand for, whether in war or in peace:*

*That all nations are equally interested in the peace of the world and in the political stability of free peoples, and equally responsible for their maintenance; that the essential principle of peace is the actual equality of nations in all matters of right or privilege; that peace cannot securely or justly rest upon an armed balance of power; that governments derive all their just powers from the consent of the governed and that no other powers should be supported by the common thought, purpose or power of the family of nations; that the seas should be equally free and safe for the use of all peoples, under rules set up by common agreement and consent, and that, so far as practicable, they should be accessible to all upon equal terms; that national armaments shall be limited to the necessities of national order and domestic safety; that the community of interest and of power upon which peace must henceforth depend imposes upon each nation the duty of seeing to it that all influences proceeding from its own citizens meant to encourage or assist revolution in other states should be sternly and effectually suppressed and prevented.*

*I need not argue these principles to you, my fellow countrymen; they are your own part and parcel of your own thinking and your own motives in affairs. They spring up native amongst us. Upon this as a platform of purpose and of action we can stand together. And it is imperative that we should stand together. We are being forged into a new unity amidst the fires that now blaze throughout the world. In their ardent heat we shall, in God's Providence, let us hope, be purged of faction and division, purified of the errant humors of party and of private interest, and shall stand forth in the days to come with a new dignity of national pride and spirit. Let each man see to it that the dedication is in his own heart, the high purpose of the nation in his own mind, ruler of his own will and desire.*

*I stand here and have taken the high and solemn oath to which you have been audience because the people of the United States have chosen me for this august delegation of power and have by their gracious judgment named me their leader in affairs.*

*I know now what the task means. I realize to the full the responsibility which it involves. I pray God I may be given the wisdom and the prudence to do my duty in the true spirit of this great people. I am their servant and can succeed only as they sustain and guide me by their confidence and their counsel. The thing I shall count upon, the thing without which neither counsel nor action will avail, is the unity of America--an America united in feeling, in purpose and in its vision of duty, of opportunity and of service.*

*We are to beware of all men who would turn the tasks and the necessities of the nation to their own private profit or use them for the building up of private power.*

*United alike in the conception of our duty and in the high resolve to perform it in the face of all men, let us dedicate ourselves to the great task to which we must now set our hand. For myself I beg your tolerance, your countenance and your united aid.*

*The shadows that now lie dark upon our path will soon be dispelled, and we shall walk with the light all about us if we be but true to ourselves--to ourselves as we have wished to be known in the counsels of the world and in the thought of all those who love liberty and justice and the right exalted.*

# ACKNOWLEDGEMENTS

The first people I'd like to thank are Pete Muldoon, Eddie Carpenter, Frank Foyston, Hap Holmes, Bernie Morris, Roy Rickey, Jim Riley, Bobby Rowe, Jack Walker, and Cully Wilson for living lives worth telling.

Next, I have to thank Paul Kim for his passion in keeping the Metropolitans story alive and for bringing it to my attention. Without him, I would never have known this story.

My wife, Michaela, and kids Annika, Anja and Lukas for providing a lifetime of fun. And, to Michaela for your incredible feedback every step along the way in this project.

My mom Rita, Grandma Joanne Nutt, Tim Burns, Paul Ticen, Andrea Ticen, Dave Ticen, Hilda Velasquez, Bob Harper, my aunts, uncles and all my cousins for making me proud every day to be part of your family. Und, meine schwiegermutter Hermi, schwester Christine und die Schedlmayers, Pösingers, Jahns, Planskys, Neubauers und alle meine Freunde und Familie in Österreich. Danke!

Greg Shaw, I still can't believe you gave me this opportunity. One of the most frustrating aspects of my life is how hard I've had to fight for everything I've ever accomplished. This was one of the first times where someone with the means to offer me opportunity, did. For that, and everything you do for our community, I'll forever be grateful.

Dave Eskenazi, I can't believe how much you did to help me. Your generosity, excitement, enthusiasm, memorabilia and incredible editing skills made this project. You are one of a kind and the type of person that makes a community amazing. I hope I conveyed my thanks to you enough over the course of this project. If not, thank you, thank you, thank you!

Doug Lorentz, it would have been a vastly different story without you. Thanks for putting in so much time to read the first completed draft and then do it again three months later with spot-on feedback! A baseball player with brains and a great role model for me.

To the editors of this book, Dan Kearney and Claudia Rowe, thank you for all your wisdom and ideas. Dan, thanks for knowing how to optimize my launch angle and exit velo. I put my best swing on this one but you got it up in the wind and made it fly. Claudia, I had no idea how to start the book before your advice got me going in the right direction and your encouragement to think "stage makeup" with everything I wrote was so incredibly valuable.

To Barbara Bonner for always making it work, for your great feedback and for always keeping our team going in the same direction.

Glenn Drosendahl, thank you for talking me off the ledge on multiple occasions. Your fantastic feedback on the first draft served as the backbone for many of the final edits.

Ralph Morton, David Blandford, Susan Treder, Tom Norwalk, Lori Magaro and everyone at Visit Seattle for your help and encouragement along the way. If they'd let me, I'd list you all. Regardless, thank you!

Katie Grad, Bobby Carlson, Amanda Streams, Lael Paul, Kevin Martinez, Art Thiel and Bret Hartnett for reading early chapters or manuscript drafts and giving me feedback.

Phil Pritchard and Mike Bolt at the Hockey Hall of Fame for coming out to our community twice to help us celebrate despite that we didn't have a hockey team.

To Pam Robenolt, Margaret O'Mara and Lisa Oberg at the University of Washington. Pam connected me with Margaret O'Mara in the UW history department. On multiple occasions, Margaret offered advice on writing, researching, understanding America at that time as well as on Woodrow Wilson. She also recommended I go to Special Collections at Allen Library where I met Lisa Oberg. Lisa responded to every long email with detailed responses and her discovery of a court document detailing the death of Bernie Morris' uncle unlocked the circumstances of his tragic early life. The University of Washington has done more to shape me than any institution in my life and I appreciate that being a Husky truly is for a lifetime.

Barbara, Kyle and Dean Daniels, Judie Sparks, Diane Keesee, Bev Parsons, and Doug Rickey for your stories and insights on your family members. Your admiration and love for them was infectious and I'm so grateful for all of the stories you shared with me.

Brian Westerman, Pete Livengood, Ethan Paul and Greg Paul for your help and encouragement.

To John Robbins for the back cover photo.

Ken Knutson, Joe Ross, Joe Weis, Frank Bartenetti and Bill Gillespie. Thanks for changing my life. You always saw what we could do rather than what we couldn't and took a talented guy without a work ethic and taught me how to compete.

Carl Malone, Mike Morrisroe, Matt McNaghten, Jay Matsudaira, Barbara

Terzieff, Mark Dickison and the entire TriFilm crew. I cut my storytelling teeth with this amazing crew.

Pete Orgill, Dominic Woody, Ryan Bundy, Bryan Williamson, Kevin Miller, Ryan Lentz and all of my Husky teammates as well as Dominic Lanza, Justin Maxhimer, Brian Neher, Jaime Hernandez, Mike Wherry, John Heywood, Bryson Galanti, Paige Brown, Jenny Grusz, Angie Baker, Cindy Merrick, Janna Boelke, Tarana Mayes, Angie Johnson, Bryan and Heidi Roth, Dave and Maggie Fields, Jay Torrell, David Gravenkemper, Jeff Bechthold, Robb Hamilton, Lisa Fraser, Jim Gregson, Geoff Kozu, Brandon Cogo, Ty Lumaco, Darren Rose, Surintr Desai, Caleb Oar, Scott Jones, Damon Farrington, Mark O'Halloran, Brett Hales and Jason Mesnick for your friendship and encouragement throughout this process.

To Dr. Phil Gold, Dr. Vivek Mehta, Dr. Steve Medwell, Alice Albright, Laura Vadman and the entire medical team at Swedish Hospital that took great care of me during a scary period of life. I will forever be grateful to you.

To Tighe Dickinson, Mike McCain, Craig Parthemer, Bobby Carlson, Tim Palmer, Walt Cougan, Mark Grandstrand, Guy Keller, Ron Omori, Jim Stewart, Ray Atkinson, Tyler Johnson, Bob Haynes, Jeff Sakamoto, Brad Conn and Darrel Sakamoto. I've been part of some amazing teams with you guys.

To all of the Edmonds Community College, University of Washington and Boys of Summer players that I have had the privilege to coach. As players, you inspired me every day with your competitiveness, commitment and talent. As people, I could not be prouder of each and every one of you. Thanks for giving me an outlet from real life. Every day I've been able to step on a field has been special – because of you.

# ABOUT THE AUTHOR

Kevin Ticen spent more than six years writing about Seattle sports as the Director of Marketing and Communications for the Seattle Sports Commission. A former catcher on the University of Washington baseball team, Ticen played professionally in the Anaheim Angels minor league system and then overseas in Austria. His sports writing career began in the off-season during his minor league days writing for one of the many Seattle startups during the dot.com boom. His post-playing days have been spent coaching baseball, first for five years on the staff at the University of Washington and now leading a high school aged summer program in the Seattle area.

Follow Kevin on Twitter @kticen

# SOURCES

A note on sources: The contents of this book were primarily researched through newspaper articles, genealogical documents, websites, photographs and limit interviews with family members. To see the full, detailed list of sources, please visit the publisher's blog at www.clydehillpublishing.com.